A BOOK OF

FAVORITE

Recipes

Compiled by

LOGAN COUNTY EXTENSION HOMEMAKERS

BUSY BEES	PADRONI
CREATIVE HOMEMAKERS	PEP AND PROGRESS
HEARTH AND HOME	PROCTOR
HIGHLAND LASSIES	RAINBOW OF HAPPINESS
HOME HUSTLERS	SHAMROCKS
KELLY	SOUTHSIDERS
NIGHT OWLS	STERLING HOMEMAKERS

X-TRA X-AMPLES X-TENSION

KELLY WOMAN'S IMPROVEMENT CLUB HISTORY

FOR

70TH ANNIVERSARY

After the organization of the Kelly Woman's Improvement
Club April 10, 1913, the club purchased and received deed for
the Kelly Community House and the land it was on September
21, 1923. The Kelly Community House was maintained by the club
until its sale March 18, 1976.

It was used for a community gathering place for community
dinners, 4H meetings, and business meetings of the local telephone
company and Farmers Union socials and business meetings. From
the establishment of the Gary DeSoto Youth Center of Logan
County. Other projects were the purchasing of car seats for babies,
Sterling Cooperative Ministries and a contribution to Save the
Depot Fund.

The 37th Anniversary of the Kelly Woman's Improvement
April, 1950, was celebrated at the Kelly Community House. At
the 45th Anniversary, 7 of the 13 charter members were present.
Five charter members were present for the 50th Anniversary.
The 60th Anniversary was celebrated at a tea at Rose Arbor. The
70th Anniversary was celebrated in April, 1983. At one time prior
to 1923, there were 36 members according to some records. From
1927 - 1982 the average membership was 15. The present membership is 9. The oldest member is 95 years 'young'. She is living with
her daughters in Greeley.

Some Club members helped a neighboring club mow and
clean the Kelly Cemetery for several years. April 1981, Club
members assisted by their husbands and cemetery board planted
30 Ponderosa pine trees in the cemetery. There were replacements
in 1982.

Several members have assisted in 4H club leadership. At
the Logan County Fair, fair booths were an outstanding activity
for many years.

Dear Friends:

In nineteen thirteen Kelly's land
Had hardly seen a plow.
It was home to many people then
But where is Kelly now?

I'd have you know there's still a club
After Seventy years have passed
Though husbands laughed at such a thing
And said it wouldn't last.

If we should tell the young folks now
They'd think it pretty strange
Of the time we spent to feed and clean
That bulky kitchen range.

Another phase of farm life
Which I'm glad was way back then,
Was if you wanted eggs and chickens
You had to set a hen.

We learned to make our cheese and soap
And lotions for our hands.
In the Fall we learned the newest ways
To get the fruit all canned.

Mary Green showed it's important
To measure when you bake.
Then Anna Rice dumped this and that
It came out angel cake.

All these work-related projects
Were not the reason that we went.
It was not just one more meeting then
But was each month's big event.

We gathered at a neighbor's home
Which on that day looked its best,
For fun and food and woman talk
An afternoon of rest.

When looking back at Kelly Club
The Community House is a must.
And no one will forget it
Who helped move out the dust.

But it could tell some stories
Of programs, dinners, plays.
Which made some entertainment
In those hard scrabble days.

Then came Highline Electric
Which freed the household slaves.
We've come as far as food processors
From there to microwaves.

You'd think with all this progress
We'd be moving straight ahead.
But what do young homemakers want?
It's making quilts and bread.

Kelly now is modern farms and homes
The school and church are gone.
Social life is now in Sterling
Which shows the world moves on.

If you went to the club or school or church
Or if your home was there.
To all who lived in Kelly
We have memories to share.

Written by Louise Schroeder
April 17, 1983

HISTORY OF THE HOME HUSTLERS E.H. CLUB

A group of homestead women in the Mt. Hope community organized a club in February, 1916 for the purpose of getting together for social time. They met twice a month, traveling by horse and buggy to their all day meetings. It was a family group with the men discussing their farm problems while the women talked about their lives as homemakers. The first meeting was held at the J.L. Ourecky home, with the following families present: Mr. and Mrs. Ed Britton, Mr. and Mrs. Lloyd Coakley, Mr. and Mrs. Ed Bishop, Mr. and Mrs. M.O. Patten, Mr. and Mrs. A.J. Britton, Mr. and Mrs. J.L. Jenks, Mr. and Mrs. Walter Dillon, Mr. and Mrs. Joseph Cavis, Mr. and Mrs. Claude Cook and Mrs. Alma Vaughn. Mrs. Jesse Jones joined in 1917.

In the first years, basic lessons were given in sewing, cooking, soap-making, bread making, darning, mending, quilting, comfort-tying, basket weaving, rug making, millinery, dress forms and pictures. Their motto was "Faith in God, Hope in the Future, and to Help One Another".

The children were organized into a 4-H Club in 1916 under the leadership of J.L. Ourecky with D.C. Bascom as County Agent and Home Agent Lucille Woodard. Highlights for the 4-H members were riding in Mr. Bascom's car, the first brought into the community and staying in Sterling for the County Fair. They stayed for two days and two nights, sleeping on cots on the top floor of the Courthouse.

In 1949, under the direction of Home Agent Roberta Lascelles, the Mt. Hope Club joined with other Home Demonstration Clubs in Logan County. The club activities were planting of trees for windbreaks, flowers and shrubs to gain color and a better appearance to their ranch homes. Much remodeling to modern conveniences, redecorating and painting. Many community projects have been done also; hearing screening, sewing cancer dressings, volunteering in the Red Cross programs, working on the hospitality center in Sterling, leading 4-H clubs, working with the handicapped, and many others.

With the addition of members from a larger area the name of the club was changed to Home Hustlers. There is only one Charter member living, Mrs. E.E. Britton who lives with her daughter. There is one fifty year member, Mrs. L.T. Stanley. We honor their pioneering spirit for giving us a start.

The club currently has fifteen members and meets on the second Friday in the members homes. The programs are on a variety of subjects. One educational or cultural trip is taken each year. The members are very active on the county level, holding office and presenting lessons.

PADRONI EXTENSION CLUB

The Padroni Home Demonstration Club was organized in 1917 as a social club. Later on it became affiliated with the Home Demonstration Clubs. The Home Demonstration Agent at that time was Velma Bourshell.

Some of the older members and possible charter members were: Mrs. W.E. Stine, L.K. Parr, Tom Higgins, J.E. Lake, Lois Parke, J.E. Northey, John Morris, Lou Pease, Roy Dunham, George Smith, Chesley Harris, Sr., Lester Smith, John Fowler, H.C. Kulbe, Daisy Gillett, and Clarence Evans.

At the beginning people were sent out from the college at Ft. Collins to present the lessons.

Over the years the club has participated in Red Cross and Cancer Fund raising drives.

The club participated in the play contests and went to Ft. Collins in 1955 and 1956, where they received white and red ribbons respectively.

The Padroni Farmerettes 4-H Club was organized by our club in 1956, the 4-H Club is now the Padroni Patriots and several of the club members are still leaders.

In former years there was a recreation park in Padroni and the club set out trees one year and kept the park up for some years.

Mrs Virgil Ballinger was H.D. County Council President in 1958 and County Historian in 1959.

Mrs. Wm. Lively was publicity chairman for the state conference held in Sterling in 1961.

Mrs. Lewis Morrison served as Colorado State Secretary for the extension Homemaker Council from 1979 to 1982 and County Council President at the present time 1983 - 1985.

(Cont.)

At the beginning, the club met at noon for a luncheon after which the business and project meetings were held. The meetings are now held in the evenings.

The club displayed a booth at the Logan County Fair, several years.

They helped with Bible School at the little community church.

It was a co-sponsor of the famous "Buffalo Suppers" held at the Padroni School for many years, some times they helped serve up to a thousand people.

The club has put together a "Padroni Extension Homemaker" calendar for 13 years. It lists all the Caliche, Sterling, and Northeastern Junior College Athletic events for each year. It obtains ads from about 30 various businesses throughout Sterling and the adjoining communities.

They have supported the Girls State activities and still suppor the Caliche Scholarship fund. They also contributed to the Harts School.

The members have acted as hostesses at the Pioneer Museum in Sterling, and have baked cupcakes and cookies for the nursing homes in Sterling, and did help take craft lessons to the nursing homes.

Each year at Christmas time the club prepares a basket of homemade candies and cookies, and fruit to take to the senior citizens that have lived in the Padroni Community.

They have been successful at the 'tire changing' contest at the Logan County Fair.

There has been an average of about 15 ladies in our group.

The club has always helped the 4-H clubs, and has helped prepare many a dinner for local family members' funerals. It is always on hand when help is needed.

STERLING HOMEMAKERS

The Sterling Homemakers Club was organized by Mrs. Louie (Nellie) Rieke on March 6, 1930. It chose for its colors blue and silver and for its flower the Delphinium.. Down through the years those who knew Nellie have been indebted to her for organizing a means of their visiting together, sharing experiences, and learning new and easier ways and methods of doing their many home-making tasks.

Many times the women would bring a covered dish and enjoy their noon meal or even a supper together. Their husbands and families enjoyed the suppers.

In 1965 we celebrated our 35th Anniversary and on March 9, 1980, the club celebrated its 50th Anniversary. At that time, Mrs. Flora Bartholomew was honored as their only living charter member. In January of 1981, Mrs. Bartholomew passed away.

The club presently has fifteen members and is second only to the Kelly Club in number of years, age wise, in the county. Mrs. Nellberdine Druyff is the present President.

PROCTOR EXTENSION HOMEMAKERS HISTORY

The Proctor E.H. Club was organized November 3, 1944 with nine charter members. They were Mesdames Ray Maiks, Norman A. Smith, Arlen Lamb, Fred Klein, Ronald Carwin, George Whitney, John Povala, Chris Schott, Jr., and Ramond Charles. They helped organize the Iliff E.H. Club in 1948. Yearly activities have included:

1949
Sent Care packages to Germany, vegetable seeds.
1950
Sent Care packages to Norway.
1951
Helped Club 19 with community sing.
1952
Made cancer dressings.
1954
Started road sign project.
1955
Put on one-act play.
1956
Member, Louise Amen, won the Western Farm Life Top Homemaker Award.

VII

(Cont.)

The club has won many first place ribbons at the Logan County Fair. We have given scissors to the outstanding freshman student at Iliff and Crook Schools for several years and now present this award at Caliche. We held a 25th Anniversary party in 1969.

The club has made self-help books for special education classes and lap robes for the elderly. In 1976 we helped make a quilt for the Historical Society. The Proctor Club won the Sweepstake Award for community booths at the 1976, 77 and 80 fairs. We have received the Logan County Outstanding Club Award.

Recent service projects have included planting trees at Caliche School, donating to the scholarship fund and girls State program, donating to the DeSoto Youth Building, and giving food and clothing to the needy. We also sponsor two residents of Rose Arbor and take them birthday and Christmas gifts. In 1981, Louise Amen received the North Star Award.

PEP AND PROGRESS HOMEMAKERS CLUB HISTORY - 1983

The club was organized October 24, 1946, at the home of Mrs. Jay Knifton. We were sponsored by the Sterling Homemakers - so decided to call ourselves the Sterling Junior Homemakers.

Charter members were: Mrs. Jay Knifton, Mrs. Albert McGruder, Mrs. Lee Swedlund, Mrs. Robert Littler, Mrs. Don Stuck, Mrs. Al Miller, Mrs. Jake Artzer , Mrs. Clifford Knudsen, Mrs. Max Coakley, and Mrs. Robert Coakley. Officers for the first year were: President, Mrs. Max Coakley; Vice President, Mrs. Don Stuck; Secretary, Mrs. Jay Knifton; Treasurer, Mrs. Albert McGruder.

We met in the afternoons, but after a few years changed to evening meetings for the convenience of the members.

After a few months we changed our name to Pep and Progress, because of the confusion of mail with the Sterling Homemakers.

The club colors are blue and white. Club flower is the Chrysanthemum. Club motto is "Ready-Willing and Able".

We don't have any charter members in our club at the present time. Two members who joined shortly after the club was organized, Mrs. Virgil Rieke, June 17, 1948, and Mrs. Harry Barthlomew, March 17, 1949, are still active in the club.

VIII

Our club has been active in promoting 4-H. We started and sponsored a 4-H club, have given 4-H trophies, helped with the Logan County Fair, often with a booth, policing, selling corn for the De Soto Building project, hearing screening , 4-H Banquet, many community projects, Red Cross, nursing home birthday parties and entertainment.

Our International Dinner is in January. February we have a card party with our husbands as guests. Our Christmas party and dinner in December. Instead of a gift exchange, we give gifts to the nursing home people, Food Bank or other needy project.

We follow the county lesson plan. Club members have been County Council Officers and County Project Ch. members have moved and dropped out, but we are still an active club. Our present membership is nineteen.

HEARTH AND HOME

The Hearth and Home Club was sponsored by the Proctor H.D. Club on April 30, 1948.

The club was officially organized on May 5, 1948, with 16 members participating. There are four charter members who are still active members of the club.

We celebrated our 25th Anniversary by hosting a tea and inviting members of Proctor H.D. Club and the Southsiders.

We have been very active in community projects as well as being represented as project leaders on the Logan County Extension Homemakers Council.

HISTORY OF THE SOUTHSIDERS E.H. CLUB

In February of 1950, the Hearth and Home E.H. Club invited ladies, south of the river, to the meeting, with the plan of starting a new E.H. Club.

Sixteen ladies did organize, elect officers and the Southsiders Club was born.

The first meeting was held on March 7, 1950. Business that day was installation of officers and choosing the second Tuesday of the month as their meeting day; colors were to be pink and white and the flower would be a pink rose. The club motto -- "Let Nothing But Your Best Satisfy You", was also chosen.

As the years have rolled by, there have been many changes-- for new members took the place of those that left-- and now only two charter members remain.

The average membership through the years has been between nine and fourteen.

In 1975, the Southsiders celebrated their 25th Anniversary.

We have had a few oddities: Four daughters-in-law and one daughter have joined the club. During the years, 59 ladies have been members. There has only been one time in 33 years that we've had two members with the same first name, and that happened in 1975, our 25th Anniversary year.

SHAMROCK

February 1, 1952, Mrs. R.J. Carroll invited a group of women to meet in her home with Miss Eisemen, Home Agent and Mrs. Harley Grubbs from the Homemakers Club. They explained the purpose and work and helped organize the club with the Homemaker Club as sponsors. The group was known as the Twenty-Eighth H.D. Club. Because the group was so large, it was decided to divide into two clubs.

Mrs. Earl Franklin was selected to present the constitution and by-laws of the Home Demonstration Clubs to the group. The charter was signed at this meeting in March 1952. There were seven charter members. The first officers were Mrs. Bruce Beavens, President; Mrs. J.J. Thompson, Vice-President; Mrs. Roy Slice, Secretary; and Mrs. Arthur Edens, Treasurer. Mrs. Barbara Spelts became a member one month later and is presently club president.

In May 1952, the group chose the Colorado Carnation as club flower, with green and white club colors. The club motto is "Better the Home for the Best" and in September 1952, the name of Shamrock was chosen. They also chose to meet in the afternoons.

In the first year it was established to have a family picnic in July and a Christmas covered dish dinner. The first year finished with 17 members.

During the second year, Shamrock Club was divided again, with most of the younger members organizing an evening club and Shamrock remaining an afternoon club. The third year finished with fourteen members.

Through the years the club qualified for the Standard Club Award. Several years won awards at the County Fair, the first being in 1956 for a Color Harmony booth.

The fifth year it was decided to have a Sweet Heart party for everybody's husband, on Valentines Day. It was enjoyed so much, it became an annual event.

Through all these 31 years we have tried to comply with all the programs, lessons and activities presented the Extension Homemakers. The changes have been many. The six remaining members are grandmothers and great-grandmothers, passing along the many things we have learned along the way.

It is our hope that Extension Homemaking may continue through the years to ever bring into the homes of the future generations all the good we have achieved through our generation.

THE NIGHT OWL EXTENSION HOMEMAKERS

Club was organized November 16, 1963, at the home of Mrs. Ernest Sonnenberg. She had been a member of the Kelly Improvement Club from 1925 to 1932. We felt the pressure of the 1930's depression and the need of cutting our mileage which was anywhere from 10 to 12 miles east to west.

Several ladies left the Kelly Club to organize the Harding E.H. Club. There were up to 15 members at one time but farms were enlarged and families moved away. This club dropped when there were only 5 or 6 left in the community.

Mr. and Mrs. Ernest Sonnenberg moved to Sterling in 1960. Mrs. Sonnenberg visited with friends and neighbors and she felt there was enough interest to start a new club. The working women could come at night so this was set for our meeting time. Thus we became The Night Owls. There were 9 starting members.

Donna Larson was County Home Agent. Our motto is " Brighten the Corner Where You Are". Club colors are pink and green, club flower is the rose.

We have enjoyed all the lessons and endeavor to learn new ways and means of doing things.

Our members have come and gone and become members among other clubs. The first officers were: President, Frances Thoren; vice-President, Carol McBride Stone; Secretary, Millie Littler; Treasurer, Millie Littler. Mrs. Ernest Sonnenberg is the present President.

1983-84 Officers are: President, Mrs. Jimmie Jones; Vice-President, Mrs. Robert Littler; Secretary, Mrs. Donald Seghi; Treasurer, Mrs. LeRoy Harms.

BUSY BEES

The Busy Bees E.H. Club was formerly known as the Senior Mrs. H.D. Club. In February, 1965, they changed their name to Busy Bees. In February 1965, the Busy Bees staged a Style Show as their first community project with proceeds going to the local chapter of the Cancer Society.

The Busy Bees were always active with fair and 4-H activities, by promoting 4-H with a booth at the fair and some years with a float. They helped with 4-H awards banquets and sponsored the Jr. Miss 4-H which later became the Jetsons 4-H Club.

In 1966, the Busy Bees sponsored a Korean boy through the Christian Children's Fund. Each member brought $1.00 each meeting and we had one correspondent.

The Busy Bees have had three members hold the office of County President for Logan County. They were: Sonia Hutt, Kathi Hutt and Marilyn Hutt.

The Busy Bees have always tried to support the County Council in all its activities along with having an active club on its own.

RAINBOWS OF HAPPINESS

Rainbows of Happiness E.H. Club was oragnized July 11, 1967 with Mrs. Birney Cox as the first President and eighteen members.

They chose rainbow colors because of the happiness they show and the rose as our flower. The club motto is: "Serving Our Community Through Our Home."

We still have four charter members. They are: Norma Penner, Iris Lambert, Eva Korrey, and Carol Lambrecht.

HISTORY OF THE HIGHLAND LASSIES

The Highland Lassies Club began with a group of neighbors, who were interested in what Extension Clubs had to offer. They are quite a new club, having just organized in 1981, with six charter members. Some of their activities have been: To plant a shrub in Pioneer Park, participating in the Logan County Fair, helping with the Diabetes Van, an annual International Dinner, Christmas cookie exchange, and a plant exchange in the spring, as well as having guest speakers on current community topics of interest.

X-TRA X-AMPLES X-TENSION

The X-tra X-amples X-tension Club was formed on March 8, 1975 with 18 charter members.

The club's colors and motto are: Red for Love, White for Law and Purity, and Blue for the Hope that our Examples and Efforts may extend to our Community and County. The club's flower is the carnation.

Our goals are to support the following: The hospital, our community, membership, 4-H and nursing homes. Also to provide a learning experience for our members and to promote better family life.

Some of our main projects have been, wall accessories at Rose Arbor Nursing Home, donated infant blood pressure machine (otoscope/opthalmoscope) to OB ward at the hospital, helped furnish the father/sibling waiting room at the hospital with childrens toys, furniture and wall accessories.

At present we have 19 members.

CREATIVE HOMEMAKERS

In January 1982, county membership chairman, Vickie Lehmkuhl, and County President, Ginny Anderson, had an organizational meeting for any interested women in starting a new E.H. Club. There were three future members present.

We met again in February with three more new women present. At the February meeting we elected our officers, chose our club name and our motto. We decided to meet in the afternoons so we wouldn't have to leave our children.

We have now grown in membership to nine women. We are looking forward to our second year as an organized club.

NOTES:

Worth Remembering

Keep a toothbrush around the kitchen sink—you will find it useful in cleaning rotary beaters, graters, choppers and similar kitchen utensils.

Instead of trying to iron rickrack on the right side of the garment, turn the article. The rickrack can be pressed perfectly.

When your hands are badly stained from gardening, add a teaspoon of sugar to the soapy lather you wash them in.

Use paper cups as handy containers for your "drippings" in the refrigerator as they take up little room and can be thrown away when empty.

Before emptying the bag of your vacuum cleaner, sprinkle water on the newspaper into which it is emptied, and there will be no scattering of dust.

To whiten laces, wash them in sour milk.

To remove burned-on starch from your iron, sprinkle salt on a sheet of waxed paper and slide iron back and forth several times. Then polish it with silver polish until roughness or stain is removed.

Dip a new broom in hot salt water before using. This will toughen the bristles and make it last longer.

Try waxing your ashtrays. Ashes won't cling, odors won't linger and they can be wiped clean with a paper towel or disposable tissue. This saves daily washing.

Plant a few sprigs of dill near your tomato plants to prevent tomato worms on your plants.

Marigolds will prevent rodents.

Spray garbage sacks with ammonia to prevent dogs from tearing the bags before picked up.

You can clean darkened aluminum pans easily by boiling in them two teaspoons of cream of tartar mixed in a quart of water. Ten minutes will do it.

Fresh lemon juice will take away onion scent from hands.

Wash old powder puffs in soapy water, rinse well and dry thoroughly. Then use them for polishing silverware, copper and brass.

Soak colored cottons overnight in strong salt water and they will not fade.

To dry drip-dry garments faster and with fewer wrinkles, hang garment over the top of a dry cleaner's plastic bag.

If a cracked dish is boiled for 45 minutes in sweet milk, the crack will be so welded together that it will hardly be visible, and will be so strong it will stand the same usage as before.

APPETIZERS, PICKLES, RELISH

SPINACH DIP
Very Good!

Esther Schuppe
Pep and Progress

1 pkg. frozen chopped spinach thawed, squeeze out (drain)
1 c. sour cream
1 c. mayonnaise
1 pkg. leek soup (dried)
1 tsp. Lawry's seasoning salt
1 1/2 c. chopped green onion
1/2 c. chopped parsley
1 tsp. dill seed
pinch of herbs (by Lawry's)
juice of 1/2 lemon

Mix all together a day ahead.

MEXICAN CHIP DIP

Reva Roland
Rainbows of Happiness

2-8 oz. pkgs. cream cheese
1-8 oz. jar picante sauce
1 green pepper, chopped
1 med. tomato, chopped
1/2 med. onion, chopped
2 avocados, chopped
chopped lettuce
grated cheese

Mix cream cheese and picante sauce together. Add green pepper, tomato, onion and avocados. Pour into 7x11 inch casserole dish. Top with finely chopped lettuce and a layer of cheese. Chill.

CHILI RELLENOS DIP

Joyce Werner
Home Hustlers

1-4 oz. can diced green chilies
1-4 1/2 oz. can chopped ripe olives
2 or 3 fresh chopped tomatoes
4 green onions, chopped
1 Tbsp. red wine vinegar
2 Tbsp. salad oil
1 tsp. garlic salt

Mix together and let stand. Serve with corn chips.

POLYNESIAN GINGER DIP

Eleanor Carlson
Home Hustlers

1 c. mayonnaise, chilled
1 c. dairy sour cream
1/4 c. chopped onion
1/4 c. minced parsley
1/4 c. finely chopped water chestnuts
1 or 2 Tbsp. finely chopped candied ginger

1

(Cont.)

2 cloves minced garlic   dash of salt
1 Tbsp. soy sauce

Combine mayonnaise and sour cream. Add remaining ingredients and mix well. Garnish with additional candied ginger bits.

CHIP DIP

Enid Lindstrom
Kelly Womans Improvement Club

1-12 oz. Phila. cream cheese
1 #602 can Snappy Tom
  tomato cocktail

1 #702 pkg. Good Seasons
  salad dressing mix

Beat all together.

HOLIDAY CHEESE BALL

Janice Grauberger
Hearth and Home

1-3 oz. pkg. cream cheese
1-5 oz. jar cheese spread
  with bacon

1-5 oz. jar cheese spread
  with pimento
1 c. crushed canned French
  fried onions

Combine softened cheeses, mixing well to blend. Stir in 1/2 cup onions. Chill. Shape into ball and roll in remaining onions.

CRUNCHY CHEESE BALL

Debbie Breidenbach
Hearth and Home

1-8 oz. pkg. cream cheese,
  softened
4 c. mayonnaise
2 c. ground, cooked ham
2 Tbsp. chopped parsley

1 tsp. minced onion
4 tsp. dry mustard
1/4 tsp. hot pepper sauce
1/2 c. chopped peanuts

Beat cream cheese and mayonnaise until smooth.
Stir in next ingredients except peanuts. Cover and chill several hours. Form into ball; roll in peanuts to coat. Serve with crackers.

CHEDDAR CHEESE AND OLIVE BALLS

Jama Marvel
X-tra X-amples X-tension Club

1/4 lb. cheddar cheese
1/4 c. butter, softened
1/4 tsp. paprika

3/4 c. flour
36 to 40 tiny stuffed Spanish
  olives

Preheat oven to 375°. Grate cheese which has been softened

to room temperature. Combine with other ingredients in order. Mix until smooth. Cover and let stand at room temperature 15 minutes. Pinch dough into small circles. Form around well drained olive. Place on ungreased cookie sheet. Chill 10 minutes in refrigerator.

Bake at 375° for 20 to 25 minutes or until lightly brown. Serve hot. Makes 36 to 40 balls.

Note: May be made in advance and frozen before baking. Bake frozen for 30 minutes. <u>Do not thaw.</u>

Can substitute pecan halves for olives. Pinch dough into small circle and press pecan half on top of ball.

CHEESE ROLL

Millie Boxler
Pep and Progress

14 oz. blue cheese
18 oz. Phila. cream cheese
1 lb. sharp cheddar cheese,
   softened
1 Tbsp. onion

1 Tbsp. parsley
1 tsp. worcestershire sauce
1/2 c. finely chopped walnuts
   or pecans

Mix all together. Form into a roll and refrigerate 3 hours. Roll in paprika. Let stand 1/2 hour before serving.

SAUSAGE COOKIES

Julie Sonnenberg
Southsiders

1 lb. hot or sweet Italian
   sausage
1 lb. sharp cheddar cheese

3 c. Bisquick
3/4 c. water

Grate cheese. Blend all ingredients together. Roll into 1 inch balls; flatten slightly. Put on ungreased cookie sheet. Bake at 400° for 12 to 15 minutes.

HORS D' OEUVRES

Mildred Littler
Night Owls

1 lb. wieners, cut into
   60 pieces

1-10 oz. jar grape jelly
1-10 oz. jar chili sauce

Mix all together and cook in crock pot on low for 3 to 4 hours.

COUNTRY DILL DIP

Sandy Schneider
Hearth and Home

16 oz. sour cream
  or 8 oz. sour cream and
  8 oz. cream cheese
1 tsp. Lawry's seasoning salt

2 tsp. parsley flakes
1 Tbsp. dill weed
1 Tbsp. grated onion

Mix the above ingredients. Use rye bread or Hawaiian Kings bread to dip. You can cut off the top of the loaf and hollow it out by pulling out bite size pieces. Then use the hollowed out loaf as a bowl to place the dip in.

GUACAMOLE DIP

Vicki Gertner
X-tra X-amples X-tension Club

4 to 6 avocados
3 Tbsp. picante sauce
  (taco sauce)
1 tsp. garlic salt

1 tsp.   onion salt or diced onion
1 c. diced tomatoes
2 Tbsp. lemon juice
1 tsp. salt

Peel and pit avocados; mash with fork or blender. Stir in remaining ingredients. Makes about 3 to 4 cups.

CHILI CON QUESO

Carole Quint
Pep and Progress

2 green pepper, diced
1 onion, chopped
1 c. canned tomatoes, chopped
    and undrained
1 can diced green chilies (4 oz.)

1 tsp. salt
1 tsp. chili powder
2 c. grated cheese
  (Old English or Velveeta)

Saute peppers and onion in shortening. Stir continuously while adding tomatoes; cook 5 minutes. Add green chilies, salt, chili powder and cheese. Cook on low heat until cheese is melted. Serve hot with tortilla or corn chips.

CHILIE CONCASO DIP

Minnie Korrey
Hearth and Home

1 box Velveeta cheese
1 pkg. cheddar cheese
1 pkg. Monterey Jack

1 can green chilie
1 can jalapeno relish
1 can evap. milk

Melt all ingredients slowly over low heat. Use as dip for vegetables and chips.

HOT SAUSAGE AND CHEESE PUFFS

Joyce Jones
Sterling Homemakers

1 lb. hot or sweet Italian
  sausage
1 lb. sharp cheddar cheese,
  shredded

3 c. Bisquick
3/4 c. water

Remove sausage from casings; cook in large skillet, breaking up the meat with a fork until no longer pink, about 8 to 10 minutes; drain off fat. Spoon sausage into large bowl and cool completely. Add cheese, biscuit mix and water. Mix with a fork just until blended. Roll into 1 inch balls. Place on large cookie sheets 2 inches apart.

Bake in hot oven at 400° for 12 to 15 minutes or until puffed and browned. Remove from cookie sheets. Cool completely on racks. These can be frozen and reheated. Delightful when served warm.

TACO DIP

Cathy Elrick
X-tra X-amples X-tension Club

1 large can refried beans
1 pt. sour cream
1 avocado or avocado dip mix
3 or 4 diced onions
3/4 lb. cheese, grated

1 small can black olives
alfalfa sprouts
1 1/2 tomatoes, diced
1 pkg. taco seasoning mix
taco chips

Mix beans and taco mix together. Spread out on pizza pan. Mix sour cream and avocado together. Spread over beans. Layer onions, cheese, olives, sprouts and tomatoes on top of sour cream mixture. Refrigerate then use the large round taco chips to scoop up dip.

VEGETABLE DIP OR SALAD

Joyce Jones
Sterling Homemakers

1 small carton sour cream
1 large carton cottage
  cheese

1 pkg. Knorr's vegetable
  soup mix
1 Tbsp. worcestershire sauce

Mix together. Serve on a lettuce leaf or as a dip for fresh vegetables.

Write your extra recipes here:

Write your extra recipes here:

SOUPS
SALADS
SAUCES
DRESSINGS

Salads and Salad Dressings

For Appeal To The Appetite

Chill ingredients before mixing—except for molded salads.

Provide tartness in the body of salad or dressing.

Use salad greens other than lettuce sometimes. Have you tried chicory, escarole, endive, kale, spinach, dandelion greens, romaine, watercress, and chinese cabbage?

Sprinkle orange, lemon, lime, or pineapple juice on fruits that may turn dark—apples, peaches, and bananas, for instance.

For tossed green salads, tear greens in fairly large pieces or cut with scissors. Larger pieces give more body to the salad.

Prevent wilting and sogginess by drying the greens used in salads, draining canned foods well before adding to salad, using just enough salad dressing to moisten. For raw vegetable salads, add dressing at the last minute.

Fruit Combinations

1. Sliced pineapple, apricot halves, sweet red cherries.
2. Watermelon balls, peach slices, orange slices.
3. Grapefruit sections, banana slices, berries or cherries.
4. Grapefruit sections, unpared apple slices.
5. Peach slices, pear slices, halves of red plums.
6. Pineapple wedges, banana slices, strawberries.
7. Cooked dried fruit, white cherries, red raspberries.

Fruit and Vegetable Combinations

1. Shredded raw carrots, diced apples, raisins.
2. Sliced or ground cranberries, diced celery and apples, orange sections.
3. Thin cucumber slices, pineapple cubes.
4. Avocado and grapefruit sections, tomato slices.
5. Shredded cabbage, orange sections, crushed pineapple.

Vegetable Combinations

1. Grated carrots, diced celery, cucumber slices.
2. Spinach, endive, or lettuce, with tomato wedges.
3. Sliced raw cauliflower flowerets, chopped green pepper, celery, pimiento.
4. Shredded cabbage, cucumber cubes, slivers of celery.
5. Cubed cooked beets, thinly sliced celery, sweet onions.
6. Cooked whole-kernel corn and shredded snap beans, sweet pickles, onion rings.

SOUPS, SALADS, SAUCES, DRESSINGS

CAULIFLOWER SOUP

Ginny Anderson
X-tra X-amples

1 head cauliflower
1/2 c. chopped onion
1 pt. milk
3 or 4 stalks celery,
   chopped

1 pt. half and half
1/2 lb. cheese (Velveeta is good)
salt and pepper to taste

Separate cauliflower flowerettes. In small amount of water, cook celery, cauliflower and onions. Mash when cooked. Add half and half, milk and then cheese; stir until melted. (Better if made ahead of time and warmed to serve).

ANDES SHRIMP AND CORN MAIN DISH CHOWDER

Debby Fehringer
Hearth and Home

1/4 c. chopped green onions
1 small clove garlic, minced
1/8 tsp. cayenne pepper
1 Tbsp. butter

2 cans cream of potato soup
1 pkg. (3 oz.) cream cheese
1 1/2 soup cans of milk
2 c. frozen, cleaned raw shrimp
1-8 oz. can whole kernel corn

In saucepan, cook onions with garlic and pepper in butter until tender. Blend in soup, cream cheese and milk; add shrimp and corn. Bring to boil; reduce heat. Cover and simmer 10 minutes or until done. Stir occasionally. Makes about 7 cups.

CREAM OF POTATO SOUP

Judy Larson
Hearth and Home

4 large stalks celery
   and leaves
2 med. onions
1 1/2 c. water
1 1/2 c. mashed potatoes

1 Tbsp. butter
2 c. milk
dash of paprika
chopped chives or parsley

Chop celery and onions; add water and simmer 30 minutes. Strain through sieve (should be about 1 cup). Stir in bouillon cubes. While hot, pour over potatoes, stirring until they dissolve. Rub through strainer to make sure no lumps remain. Add butter, milk, and paprika and heat. Serve with chopped chives or parsley. Makes 4 to 6 servings.

CHUNKY TACO SOUP

Darlene Denton
X-tra X-amples X-tension Club

1 lb. ground meat
1/2 large chopped onion
2 1/2 c. water
1-16 oz. can stewed tomatoes,
   cut up

1-16 oz. can kidney beans
1-8 oz. can tomato sauce
1 env. taco seasoning mix
shredded cheddar cheese
   (for topping)

In large pan, brown meat and onion; until meat is brown and onion is tender; drain grease. Add all ingredients except cheese. Simmer, covered 15 to 20 minutes. Top each bowl with desired amount of cheese. Serves 6 to 7.
Note: This is an excellent base for "Hobo Stew" if your having a gathering or party of some kind, you can ask each person attending to bring one can of vegetables to add to the pot. This is a Mexican dish.

CHILI

Jill Distel
Creative Homemakers

1 lb. ground beef
1 c. chopped onion
2-15 1/2 oz. cans chili beans
1 can tomato soup

1/2 c. water
2 Tbsp. chili powder
1/2 tsp. salt
dash of pepper

Brown ground beef and onion in large heavy saucepan; pour off grease. Add remaining ingredients; cover and simmer 1 hour.

CANADIAN CHEESE SOUP

Alice E. Lindstrom
Kelly Women's Improvement Club

2 Tbsp. butter or oleo
2 Tbsp. chopped onion
2 Tbsp. flour
2 tsp. cornstarch
pinch of paprika
salt and pepper to taste

2 1/4 c. warm milk
2 1/4 c. chicken broth
1/3 c. cooked diced carrots
1/3 c. cooked diced celery
1/3 lb. cheese, grated
   (sharp, cheddar or American)

Melt butter or oleo. Add onions and saute until brown. Add flour, cornstarch, paprika, salt and pepper, stirring together. Add chicken broth and cook until thick. Add cooked vegetables. Just before serving, add warm milk and cheese. Heat to serving temperature. Makes 5 or 6 cups.

NEW ENGLAND CLAM CHOWDER

Rosabelle Smith
Kelly Woman's Improvement Club

2-7 or 7 1/2 oz. cans minced
  clams or equal amt. of
  baby clams
1/4 lb. salt pork
2 c. water
5 med. potatoes
1/2 c. chopped onion

2 c. milk
1 c. light cream
1 1/2 tsp. salt
1/4 tsp. pepper

Drain clams, reserving liquor. Fry salt pork till crisp in large saucepan. Remove and add water, potatoes, onion and reserved clam liquor to fat in the saucepan. Cook, covered, until potatoes are tender. Add milk, cream, clams, salt and pepper. Let steep for several minutes to blend flavors. Then serve with dabs of butter and salt pork floating on top.

COUNTRY STYLE HAM AND BEAN SOUP

Rosabelle Smith
Kelly Woman's Improvement Club

1 c. diced cooked ham
1/2 tsp. rubbed sage
2 Tbsp. butter or margarine
1-10 3/4 oz. can condensed
  chicken gumbo soup
1-10 3/4 oz. can condensed
  chicken and noodle soup

1 1/2 soup cans of water
1-10 oz. pkg. frozen mixed
  vegetables
1-15 1/2 oz. can kidney beans,
  drained

In a large saucepan, brown ham with sage in butter. Add remaining ingredients. Bring to boil; reduce heat. Simmer 10 minutes or until done, stirring occasionally. Makes about 4 servings.

SAUSAGE SOUP

Julie Sonnenberg
Southsiders

1 1/2 lbs. sausage
1 med. onion
1 can waxed beans
1 can green beans
1 can chile beans

1 can pork and beans
3/4 c. sugar
1-12 oz. can tomato paste
2 tsp. mustard

Fry sausage along with onion (grated); drain. Add all beans, sugar, tomato paste, mustard and enough water to make your favorite soup consistency. Simmer on low or cook in crock pot on low for 6 to 8 hours. (Can use brown sugar or molasses in place of sugar.)

POTATO CHEESE CHOWDER

Esther Nelson
Sterling Homemakers

2 c. diced potatoes
1/4 c. chopped onion
1 1/4 tsp. salt
2 c. boiling water
1/4 c. butter or margarine

1/4 c. flour
2 c. milk
2 c. grated shredded sharp
  cheddar cheese
2 1/2 tsp. worcestershire sauce

Combine potatoes, onion, salt and water in medium sized pan. Bring to boil; reduce heat and simmer, covered until potatoes are done. (Don't drain off liquid.)

In another medium sized pan, melt butter. Add flour. Cook over moderate heat, stirring a few minutes. Gradually add milk. Cook over moderate heat, stirring constantly until thickened. Remove from heat. Add cheese. Stir until cheese melts. Add vegetables and their cooking liquid and worcestershire sauce. Heat to serving temperature. Don't boil. Makes about 5 cups.

CORN CHOWDER

Mrs. Lorin Lindstrom
Kelly Woman's Improvement E.H.C.

4 c. hot water
3 c. diced raw peeled
  potatoes
2 c. creamed style corn
1 c. diced ham
1/2 c. diced onion

1/4 c. chopped celery and leaves
1/2 tsp. black pepper
1/4 c. chopped green pepper (opt.)
1 c. cream or rich milk

Cook potatoes and onion until tender. Add corn, ham, celery and leaves and green pepper. After the mixture is real hot and just before serving, stir in black pepper and milk.

SPAGHETTI SEASONING MIX

Patty Craven
Creative Homemakers

1 Tbsp. instant minced onion
1 Tbsp. parsley flakes
1 Tbsp. cornstarch
2 tsp. green pepper flakes
1 1/2 tsp. salt

1/4 tsp. instant minced garlic
1 tsp. sugar
3/4 tsp. Italian seasoning
  or combination of Italian herbs
  (oregano, basil, rosemary, thyme,
    sage, marjoram)

Combine all ingredients in a small bowl until evenly distribut-
Spoon mixture onto a 6 inch square of aluminum foil and fold to make air tight. Label. Store in a cool dry place. Use within 6 month
Makes 1 package (about 1/3 cup).

MINT SAUCE

Mildred Littler
Night Owls

1/2 c. sugar
1/2 c. water

2 Tbsp. crushed mint
juice of 1 lemon and 1 orange

Boil sugar and water for 5 minutes, then add crushed mint and juices.

MINT SAUCE

Amelia Vendegna
Pep and Progress

1/4 c. water
1/4 c. sugar

finely chopped mint
1/2 Tbsp. vinegar

Boil water and sugar a few minutes. Add vinegar. Let come to a boil then add mint leaves. Do not boil after mint leaves. have been added. Use sauce on lamb roast.

SPICY BARBECUE SAUCE

Janet Weingardt
Rainbows of Happiness

1 med. onion
1 tsp. salt
1 Tbsp. vinegar
1 Tbsp. brown sugar
1 Tbsp. worcestershire sauce

1/2 tsp. chili powder
1/4 tsp. black pepper
1/2 c. catsup
1/4 c. water

Combine all ingredients in a saucepan. Simmer 15 minutes, stirring 2 or 3 times. Good on barbecued spareribs, Swiss steak, barbecued chicken, hamburgers, etc.

CASSEROLE SAUCE MIX (IOWA)

Jan Nixon
Extension Home Economist

2 c. non fat dry milk
3/4 c. cornstarch
1/4 c. instant chicken bouillon
2 Tbsp. dried onion flakes

1 tsp. dried basil, crushed (opt.)
1 tsp. dried thyme, crushed (opt.)
1/2 tsp. pepper

Combine all ingredients; mix well. Store in airtight container. Makes 3 cups.
To use, combine 1/3 cup mix with 1 1/4 cup water. Cook and stir until thickened. If desired, add 1 tablespoon margarine. Use in place of canned soups in recipes.

MUSTARD SAUCE

Ginny Anderson
X-tra X-amples X-tension Club

3 eggs, beaten
1/2 c. mustard
1/2 c. sugar

1/2 c. tomato soup
1/2 c. vinegar
1/2 c. butter

Beat eggs in top of a double boiler, then add all the other ingredients. Cook over hot water until thick. This can also be made in the microwave. Cook on high power, stirring every 2 minutes until thick. This is great with ham.

LEMON SAUCE

Luverta Wilson
Sterling Homemakers

1 egg
1 Tbsp. water
3/4 c. sugar

1 Tbsp. lemon juice
1 tsp. vanilla

Boil one minute. Stir continually and watch carefully, it burns easily. Can add rum or brandy. Can be used on date or any pudding type cake.

BAKED PINEAPPLE

Thelma Davis
Sterling Homemakers

1-16 oz. can pineapple chunks
1 Tbsp. flour

2 Tbsp. butter
2/3 c. sugar

Drain pineapple. Make a sauce with pineapple juice that was drained from pineapple, flour, sugar and butter. Mix together well. Put pineapple in baking dish and pour over sauce.

Bake in 325° oven for 30 minutes. Serve warm with ham or turkey. Good over angel food cake also for a dessert.

MICROWAVE SPAGHETTI SAUCE

Patty Ament
Proctor

2 Tbsp. salad oil
1 1/2 lbs. ground beef
2 large onions, sliced
  or 2 Tbsp. dried onion flakes
3 cloves garlic, minced or
  1/2 tsp. garlic powder

1-15 oz. and 1-8 oz. can tomato
  sauce
1-6 oz. can tomato paste
3 tsp. chili powder
1 tsp. salt
1 tsp. sugar

Combine all ingredients in a 3 quart casserole. Cover with plastic wrap; leaving a 2 inch vent. Microwave at high for 20 to 25 minutes, stirring every 8 minutes. Serve over cooked spaghetti.

Pass the grated Parmesan cheese and garlic toast. Makes 6 generous servings.

BLUE CHEESE SALAD DRESSING

Lillian Sitarski
Highland Lassies

1 can cream of celery soup	3 eggs
1/8 c. white vinegar	1 tsp. dry mustard
1 tsp. sugar	1 1/2 c. salad oil
1/4 tsp. salt	8 Tbsp. sour cream
1-4 oz. pkg. bleu cheese	dash of cayenne

In blender combine soup, vinegar, eggs and seasonings. Add the oil. Gradually stir the basic dressing into the sour cream. Add the bleu cheese. Chill and serve on salad greens or vegetable salads.

FRENCH DRESSING

Connie Lechman
Proctor E.H. Club

1 c. Mazola Oil	1 c. sugar
1/2 c. vinegar	1 can tomato soup
1 tsp. dry mustard	1 tsp. salt
1 tsp. paprika	1 small onion
1 small green pepper	

Put all ingredients in a quart jar. Shake well. Refrigerate.

SALAD DRESSING

Lakie Taylor (deceased)
Kelly Woman's Improvement Club

butter (1/2 size of an egg)	1/2 c. sugar
1 heaping Tbsp. flour	1 egg
1 c. boiling water	1/4 tsp. dry mustard
2/3 c. vinegar	1/4 tsp. pepper

Melt butter and stir in flour. Add water and vinegar, beaten egg and sugar and spices. Bring to boil, stirring constantly.

This is very good when mixed half and half with a commercial dressing and used on potato salad or cabbage.

PISTACHIO SALAD

Emma Acre
Pep and Progress

-9 ox. tub Cool Whip	1 lb. can crushed pineapple
box instant pistachio pudding	1 c. miniature marshmallows
c. milk	chopped nuts

Prepare the pudding mix with 1 cup milk. Add marshmallows, pineapple, nuts and Cool Whip. Refrigerate until set.

PISTACHIO-NUT FRUIT SALAD

Judy Larson
Hearth and Home

1 pkg. Jell-0 pistachio
  pudding
1 c. nuts
1 c. marshmallows

1 #303 can crushed pineapple
  with juice
1-9 oz. Cool Whip

Combine and refrigerate 1/2 hour.

WATERGATE SALAD

Esther Nelson
Sterling Homemakers

1-20 oz. can crushed pineapple
1-3 1/2 oz. box instant
 pistachio pudding mix
1-9 oz. tub non dairy
  whipped topping

1 c. miniature marshmallows
1/2 c. finely chopped pecans
  or walnuts

Drain pineapple and reserve syrup. Place pudding mix in large bowl. Add about 4 tablespoons of the pineapple juice or enough to make a soft paste (and pudding mix turns bright green); mix well. Add drained pineapple, whipped topping, marshmallows and chopped nuts. Mix well until mixture is fluffy and increases in volume. Refrigerate until thoroughly chilled. Serve as a salad or dessert. Makes 8 or more servings.

EASY FRUIT SALAD

Emma Acre
Pep and Progress

1 large can fruit cocktail
1 can mandarin oranges

2 c. miniature marshmallows
1 c. sour cream

Drain the fruit cocktail and oranges. Mix all ingredients together. Refrigerate 2 hours before serving.

CHRISTMAS CRANBERRY SALAD

Ruth Reed
Padroni E.H.

4 apples
1/2 lb. miniature marshmallows
1 pt. heavy cream, whipped

1 lb. cranberries
2 c. sugar

Core apples; do not peel. Put apples and cranberries through coarse food grinder. Combine with marshmallows and sugar; refrigerate overnight. Fold in whipped cream. Serve.

WHITE CHRISTMAS SALAD

Cheryl Monheiser
X-tra X-amples X-tension Club

1/4 tsp. dry mustard
1/2 c. milk
4 well beaten egg yolks
juice of one lemon
1 pt. whipped cream or
  1-8 oz. tub Cool Whip

1 lb. red grapes, seeded
1 small can crushed pineapple
1 c. pecans

Add mustard to milk and heat to boiling point. Pour slowly into egg yolks. Cook mixture until it makes a thick custard. When cool, add lemon juice, then whipped cream. Then add marshmallows, grapes, pineapple and nuts. Chill overnight.

PINK SALAD

Sandy Schneider
Hearth and Home

1 can Eagle Brand sweetened
  condensed milk (8 oz.)
1-9 oz. tub Cool Whip
1-21 oz. can cherry pie filling

1 can pineapple tidbits
1 can mandarin oranges
2 c. miniature marshmallows

Beat milk and Cool Whip together. Stir in pie filling. Add rest of the ingredients and refrigerate. Make sure fruits are drained well.

CRANBERRY SALAD

Emma Acre
Pep and Progress

1 small can crushed pineapple
1 lb. cranberries
1 1/2 c. sugar

1 pt. whipping cream, whipped
1 bag small marshmallows

Grind cranberries. Add sugar, pineapple and marshmallows. Stir in whipped cream.

FRUIT SALAD

Bertha Luft
Pep and Progress

2 c. cooked spaghetti
 (small, measure before cooking)
6 apples, peeled and cut fine
1 #2 can pineapple tidbits
2 c. Dream Whip

Sauce:
1/2 c. lemon juice
2 c. powdered sugar
4 eggs, beaten
 (cook until thick,)

(Cont.)

Cool sauce and add to salad. Add 2 cups prepared Dream Whip before serving.

FRUIT SALAD

Lena Cummins
Shamrock

1 can strawberry pie filling
  (cherry is good too)
1 can crushed pineapple (#303)

1 can Eagle Brand milk
1 large Cool Whip
pecans

Mix all together. Freeze or refrigerate overnight.

TWENTY FOUR HOUR SALAD

Luverta Wilson
Sterling Homemakers

1 lb. marshmallows
1-1 lb. 4 oz. large can
  pineapple tidbits
1 lb. white or red grapes,
  halved and seeded

juice of 2 lemons
4 egg yolks
1 1/2 c. (approx.) whipped
  cream or Dream Whip

Cook egg yolks, lemon juice to custard; cool. Fold in rest of ingredients. Refrigerate and let stand for about 24 hours.

QUICK FRUIT SALAD

Pam Clark
X-tra X-amples X-tension Club

1 small carton cottage cheese
1 small carton Cool Whip
1 small can mandarin oranges,
  drained

1 small can chunk pineapple
  drained
1 small size box orange jello
  (dry)

Mix together and refrigerate for 1 hour before serving.

FRUIT COCKTAIL SALAD

Gail Wagner
Pep and Progress

1-2 1/2 can fruit cocktail
1 small pkg. lemon jello
3/4 c. boiling water
2-3 oz. pkgs. cream cheese

8 large or 1 c. small marshmallows
1 c. whipped cream or Cool Whip

Drain fruit cocktail. Boil water and fruit juice; add jello. Stir in cream cheese and marshmallows until smooth. Cool in refrigerator until slightly set. Add fruit and Cool Whip. Chill.

FRUIT SALAD

Nora Karg
Shamrock

1-16 oz. can fruit cocktail
1 can mandarin oranges
1 med. can pineapple tidbits

1/2 c. coconut
3 oz. box lemon instant pudding

Mix together undrained fruit and fold in coconut. Sprinkle in pudding. Refrigerate. Just before serving, add one chopped large banana.

AMBROSIA

Irene Golgart
Kelly Woman's Improvement Club

1-8 1/2 oz. can pineapple tidbits
1-11 oz. can mandarin oranges
1-17 oz. can fruit cocktail, undrained
2 or 3 bananas

2 Tbsp. lemon juice
1/2 c. flaked coconut
1 large box instant lemon pudding mix

Into a large bowl, combine undrained pineapple, cocktail, mandarin oranges, lemon juice and coconut. Mix and put into a 9x12 inch pan. Sprinkle the pudding mix over this mixture and toss lightly. Chill until set. Just before serving cube the bananas and add to the above mixture and stir slightly. Serve in sherbet glasses. Put whipped topping on top and add a slice of orange for garnish.

FROZEN SALAD

Nell Berdine Druyff
Sterling Homemakers

8 oz. pkg. cream cheese
2 1/2 Tbsp. milk
1 tsp. vanilla

1 c. powdered sugar
1 large can fruit cocktail, drained
1 small bottle maraschino cherries, drained

Cream the cheese, milk, vanilla, powdered sugar together and add cocktail and cherries. Line bread pan with foil and pour in salad. Cover with foil and freeze. After frozen can remove from pan and slice off desired servings. Keep remainder frozen.

HOLIDAY SALAD DESSERT

Dorothy A Harms
Home Hustlers

1-3 to 3 5/8 oz. pkg. vanilla pudding and pie filling
1 3/4 c. milk
1-11 oz. can mandarin oranges, drained

1-15 1/4 oz. can pineapple chunks or tidbits, drained
1 c. halved sweet grapes
2 c. miniature marshmallows

17   (Cont.)

1 1/2 to 2 c. whipped cream
   topping

10 to 12 halved
   maraschino cherries

    Use 2 quart microwave cooking bowl. Combine pudding mix and milk. Cook on high until just boiling, stirring at one minute intervals. Let stand until cool. Gently fold in whipped cream or dairy topping and mix only to blend. Add all the fruits and marsh-mallows, gently mixing just enough to coat all. Fold in cherries last with only one or two motions. Cover and refrigerate for at least 12 hours. (Various fruits can be used in this, including bananas, fruit cocktail, canned peaches, etc.) Especially good as filling for Cream Puffs.

CIRCUS PEANUT SALAD

Katherine Kalinowski
Sterling Homemakers

14 pieces Circus Peanut
  candy
1-3 oz. pkgs. orange gelatin
2 c. hot water
1-1 lb. 4 1/2 oz. can
  crushed pineapple, drained
    (save the juice)

2 c. celery, chopped fine
1/2 c. chopped nuts
1 small tub whipped topping

    Melt and dissolve Circus Peanut candies in hot water and add gelatin. Measure pineapple juice and add cold water to make 2 cups. Add to gelatin mixture. Chill until partially set. Add pineapple, celery and nuts; stir well. Fold in whipped topping. Put in 9x13 inch pan and refrigerate.

CIRCUS PEANUT SALAD

Nora Karg
Shamrock

15 Circus Peanuts (candy)
1-3 oz. pkg. orange jello

1 can pineapple, crushed
1 pkg. prepared Dream Whip

    Dissolve Circus Peanuts and jello in 1 cup boiling water; drain juice from pineapple and add enough cold water to make one cup. Chill. Add Dream Whip and let set. Serve.

ORANGE TAPIOCA SALAD

Barb Schaefer, Home Hustlers
Julie Schaefer, X-tra X-amples X-tension Club

2-3 oz. pkgs. tapioca pudding
1-3 oz. pkg. orange jello
1 can mandarin oranges

3 c. boiling water
1-8 oz. tub Cool Whip

Cook pudding in water until thick. Stir in jello and cool. Before it chills too firm, add oranges and Cool Whip.
Note: Strawberry jello and strawberries may be substituted for oranges.

ORANGE DELIGHT

Kenda Stoltenberg
Padroni E.H.

1 small pkg. instant vanilla pudding
1 small pkg. orange jello

1 small pkg. tapioca pudding

Add 2 cups warm tap water and bring to boil for 5 minutes. Let cool and then add one can of drained mandarin oranges and 9 ounce tub Cool Whip.

ORANGE SALAD

Lena Cummins, Shamrock
Esther Pace, Night Owls Club

1 small can mandarin oranges
1 small can pineapple tidbits
1 1/2 c. mini-marshmallows
small tub Cool Whip

1 small pkg. orange jello
1 pkg. instant vanilla pudding
1 pkg. vanilla tapioca pudding

Drain liquid from fruits and add water to equal 2 1/4 cups. In pan, combine jello and puddings. Add liquid and bring to a full boil. Remove from heat. Add marshmallows. Stir until dissolved. Let cool, about 30 to 45 minutes in freezer is usually ok. Add fruit and Cool Whip (one or two sliced bananas can also be added at this time if desired.) Refrigerate until completely set. Also good as a dessert.

STRAWBERRY SUPREME

Vickie Lehmkuh
X-tra X-amples X-tension Club

1-6 oz. pkg. strawberry jello
2 mashed bananas
2 c. boiling water

1-10 oz. pkg. frozen strawberries
1-12 oz. carton sour cream

Dissolve jello in boiling water. Add frozen strawberries; mix in the bananas. Pour half the jello mixture into a 9x13 inch dish. Refrigerate until set. Keep the other half of jello mixture soft on counter. When the jello in the pan is set, spread on the sour cream over the set jello. Pour the other half of jello mixture over sour cream and return to refrigerator and let set a couple hours. Makes 12 servings.

EASY FRUIT SALAD

Juanita Pyle
Proctor E.H. Club

1 pkg. instant vanilla or lemon
    pudding
2 or 3 bananas

1 c. fruit cocktail
any other fruit, if desired

Mix up pudding as directed on package. Drain fruit cocktail and add to the pudding. Slice the bananas and add them to the mixture. You may add any other fruit, canned or fresh, or you may serve as is. Double this recipe according to the amount of people you are serving.

PARTY JELLO SALAD

Lorene Freemon
Southsiders

2-3 oz. pkgs. orange jello
1 small can crushed pineapple
2 2/3 c. hot water

1-6 oz. can frozen orange juice
2 small cans mandarin oranges,
    drained

Dissolve jello in hot water; add frozen orange juice. Stir until dissolved. Let cool. Add pineapple and oranges. Pour in 9x13 inch pan and let set until firm.

BLUEBERRY SALAD

Shirley Herzog
Padroni E.H.

2-3 oz. pkgs. black cherry gelatin
2 c. boiling water
1 c. sour cream

1-15 oz. can wild blueberries,
    reserve 1/2 c. juice
1-3 1/4 oz. can crushed
    pineapple and juice

Dissolve gelatin in hot water; add blueberry juice and 8 ice cubes. When partially set, add blueberries and pineapple. Gently swirl sour cream throughout mixture. Refrigerate in 8 inch pan. Serves 8 to 10.

CHERRY SALAD

Olive Myers
Sterling Homemakers

1 pkg. cherry jello
1 c. hot water
1 can cherry pie filling

1-3 oz. pkg. cream cheese
1-8 oz. can crushed pineapple,
    slightly drained

Dissolve jello in hot water; add pie filling and let set. Top with cream cheese and crushed pineapple, slightly drained, and whipped together.

KRAVEMORE SALAD

Nora Karg
Shamrock

3/4 c. hot water
1-3 oz. pkg. lime jello
1-3 oz. pkg. Phila. cream cheese
1 pkg. prepared Dream Whip

1/2 c. chopped pecans
1/2 c. chopped celery
10 maraschino cherries
1 small can crushed pineapple

Dissolve jello and cream cheese in the hot water until cheese melts. Add pecans, celery, cherries and pineapple. Fold in Dream Whip and refrigerate.

CHEESE AND PINEAPPLE SALAD

Carol Atkin
Home Hustlers

1-8 oz. can crushed pineapple
1/2 c. sugar
1 env. gelatin

1 c. shredded American cheese
1 c. cream, whipped

Drain pineapple; reserve syrup. Mix sugar and gelatin together. Add hot water to syrup to make 3/4 cup. Add to sugar mixture. Heat till dissolved. Chill till partially set. Add pineapple and cheese. Fold in whipped cream.

SALAD

Werdna Montgomery
Shamrock

1-3 oz. pkg. lemon jello
1-3 oz. pkg. lime jello
2 c. hot water
1 can crushed pineapple
   (16 oz., undrained)

1 carton small curd cottage
   cheese
1 can Eagle Brand milk
1 c. Miracle Whip salad
   dressing
1 tsp. horseradish
1 c. nuts

Combine the first 4 ingredients and let set until it begins to thicken. Then add the remaining ingredients.

PINEAPPLE CHEESE MOLD SALAD

Opal Vance
Sterling Homemakers

3 oz. pkg. lime flavored
   gelatin
1 c. boiling water
1 c. evap. milk
1 c. cottage cheese

1 lb. 4 1/2 oz. can crushed pineapple,
   well drained
1/2 c. mayonnaise
1/4 c. chopped celery
1/4 c. chopped nuts (opt.)

(Cont.)

Dissolve gelatin in boiling water. Stir in evaporated milk, cottage cheese, crushed pineapple, mayonnaise, chopped celery, and chopped nuts. Chill until firm or overnight. Makes 8 servings.

EMERALD SALAD

Marlene Allen
Padroni E.H.

1-3 oz. pkg. lime jello
1/2 c. chopped walnuts
1 c. whipped cream

1/2 c. cottage cheese
1 c. crushed pineapple
1 c. boiling water

Dissolve jello in boiling water. Add cottage cheese. Chill until slightly thickened. Add remaining ingredients. Chill until firm.

SPRING WHIP

Helen Vaughn
Padroni E.H.

1-3 oz. pkg. orange jello
1 c. orange and pineapple
    juice
3 Tbsp. sugar
1 small can crushed pineapple,
    drained

1 c. hot water
1/2 c. whipped cream
2 sliced bananas
1/2 c. chopped nuts (opt.)

Mix jello, water and juice and let stand until syrupy. Whip cream with sugar, then add to jello and whip together. Add bananas, pineapple and nuts. Pour into angel food cake pan or square pan of jello mold.

YUM YUM SALAD

Helen Vaughn
Padroni E.H.

1-3 oz. pkg. lemon jello
1 c. crushed pineapple
1 c. grated American cheese
1 c. whipped cream

1 c. cold water
1 c. sugar
1 c. nuts

Dissolve jello in 1 cup cold water. Cook crushed pineapple and sugar until a thread is spun. Mix the two mixtures together. Cool until it has consistency of soft jelly. Add grated cheese, nuts and whipped cream.

SUNNY WHIP SALAD

Janet Kloberdanz
X-tra X-amples X-tension Club

1 pkg. orange jello
1 c. boiling water

3/4 c. cold orange juice

Dissolve jello in boiling water. Then add orange juice. Chill until slightly set. Then whip at low until fluffy and doubled in volume. Chill until set. Perfect on a hot summer day!

CRYSTAL SALAD

Mabel Karg
Southsiders

1-3 oz. pkg. lemon jello
1/2 c. pineapple juice
1/2 c. salad dressing
1/2 c. diced celery
6 marshmallows, cut fine

1 1/4 c. hot water
1/2 c. whipping cream, whipped
1/2 c. diced pineapple,
    drained
1/2 c. diced apples, unpeeled

Dissolve gelatin in hot water, adding pineapple juice. When it begins to congeal, fold in whipped cream. Combine remaining ingredients and fold into gelatin mixture. Chill until firm. Serves 10.

GREEN PINEAPPLE SALAD

Mrs. Lorin Lindstrom
Serves 10 to 12   Kelly Woman's Improvement Extension H.C.

2 pkgs. lime flavored gelatin
2 c. hot pineapple juice
    and water
1-8 oz. pkg. cream cheese
1/2 c. chopped pecans

1 c. chopped celery
1 c. crushed pineapple
1 small jar pimento, chopped

Dissolve gelatin in hot liquid. Stir until dissolved. When cooled to warm, blend in the cream cheese. Stir until smooth. When cool add pineapple, celery, pecans and pimento. At last, fold 1 cup whipped cream. Top with 1/2 cup mayonnaise with some of the dissolved gelatin mixture.

RED SALAD

Sadie Slice
Shamrock

1 pkg. cranberries
2 large apples
1 small can pineapple
2 c. sugar

1 large pkg. lemon jello
2 c. hot water
1/2 lb. marshmallows
1/2 c. walnuts

Grind cranberries and peeled apples together. Mix in 2 cups

23   (Cont.)

sugar and pineapple and let stand. Mix lemon jello and 2 cups hot water; stir in marshmallows until melted. Mix both mixtures together and add nuts (chopped); chill. A good salad to serve with turkey or pork.

STRAWBERRY BAVARIAN CREAM

Debbie Breidenbach
Hearth and Home

1-10 oz. pkg. frozen
  strawberries
1 c. boiling water

1-3 oz. pkg. strawberry gelatin
1 c. chilled whipped cream or
  1 env. Dream Whip

Drain strawberries; reserve syrup. Pour boiling water over gelatin and stir until dissolved. Add enough cold water to syrup to make 1 cup. Stir into dissolved gelatin. Chill until almost set.

In chilled bowl, beat cream until stiff. Beat gelatin until foamy. Fold gelatin and strawberries into cream. Pour into 1 quart mold. Chill until firm. Garnish with whipped cream and strawberries. Serves 6 to 8 people.

CRANBERRY CRUNCH SALAD

Dorothy Smith
Kelly Woman's Improvement Club

1 large pkg. raspberry jello
2 c. boiling water
1 c. cold water
2 Tbsp. lemon juice

1 2/3 c. whole cranberry sauce
  (1 lb. can)
1 c. sliced celery
1/2 c. chopped pecans

Dissolve jello in hot water; add cold water and lemon juice. When thickened, add other ingredients. Pour into a 2 quart mold. Chill.

CRANBERRY SALAD

Luverta Wilson
Sterling Homemakers

2 small pkgs. cherry jello
2 c. hot water
1 c. pineapple juice
1 c. sugar
2 c. ground cranberries

1 orange, ground
1 c. drained pineapple
1 c. celery or apples
1/2 c. walnuts
1 tsp. lemon juice

Dissolve jello and sugar in hot water. Add pineapple juice, then rest of ingredients when partially set.

RASPBERRY SALAD

Norma Penner
Rainbows of Happiness

1 pkg. raspberry jello
1 c. hot water
1 pkg. frozen raspberries

1-16 oz. can applesauce
1 c. sour cream
2 c. small marshmallows

24

Prepare first 4 ingredients and let set. Top with sour cream and marshmallows.

CINNAMON APPLE CHEESE SALAD — Alice E. Lindstrom
Kelly Women's Improvement Club

1-3 oz. pkg. lemon jello
1/2 c. red cinnamon candies
1 c. boiling water
1 1/2 c. applesauce

8 oz. cream cheese
1/2 c. chopped nuts
1/2 c. fine cut celery
1/2 c. salad dressing

Dissolve red cinnamon candies in boiling water, then add lemon jello. Stir until dissolved. Add the applesauce and mix. Divide in two equal parts. Let one part set until jelled. Mix the cream cheese, chopped nuts, celery and salad dressing and when the jello is set firm. spread cheese mixture on top. Add remaining jello as the third layer and let set until firm.

STRAWBERRY-BANANA SALAD — Lena Cummins
Shamrock

1-3 oz. pkg. strawberry jello
1 c. boiling water
1 pkg. frozen strawberries

1-3 oz. pkg. cream cheese
2 small bananas
1 c. whipped cream or
    Cool Whip

Pour boiling water on jello and stir. Add strawberries and let stand until it starts to congeal. Mix whipped cream and cheese together. Add bananas to jello. Add cream mixture and mold in a 9x9 inch flat dish and refrigerate. Different kinds of jello and fruits can be substituted.

CRANBERRY WALDORF SALAD — Alice Folladori
Proctor

2 c. cranberry juice cocktail,
    divided
1-3 oz. pkg. lemon jello
1/4 tsp. salt
1 c. chopped apple

1/2 c. chopped celery
1/4 c. chopped pecans or
    walnuts
1/3 c. mayonnaise
2-3 oz. pkgs. cream cheese

Bring to boil 1 cup juice. Add jello; stir until dissolved. Stir in salt and remaining 1 cup juice; chill. Combine cream cheese and mayonnaise, then blend until smooth. Add remaining ingredents with jello mixture and chill until firm.

25

STRAWBERRY 'NANA SALAD

Lillian Sitarski
Highland Lassies

1-3 oz. pkg. strawberry gelatin
1-8 oz. can crushed pineapple
  (with juice)
1 ripe banana, sliced

1/2 c. boiling water
1-10 oz. pkg. frozen
  strawberries

Dissolve gelatin in boiling water. Add crushed pineapple, strawberries and banana. Pour into mold and refrigerate until set.

FROSTED SALAD

Helen Fahringer
Hearth and Home

2 pkgs. lemon jello
2 c. hot water
2 c. 7-Up
1 #2 can pineapple

1 c. marshmallows
2 bananas
2 oranges

Mix together ingredients for salad, saving juice from pineapple. Boil together ingredients in the frosting and let cool.

FROSTED JELLO

Alice Folladori
Proctor

1-6 oz. pkg. orange jello
2 c. boiling water
1 c. cold water
1 env. unflavored gelatin

1-6 oz. can frozen orange
  juice, thawed and
  undiluted
1 small can mandarin oranges,
  drained
1 #2 can crushed pineapple,
  drained

Dissolve orange gelatin in boiling water. Soften unflavored gelatin in cold water. Heat at low temperature, stirring until unflavored gelatin is dissolved. Add to orange gelatin. Stir in orange juice until thickened. Add oranges and pineapple. Chill until set. Frost with Cooked Dressing.

Cooked Dressing:

1/2 c. sugar
1 c. mixed fruit juices
  (orange and pineapple)
3 Tbsp. flour

2 Tbsp. butter
1 egg, well beaten
1/2 pt. heavy cream
grated cheddar cheese

Mix together sugar and flour in top of double boiler. Stir in egg and fruit juices. Cook over boiling water, stirring until thickened. Stir in butter; cool. Whip cream until stiff. Fold cream into cooked mixture and frost jello. Sprinkle grated cheese over top.

LIME-PEAR DELITE
Serves 8

Yvonne Davidson
Night Owls

1-3 oz. pkg. lime jello
1 large can pear, chopped
12 oz. cream cheese

1 pkg. Dream Whip
3/4 c. coconut (opt.)
1/2 c. chopped nuts (opt.)

Dissolve jello in hot pear juice adding enough water to make 1 3/4 cup. Add softened cream cheese; beat with mixer to melt cheese. Cool to a light thickness, add chilled diced pears, nuts and coconut. Fold in whipped Dream Whip. Chill.

TRIPLE ORANGE AMBROSIA SALAD

Fran Hofmann
Hearth and Home

2 c. boiling liquid (water)
1-6 oz. pkg. orange jello
1 pt. orange sherbet
1 c. dairy sour cream

2-11 oz. cans mandarin
    oranges, drained
1-13 1/2 oz. can pineapple
    chunks, drained
1 c. flaked coconut
1 c. miniature marshmallows

Pour boiling liquid over jello in bowl; stir until dissolved. Add sherbet and stir till melted. Stir in 1 can of orange segments; pour into 6 cup ring mold. Chill until firm.

Combine remaining orange segments, pineapple, coconut and marshmallows; fold in sour cream. Chill at least 3 hours. Fill center of unmolded salad with fruit mixture.

DESSERT SALAD

Rachel Schuppe
Proctor

1-3 oz. pkg. lemon jello
1 #2 can crushed pineapple
1-3 oz. pkg. Phila. cream cheese
1/2 c. water
1 Tbsp. pimento (opt.)

1 c. diced celery
1 c. chopped walnuts
1 small env. Dream Whip
Miracle Whip to taste

Drain pineapple and heat juice, adding water. Dissolve jello in hot juice. Soften cheese in a little milk and add to jello. Cool. Add pimento if desired. Add remaining ingredients and chill.

TABOULI

Mary May
Hearth and Home

3/4 c. bulgar
1/2 bunch green onions,
   chopped
2 tomatoes

1 cucumber, finely chopped
1 c. chopped parsley
salt and pepper
chopped mint

Rinse bulgar and drain. Squeeze out excess water. Add all ingredients. Add 1/2 cup lemon juice and 1/2 cup olive oil and mix.

GLORIFIED RICE SALAD

Nell Berdine Druyff
Sterling Homemakers

2/3 c. Minute rice
1/2 c. water
1/4 c. pineapple juice
1/2 tsp. salt
1 small tub whipped topping

1/2 bag miniature marshmallows
6 diced maraschino cherries
3/4 c. crushed pineapple
1 diced banana (opt.)

Combine in saucepan the rice, water, pineapple juice and salt . Bring to boil; cover and simmer 3 minutes. Remove from heat and let stand 10 minutes. Add marshmallows, cherries, pineapple and banana. Fold in whipped topping into rice mixture and chill.

MAKE AHEAD TANGY SWEET MACARONI SALAD

Glennis Lechman
Sterling Homemakers

1/2 c. sugar
1/2 c. mayonnaise
1/4 c. vinegar
2 small scallions or
  green onions and some tops

1-7 oz. pkg. small macaroni
chopped green peppers
chopped hard boiled eggs
chopped pimento

Mix well with wire whisk the sugar and mayonnaise. Add vinegar and mix till it no longer looks curdled. Stir in scallions. Cook macaroni according to directions. While warm, add dressing and mix well. Refrigerate covered about 24 hours. Let salad stand at room temperature about 30 minutes before serving. Just before serving, add egg, pepper and pimento to taste.

MACARONI CHEESE TOSS

Mrs. Walter Browner
Sterling Homemakers

1/2 lb. (2 c.) small
  shell roni
3 Tbsp. clear French dressing
3 hard boiled eggs, chopped
1 c. cubed sharp cheddar
  cheese (1/4" cubes)
1 c. drained canned peas
1/2 c. chopped celery

1/4 c. chopped green onion
1/3 c. salad dressing
1 Tbsp. prepared mustard
1 1/2 tsp. horseradish
1/2 tsp. worcestershire sauce
salt and pepper to taste

Cook macaroni in boiling water until tender; drain and cool. Pour French dressing over macaroni and set aside.

Combine cheese, vegetables and chopped eggs. Blend mayonnaise, horseradish, mustard and seasoning. Pour over cheese mixture. Add macaroni and toss to mix. Chill. Serves 8 to 10.

MACARONI SALAD

Janet Weingardt
Rainbows of Happiness

2 c. shell macaroni,
  cooked
6 hard cooked eggs
1 small onion, chopped
1 c. Miracle Whip
1/2 c. pickle relish

1 Tbsp. vinegar
1 tsp. prepared mustard
1 tsp. salt
1/4 tsp. pepper

Combine cooked macaroni and chopped eggs and onion. Mix Miracle Whip, pickle relish, vinegar, mustard, salt and pepper. Pour over macaroni mixture and mix well. Chill.

TUNA VEGETABLE MOLD

Eva Korrey
Rainbows of Happiness

1-3 oz. box lemon flavored
  gelatin
2 Tbsp. vinegar
2 Tbsp. minced onion
1/2 tsp. salt
1-6 1/2 to 7 oz. can tuna,
  drained and flaked

3/4 c. diced celery
3/4 c. diced carrots
1/4 c. diced sweet pickle
salad greens
mayonnaise

Dissolve gelatin in 1 cup hot water. Add 1 cup cold water, vinegar, onion and salt; chill until thickened, but not firm. Fold in tuna, celery, carrots and sweet pickle. Pour into 1 to 1 1/2 quart mold and chill until firm. Unmold on salad greens and serve with mayonnaise. Makes 4 to 6 servings.

TUNA-MACARONI SALAD CUP

Charlotte Lambrecht
Rainbows of Happiness

1 c. elbow macaroni
2 hard cooked eggs,
  chopped
1/4 c. chopped celery
2 Tbsp. chopped green pepper
1 tsp. minced onion
1/4 c. chopped sweet pickle
1-7 oz. can tuna, flaked

1/2 c. mayonnaise
1 Tbsp. prepared mustard
1/2 tsp. salt
1/4 tsp. pepper

Cook macaroni in boiling salted water until tender; drain and rinse. Mix macaroni with remaining ingredients and refrigerate. Press salad into a 1 cup measuring cup to mold. Unmold and serve on a lettuce leaf. Serves 6.

CHICKEN SALAD ORIENTAL

Elma Dickinson
Sterling Homemakers

3 c. diced, skinned,
  cooked chicken
1 c. drained pineapple tidbits
2 Tbsp. sliced onion
1-5 oz. can water chestnuts,
  drained and sliced
3/4 c. dairy sour cream

1 tsp. ground ginger
1/2 tsp. salt
pepper to taste
lettuce
1/2 c. toasted slivered almonds
chopped pimento, to taste

In large bowl, mix together chicken, pineapple, onions and water chestnuts. Refrigerate mixture covered until chilled. Thoroughly stir together sour cream, ginger, salt and pepper. Mix lightly but thoroughly. Serve salad on lettuce. Sprinkle with almonds and pimento. Makes 4 to 6 servings.

CHICKEN SALAD

Lakie Taylor (deceased)
Kelly Woman's Improvement Club

1 chicken, cooked and cubed
1 bunch celery, sliced
1 c. chopped nuts

6 hard cooked eggs
1 #2 can ripe olives
1 pt. homemade salad
    dressing

Mix ingredients well and refrigerate for several hours to allow flavors to blend. Serve on a lettuce leaf with crackers, rolls or hot biscuits.

SHRIMP MOLD

Lorraine Johnston
Home Hustlers

1 can tomato soup
1 pkg. gelatin
1/2 c. cold water
1-8 oz. pkg. cream cheese
1 c. mayonnaise
1/2 c. each chopped onion,
  celery and green pepper

1 can small shrimp
1 can crab
1 can lobster or use
  2 cans shrimp
1 can tuna

Heat soup to boiling point. Add gelatin. Mix cheese and mayonnaise. Add to soup and beat with beater until cool. Add vegetables and fish. Refrigerate until firm. Serve with crackers.

TROPICAL CHICKEN SALAD

Mrs. Oscar Marks
Harding Extension H.C.

4 c. diced cooked chicken
8 slices pineapple
2 c. chopped celery
1 tsp. salt

4 Tbsp. lemon juice
2/3 c. mayonnaise
4 bananas, diced

Mix chicken, diced pineapple and chopped celery with mayonnaise and salt. Refrigerate until ready to serve, then add diced bananas that have marinated in lemon juice. Serves 12 to 16.
Note: Recipe submitted by Mrs. Lorin Lindstrom.

MEAT SALAD

Bette McBride
Proctor

1-3 oz. pkg. lemon jello
3/4 c. mayonnaise
1 c. corned beef
1 c. diced celery
3 hard cooked eggs, chopped

1 c. consomme soup
2 Tbsp. lemon juice
1 tsp. worcestershire sauce

Heat soup and jello. Cool until slightly set. Combine remaining ingredients and stir into jello.

CHICKEN AND RICE SALAD

Thelma Davis
Sterling Homemakers

1 1/2 c. cooked rice
1 1/2 c. cooked cubed chicken
1/3 c. diced onion
1/3 c. chopped green pepper
1 1/2 c. chopped celery

2 Tbsp. salad oil
1 tsp. curry powder
3/4 c. salad dressing
1 Tbsp. vinegar

(Cont.)

Toss together lightly in bowl all ingredients except salad dressing. Cover and chill 3 to 4 hours. Just before serving, blend in salad dressing.

HOT CHICKEN SALAD
Judy Armstrong
Southsiders

4 c. cooked chicken, cubed
1 c. diced celery
1 tsp. minced onion
1 can cream of mushroom soup, undiluted
3/4 c. mayonnaise

1 c. milk
1-8 oz. can water chestnuts, sliced
2 c. cooked rice
1 Tbsp. lemon juice
3 hard cooked eggs, diced

Mix milk, mayonnaise and soup. Add to rest of ingredients. Put into 9x13 inch casserole. Top with 1 cup crushed corn flakes and 1/2 cup slivered almonds (optional). Mix almonds in 1/4 cup melted butter. Bake at 350° for 35 to 40 minutes.

HOT CHICKEN SALAD
Nona Amen

2 c. cooked cubed chicken
2 c. sliced celery
3/4 c. mayonnaise
1 pkg. slivered almonds
1 onion, chopped

2 Tbsp. lemon juice
1/2 tsp. Accent
1/2 tsp. salt
1/2 c. shredded cheese
1 c. crushed potato chips

Combine everything. Bake at 350° for 30 minutes. You can add potato chips to the top also.

HOT CHICKEN SALAD
Rosabelle Smith
Kelly Woman's Improvement Club

1 whole chicken, cooked and cubed
2 cans cream of chicken soup
1 small jar pimento
6 hard cooked eggs
1/4 tsp. celery salt

4 tsp. chopped onion
2 tsp. lemon juice
1 c. mayonnaise
4 c. crushed potato chips (save some for topping)

Mix together and put into a 9x12 inch baking pan. Sprinkle reserved chips on top. Bake in a 400° oven for 30 minutes.

TACO SALAD (MICROWAVE)   Kathy Martinez

1 lb. ground beef
1 med. onion, chopped
1-15 oz. can kidney beans,
  drained
1/2 c. water
1-1 1/4 oz. pkg. taco
  seasoning mix
1/2 med. head lettuce,
  torn into bite sized pieces

2 med. tomatoes, cut in chunks
1/2 med. green pepper, chopped
1/2 c. shredded cheddar cheese
1/2 c. Monterey Jack cheese,
  shredded
1 c. broken corn chips

Crumble ground beef into 2 quart casserole; add onion. Microwave at high power for 4 1/2 to 6 1/2 minutes or till meat loses
its pink color. Stir to break up meat after half the cooking time;
drain. Stir in beans, water and taco seasoning. Microwave uncovered
at medium power for 10 to 13 minutes, or till thick and bubbly,
stirring once. Combine lettuce, tomatoes and green pepper in
salad bowl while meat and beans cook. Spoon mixture over lettuce.
Top with cheeses, then corn chips. Serve immediately with chili
sauce or taco sauce. Serves 4 to 6.

TACO SALAD   Mary Beam
                                            Proctor

1 lb. ground beef, browned
1 med. onion, chopped
1 chopped green pepper
1 can pinto beans, drained
1 bottle Italian dressing (small)

salt and garlic salt (seasonings)
1 small head lettuce, torn
1 or 2 chopped tomatoes
1/4 lb. grated cheese
1/2 pkg. taco chips

Mix browned beef, beans, dressing, onion, green pepper and
seasonings. Let stand in refrigerator overnight. Just before serving,
add the rest of the ingredients.

CARROT RAISIN SALAD   Ruth Reed
                                            Padroni E.H.

1 1/2 c. shredded carrots
1 1/2 c. diced oranges

1/2 c. seedless raisins
mayonnaise

Toss carrots, raisins and orange pieces together; moisten
with mayonnaise. Serve on lettuce.

CARROT SALAD

Hazel Korrey
Hearth and Home

2 pkgs. orange jello (3 oz.)
50 miniature marshmallows
1-8 oz. pkg. cream cheese
2 c. boiling water

1 c. crushed pineapple,
  undrained
1/2 c. chopped nuts
1 c. grated carrots
1 c. whipped cream

Dissolve ingredients in left column in boiling water. Use beater to make it easier to blend. Let cool until it starts to congeal. Fold in rest of ingredients. Mold in 8x9 inch square pan.

CUCUMBER SALAD

Connie Lechman
Proctor E.H. Club

2 med. cucumbers
1 Tbsp. white vinegar
2 tsp. sesame seed oil
1/2 tsp. salt

1 tsp. soy sauce
1 Tbsp. sugar
1/4 tsp. tabasco

Peel cucumbers and cut them in half lengthwise. With a spoon, scrape out all seeds. Cut cucumbers in 1/4 inch slices. In glass bowl, combine soy sauce, vinegar, sugar, sesame seed oil, tabasco and salt. Add cucumbers. Toss to coat each slice thoroughly. Chill before serving.

MARINATED CUCUMBER SLICES

Debby Fehringer
Hearth and Home

2 small or 1 large cucumber
  unpeeled, halved, seeded
  and thin sliced
1 1/2 tsp. salt

1/2 c. white vinegar
1/4 c. parsley
1/2 tsp. sugar
1/4 tsp. white pepper

Layer cucumber slices with 1 teaspoon of the salt in a 8 inch pie plate; let sit for 10 minutes. Press cucumbers into plate and pour off liquid that accumulates. Sprinkle vinegar, parsley, sugar, pepper and remaining salt over cucumbers, tossing gently to mix well. Marinate, covered, for at least 30 minutes, to let flavors blend before serving.

WILTED LETTUCE (MICROWAVE)

Jill Distel
Creative Homemakers

3 thin strips bacon
1 Tbsp. sugar
1/4 tsp. dill
1/4 tsp. seasoned salt
dash of pepper
1/4 c. vinegar

1/4 c. chopped celery
1 Tbsp. sliced green onion
1 med. head lettuce (torn)
2 hard boiled eggs, peeled
and sliced thin

Place bacon in a 3 quart casserole. Microwave on high (100%) for 3 to 4 minutes or until crispy. Remove bacon to paper towels to drain. Crumble and set aside.

Stir sugar, seasonings and vinegar into drippings. Microwave on high (100%) for 2 to 3 minutes or until boiling. Stir in celery and onion. Toss lettuce into hot dressing until thoroughly coated and slightly wilted. Top with egg slices and bacon pieces. Serve immediately. Makes 8 to 10 servings.

OVERNIGHT VEGETABLE SALAD

Betty Robinett
Highland Lassies

1-10 oz. pkg. frozen green
peas, thawed
1-15 to 16 oz. can red kidney
beans, drained
1-16 oz. can cut green
beans, drained
1-12 oz. can white whole kernel
corn, drained
1 c. diced celery
1 med. onion, diced
1/2 c. diced green pepper

1-2 oz. jar pimento, chopped
3/4 c. white vinegar
1/2 c. sugar
2 Tbsp. salad oil
1 1/2 tsp. salt
2 tsp. water
1/2 tsp. paprika

In a large bowl, combine all the vegetables and pimento. In small bowl, combine remaining ingredients and stir until sugar is dissolved. Pour over vegetables and toss. Cover and refrigerate at least 24 hours, stirring occasionally. Makes 14 to 16 servings. Contains 120 calories per 14 servings.

MARINATED VEGETABLE SALAD

Dorothy J. Robinson
Home Hustlers

avocado slices
tomato slices
red onion slices
2 Tbsp. parsley

1/3 c. vegetable oil
1 Tbsp. worcestershire sauce
1 Tbsp. lemon juice
1 tsp. basil leaves, crumbled

35 (Cont.)

1 tsp. salt   1/2 tsp. sugar

Lay slices of avocados, tomatoes and red onions in 9x12 inch dish overlapping each slice. Pour the marinating mixture over the top and let set in refrigerator for several hours before serving. Sprinkle with parsley just before serving. Combine the liquid ingredients into quart jar and shake well before pouring over the vegetables.

VEGETABLE SALAD

Cathy Elrick
X-tra X-amples X-tension Club

1 large head cauliflower	2 Tbsp. sugar
1 large green pepper	1/2 tsp. salt
1 can ripe olives	1/2 tsp. garlic salt
1 1/2 c. salad oil	1/2 tsp. basil leaves
1/3 c. vinegar	1/2 tsp. oregano leaves

Separate cauliflower and slice. Soak in oil and spices mixture for 2 hours or overnight. Then add sliced green pepper and drained olives, sliced into cauliflower mixture.

FROZEN CABBAGE

Phyllis Jones
Night Owls

1 med. size head of cabbage	1 tsp. salt
2 c. sugar	1 tsp. mustard seed
1/4 c. water	1 tsp. celery seed
1 c. vinegar	red or green peppers
carrots	

Shred cabbage and sprinkle salt over it. Let stand 1 hour. Squeeze water out good. Combine sugar, mustard seed, celery seed, water and vinegar in saucepan and boil 1 minute to dissolve sugar. Cool. Add red or green peppers and carrots (for color). Mix all ingredients together and put in containers and freeze. May be eaten before freezing.

FREEZER SLAW

Fran Hofmann
Hearth and Home

1 med. cabbage	1 tsp. whole mustard
1 carrot, grated	1 green pepper, chopped
1 c. white vinegar	1 tsp. salt
1/4 c. water	

36

1 tsp. celery seed   1 c. sugar

Mix salt and cabbage. Let stand for 1 hour. Squeeze excess moisture from cabbage. Add carrot and green pepper.

Mix together in a saucepan the vinegar, water, mustard, celery seed and sugar; boil 1 minute. Cool to lukewarm. Pour over cabbage and mix. Serve. This slaw freezes very well.

COLE SLAW
Barbara Spelts
Shamrock

1 med head cabbage
  (1 1/2 lbs.)
3 med. carrots
2 green peppers or
  1 red and 1 green

1 c. Crisco oil
1/2 c. honey
1/2 c. sugar
1/2 c. vinegar
1 tsp. celery seed
1 tsp. salt

Shred cabbage, carrots and green peppers. Place in one gallon container. Combine in a 3 quart saucepan the oil, honey, sugar, vinegar, celery seed and salt. Bring to a hard boil and pour over cabbage mixture. Cover and chill overnight. Freezes well and will keep indefinitely in refrigerator.

FROZEN PEA SALAD
Bertha Luft, Pep and Progress
Lena Cummins, Shamrock Club

1 small head of lettuce
1 c. chopped celery
5 hard boiled eggs,
  chopped or sliced
cheese, grated

1-10 oz. pkg. frozen peas
1/2 c. chopped green pepper
8 slices crisp crushed bacon
2 c. mayonnaise
2 Tbsp. sugar

In pan, layer the ingredients as follows:

layer of torn lettuce
1 c. chopped celery
hard boiled eggs
frozen peas

chopped pepper
crushed bacon
mixture of 2 c. mayonnaise
  and 2 Tbsp. sugar

Spread over top and sprinkle cheese over top. Can be made day ahead of serving time.

MAJESTIC SPINACH SALAD
Mary Ellen Breidenbach
Hearth and Home

1 c. (4 oz.) Kraft Swiss
  cheese, cubed

1 qt. torn spinach leaves
1-8 oz. cream cheese

(Cont.)

1/2 c. dairy sour cream
4 crisply cooked bacon
  slices, crumbled
4 hard cooked eggs, sliced
2 c. mushroom slices

3 tsp. milk
2 tsp. lemon juice
2 tsp. sugar
1/4 c. green onion slices

In 2 quart bowl, layer the Swiss cheese, spinach, eggs and mushrooms. Combine cream cheese, sour cream, milk, lemon juice and sugar mixing until well blended. Stir in green onion. Spread over salad to seal. Cover and chill several hours or overnight. Top with bacon before serving.

SPINACH SALAD

Margaret Lueck
Hearth and Home

20 oz. fresh spinach
1 c. pecans

12 oz. dry curd cottage cheese

Dressing:

1 c. sour cream
1/2 c. sugar
3 Tbsp. vinegar

1 1/2 tsp. dry mustard
1/2 tsp. salt
3 tsp. horseradish

Let stand 1 to 2 hours before serving.

SPINACH SALAD

Charlotte Lambrecht
Rainbows of Happiness

1 c. vegetable oil
1/2 c. vinegar
1/2 c. sugar
1 Tbsp. must
1 tsp. salt

1/2 tsp. pepper, coarsely
  ground
1 tsp. celery seed
1 small onion, minced
fresh spinach

Blend all ingredients except spinach in blender until creamy. Toss with fresh spinach, six slices fried bacon, crisp fresh mushrooms and croutons. Also can add slivered Swiss cheese if desired. Serves 6 to 8.

SPINACH SALAD

Earlene Schuppe
Proctor

10 oz. fresh spinach
10 mushrooms
1 c. fresh green sprouts
1 c. sliced water chestnuts

4 or 5 chopped scallions
1/2 c. Baco's or crisp
  fried bacon

Dressing:

1/2 c. catsup

1/2 c. salad oil

1/2 c. sugar

2 Tbsp. vinegar

1 Tbsp. worcestershire sauce

Tear spinach into bite size pieces and slice mushrooms. Toss salad ingredients together.

Dressing: Mix together well and pour over salad. Use immediately. Does not keep well.

GARBANZO BEAN SALAD

Sandy Ils
Home Hustlers

2-15 oz. cans garbanzo beans, drained and rinsed

2 med. tomatoes, chopped

3 green onions, thinly sliced

3/4 c. finely cubed cheddar cheese

1/2 c. lemon juice

1/3 c. salad oil

1/2 tsp. ground cumin seed

1/2 tsp. salt

1/4 tsp. freshly ground black pepper

Combine all ingredients. Cover and refrigerate at least 1 hour.

BEAN SALAD

Deana Rasmussen
Rainbows of Happiness

1-15 to 16 oz. can red kidney beans

1-16 oz. can yellow wax beans

1-16 oz. can cut green beans

1-15 to 16 oz. can garbanzo beans

1 small onion, cut in rings

1 sliced green pepper

1/4 c. vinegar

1/4 c. water

3/4 c. sugar

Drain and add the cans of beans together with the onion and pepper. Mix vinegar, sugar and water together and stir until sugar is partly dissolved. Pour over bean mixture and let stand overnight. Stir once in awhile if desired. Serve with small chunks of cheddar cheese on top.

LAYERED LETTUCE SALAD

Ginny Anderson
X-tra X-amples X-tension Club

1 small head lettuce

1 1/2 c. cheese, grated

1/2 c. celery, chopped

1/2 c. onion, chopped

1/2 c. green pepper, chopped

1 box frozen peas, cooked

8 slices bacon, fried, drained and broken up

1 1/2 c. sour cream

1/2 c. salad dressing(Miracle Whip)

2 Tbsp. sugar

Shred lettuce fine and put in bottom of a 9x9 inch pan. Sprinkle chopped celery, onion, green pepper and peas on top of lettuce. Mix sour cream and salad dressing together then pour over layers. Sprinkle 2 tablespoons sugar on dressing. Sprinkle on bacon then top with cheese. Cover and let set overnight in refrigerator.

RAW VEGETABLE SALAD

Margaret Ann Stieb
Hearth and Home

2 c. carrots
2 c. celery
2 c. cucumber

1 or 2 heads of cauliflower
1 sliced onion
1 pt. cherry tomatoes

Dressing: Combine and pour over vegetables.

1 Tbsp. sugar
1/2 c. vinegar
3/4 c. oil
1 1/2 tsp. salt

1/4 tsp. pepper
1/2 tsp. dry mustard
1 clove garlic
1/2 c. parsley

Let stand in refrigerator overnight. Keeps very well.

CREAMY CAULIFLOWER SALAD

Margaret Ann Stieb
Hearth and Home

1 med. head cauliflower,
    broken
1 bunch green onion, sliced
1 c. sliced radishes

1 c. mayonnaise
1-7 oz. pkg. garlic cheese
    dressing
2 tsp. caraway seeds

Combine first 3 ingredients in medium bowl. Combine the remaining ingredients and pour over the vegetables. Toss to coat. Cover and refrigerate overnight.

BEAN SALAD

Mrs. R. Burkholder
Kelly Woman's Inprovement Extension H.C.

1-1 lb. can wax beans
1-1 lb. can green beans
1-1 lb. can kidney beans
1/2 c. green chopped pepper

1/2 c. sugar
2/3 c. vinegar
1/3 c. salad oil
1 tsp. salt
1 tsp. pepper

Drain all the beans. Mix sugar, vinegar, salad oil, salt and pepper. Pour over vegetables. Refrigerate 24 hours before using. Salad will keep for a week under refrigeration.
Note: Recipe submitted by Mrs. Lorin Lindstrom.

FROZEN PEA SALAD

Eva M. Guenzi
Home Hustlers

8 oz. sour cream
1/2 c. chopped celery

1/2 c. chopped onion
20 oz. pkg. frozen peas,
   uncooked

Mix together and marinate overnight or for several hours. Before serving, add 1/2 cup chopped almonds and 1/2 cup bacon crumbs.

GREEN RAW SALAD

Margaret Ann Stieb
Hearth and Home

2 c. frozen broccoli, cut up
2 c. frozen peas
1 c. chopped onion
2 c. fresh cauliflower
1 c. sour cream

1 c. mayonnaise
2 tsp. sugar
1 tsp. vinegar
dash of salt and tabasco

Mix broccoli, peas, cauliflower and onion in large bowl. Mix other ingredients and pour over vegetables. Let stand 8 to 12 hours in refrigerator.

PROSPECTER SALAD

Traci McGeehan
Creative Homemakers

1 basket cherry tomatoes
1-16 oz. can pitted black olives,
   drained
1 med. head broccoli
1/2 lb. fresh mushrooms,
   sliced

1 med. head cauliflower
1-8 oz. bottle Italian dressing
1/2 c. sugar (opt.)

Cut broccoli and cauliflower into bite size pieces. Combine with all the other ingredients. Pour on the dressing and mix well. Refrigerate.

FRESH SALAD

Norma Nab
Pep and Progress

med. cauliflower, cut in
  bite size pieces
lb. broccoli, cut in
  bite size pieces
/2 lb. fresh mushrooms,
   sliced

1 c. chopped celery
1 green pepper, diced
2 onions, cut in rings
1 can black olives, cut in half
1 c. green stuffed olives
1 pkg. Hidden Valley dressing
       mix

1 c. mayonnaise
  (not salad dressing)

1 c. milk

Put vegetables in large salad bowl. Mix dressing with mayonnaise and milk. Let sit till thickened. Pour over vegetables and marinate 15 minutes. Serves 10 to 12.

WINTER HOLIDAY SALAD

Thelma Davis
Sterling Homemakers

9 c. torn Iceberg lettuce
  leaves
2 ripe avocados
1 Tbsp. lemon juice

4 oranges, peeled and
  sectioned
1 red onion, peeled and
  sliced thinly
1 c. seasoned croutons with
  herbs and cheese

Lemon Dressing:

3 oz. honey
3 oz. vegetable oil

2 1/2 Tbsp. fresh lemon juice

Wash lettuce and dry well; tear into bite sized pieces. Cut avocado in half lengthwise. Twist halves in opposite direction; remove seed and peel. Slice avocado; sprinkle with lemon juice.

In a large bowl, combine lettuce, avocado slices, orange sections, onions and croutons. Add fresh lemon dressing and toss to mix well. Serve immediately.

Fresh Lemon Dressing : Blend honey and vegetable oil and fresh lemon juice with blender.

SEVEN LAYER SALAD

Lena Cummins
Shamrock

1 layer of lettuce
1 layer of frozen peas,
  thawed
1 layer of onion
1 layer boiled eggs

1 layer of crisp bacon
1 layer of sour cream
  and mayonnaise
1 layer of grated cheese on top

Mix well.

Write your extra recipes here:

How To Carve Turkey

1. Remove leg: Hold drumstick firmly, pulling gently away from body. Cut skin between leg and body. Press leg downward and cut from body. Separate drumstick and thigh; slice meat from each piece.

2. Cut into white meat parallel to wing, making a cut deep into the breast to the body frame, as close to the wing as possible.

3. Slice white meat. Beginning at front starting half way up breast, cut thin slices of white meat down to the cut. Slices will fall away from turkey as cut. Continue until enough meat has been carved for first servings. Carve more as needed.

Tips
TO THE CARVER

- Convention doesn't forbid your standing up to carve, so, if it's easier, stand up.

- The bones get in your way if you don't know where to expect them; a little investigation tells you just where they are.

- Carving is unduly complicated by a dull knife.

- And remember the first rule of carving . . .
  "Cut across the grain"
  If you cut with the grain, long meat fibers give a stringy texture to the slice. Steaks are the exception.

Tips
TO THE HOSTESS

- A large roast can be carved more easily after it stands for about thirty minutes.

- When garnishing, don't be over-generous; leave space for the work to be done.

- Servings cool quickly so plates and platter *must* be heated.

- An inexperienced carver will appreciate a hostess who keeps the guests' attention diverted from his carving.

MAIN DISHES--
MEAT, SEAFOOD, POULTRY

BATTER FOR FRYING FISH Ann Ruf
Pep and Progress

2 eggs, beaten
1/2 c. beer
1/2 c. flour

1/2 c. cornstarch
2 tsp. salt
1/2 tsp. pepper

Fry fish in oil at 380° on an electric frying pan.

BAKED TROUT Traci McGeehan
Creative Homemakers

trout, to fit a 9x13" pan
  (glass preferable)
1/2 stick butter
1 lemon (lemon juice may
  be substituted)

1 small pkg. slivered almonds
seasoning salt

Wash and scale trout leaving heads on. Place in baking dish with butter and lemon squeezed over all fish. Season with seasoning salt and sprinkle on almonds. Bake at 350° until fork tender. Remove heads before serving.

LAMB STEW Sandy Ils
Home Hustlers

2 lbs. lamb shoulder, cubed
1 onion
1 clove garlic
4 c. water
1 Tbsp. salt
1 Tbsp. lemon juice
1 tsp. sugar

1 tsp. worcestershire sauce
1/2 tsp. pepper
1/2 tsp. paprika
1 bay leaf
dash allspice
6 carrots, sliced
4 potatoes, cubed

Brown meat very slowly in small amount of salad oil. Slice onion and add to browned meat. Saute slightly. Add remaining ingredients except for carrots and potatoes. Cover and simmer gently for 2 hours or until meat is tender. Add vegetables and simmer 30 minutes longer. Discard bay leaf and garlic. Thicken stew with mixture of 1/2 cup water and 1/4 cup flour.

BARBECUED CHICKEN

Debbie Garcia
Creative Homemakers

1 cut up chicken
1 c. oleo
1/2 c. brown sugar
1/2 c. catsup

1/2 c. vinegar
1/2 c. water
dash worcestershire sauce

Place chicken in roaster or deep pan. Mix remaining ingredients and pour over chicken. Place in 325° oven for 3 to 6 hours. Chicken just gets more tender and delicious. Also may be used on ribs.

DELUXE CHICKEN

Pam Clark
X-tra X-amples X-tension Club

5 whole chicken breasts,
  deboned and skinned
10 slices bacon
4 oz. dried beef

2 cans cream of mushroom soup
1 1/2 c. sour cream

Grease a 9x13 inch pan. Place beef on bottom of pan. Wrap chicken with bacon. Mix soup and sour cream together and pour over chicken. Bake 3 hours at 275°, uncovered.

YOGURT-GLAZED CHICKEN

Hazel Korrey
Hearth and Home

1/4 tsp. garlic powder
1/2 tsp. paprika
1/2 tsp. basil
1-2 1/2 lb. fryer, cut in
  pieces and skinned

1/2 c. plain yogurt, at room
  temp.
1 tsp. soy sauce or
  worcestershire sauce
1/2 c. plain yogurt, at
  room temp.
1 tsp. flour
3 tsp. Parmesan cheese

Preheat oven to 400°. Sprinkle garlic, papirka and basil over chicken. Stir 1/2 cup yogurt and soy or worcestershire sauce till creamy. Place chicken in shallow baking dish. Brush with yogurt mixture. Bake uncovered 20 minutes. Turn chicken over and baste with juices. Bake another 20 minutes. Reduce oven temperature to 350°. Stir 1/2 cup yogurt and flour until creamy. Spread over chicken; sprinkle cheese over chicken. Bake 3 to 5 minutes longer.

BEST EVER CHICKEN AND DUMPLINGS

Rosalie Wolfe
Home Hustlers

4 to 5 lb. stewing chicken
4 c. water
1 large onion, sliced
2 stalks celery, diced
1 Tbsp. salt

1 bay leaf
1/2 c. flour
1/2 c. water
2 to 3 c. frozen peas
    and carrots

In large saucepan, combine first 6 ingredients. Simmer, covered, for 1 1/2 to 2 hours until chicken is tender. Cool; remove chicken from bones and cut into pieces. Skim fat from broth. Reheat broth, about 5 cups. Blend flour into 1/2 cup water until smooth; stir into hot broth, stirring constantly. Add vegetables and chicken pieces and heat to boiling; lower heat and prepare Dumplings.

Dumplings:

1 1/2 c. flour
2 tsp. baking powder
1/2 tsp. salt

2/3 c. milk
2 Tbsp. cooking oil
1 egg, slightly beaten

In medium bowl, combine first 4 dumpling ingredients. Stir to blend. Combine milk, oil and egg; add to flour mixture. Stir just until dry ingredients are moistened. Drop dumplings by rounded tablespoons onto hot soup. cover tightly. Boil gently 12 to 15 minutes until dumplings are fluffy and dry. Serve immediately. Makes 6 servings.

CHICKEN WITH MUSHROOMS AND TARRAGON

Patty Ament
Proctor

6 chicken breasts, skinned
2 to 3 peeled fresh tomatoes
mushrooms, drained
tarragon

salt
pepper
1/4 c. butter

Salt and pepper chicken pieces generously. Brown in melted butter in a skillet. Sprinkle generously with tarragon. Cook until done. Cut peeled tomatoes into fourths or sixths. Remove chicken to warm platter and brown tomatoes in drippings, quickly. Remove to separate dish. Brown mushrooms quickly and remove to separate dish. Return chicken to skillet. Add cooked tomatoes and mushrooms on top of chicken. Heat through and serve from skillet or remove to platter. Pour drippings over. Figure about 1 chicken breast per person. Delicious with wild rice.

HAWAIIAN CHICKEN

Dorothy A. Harms
Home Hustlers

1 large chicken, cut up
1/4 c. flour with 1/4 tsp.
  ginger added
cooking oil
2 c. spring onions
1/2 lb. mushrooms
2 Tbsp. soy sauce
1 small can apricot nectar or
  papaya juice
1 can consomme or chicken broth
1 can sliced water chestnuts
1 can bamboo shoots
1 can pineapple chunks
salt and pepper
1 c. rice, cooked in
  2 c. water with salt
1 c. coconut, browned under
  broiler

In large skillet, place chicken which has been covered with flour. Fry until browned thoroughly. Drain all but 2 tablespoons of oil. Remove chicken. In oil, fry onions and mushrooms until liquid is dissolved. Return chicken to skillet.

In bowl, mix remaining ingredients except pineapple and rice. Pour over chicken and simmer for one hour. Ten minutes before finished, add pineapple.

Cook rice. When cooked, add coconut. Serve chicken over rice. (Leftover rice may be mixed later with Dream Whip to make a dessert.)

SUNSET'S FRIED CHICKEN
(Can also be used for pork chops.)

Dorothy J. Robinson
Home Hustlers

3 to 3 1/2 lbs. chicken
1 Tbsp. each garlic salt
  and seasoned salt
1/4 tsp. each pepper, sage,
  and thyme leaves and basil
2/3 c. all purpose flour
1/2 tsp. paprika
3 c. oil (approx.)

Remove excess lumps of body fat from chicken. Rinse chicken and set aside but do not dry. In plastic bag, combine flour, garlic salt, seasoned salt, paprika, pepper, sage, thyme and basil.

In deep electric skillet, pour 1/2 inch of salad oil. Shake each piece of chicken in flour mixture and place in cold oil. Cover pan and turn control to 350°. When you hear the chicken sizzling loudly, set a time and cook the chicken 15 minutes. Remove cover and turn chicken over; cook, uncovered for 10 minutes longer. Drain briefly on paper towels. (Sometimes takes a bit longer to brown before turning over.)

OVEN FRIED CHICKEN

Esther Nelson
Sterling Homemakers

1 Tbsp. shortening
2/3 c. biscuit mix
1 1/2 tsp. paprika

1 1/4 tsp. salt
1/4 tsp. pepper
1 cut up chicken

Melt shortening in 9x13 inch pan. Mix biscuit mix, paprika, salt and pepper. Coat chicken in mixture. Place skin side down in pan. Bake at 425° for 35 minutes; turn chicken and bake 15 minutes longer. High altitute: Bake 40 minutes and 20 minutes.

CUCUMBER PORK CHOPS

Iris Lambert
Rainbows of Happiness

pork chops
liquid mustard
1/2 c. chopped onion

1 diced unpeeled cucumber
1 can beef consomme
1/2 c. milk

Spread liquid mustard on pork chops. Brown in butter; remove from pan. Saute chopped onion and cucumber. Add beef consomme and milk. Add chops and simmer 20 minutes.

PORK CHOP SKILLET MEAL

Katherine Kalinowski
Sterling Homemakers

4 Tbsp. lard
4 pork chops, 1" thick
4 slices onion
4 rings green pepper

1/2 c. uncooked rice
3 c. canned tomatoes
1 c. diced celery

Brown chops on both sides. Place slice of onion and ring of pepper on each   chop. Add a tablespoon of rice to each ring and pour tomatoes around meat. Add diced celery. Cover and simmer for 60 minutes.

GRAVY-BAKED PORK CHOPS

Doris Harms
Night Owls

4 lean pork chops, 1/2 to 3/4"
      thick
1/4 tsp. salt
1 can cream of chicken or
   mushroom soup
1/3 c. water

1 Tbsp. hot shortening
1/8 tsp. pepper
3/4 c. evap. milk (1 small can)

Sprinkle pork chops with salt and pepper. In a 10 inch skillet, brown chops in hot shortening. Pour off drippings. Pour around chops a mixture of soup, evaporated milk and water.

Bake in 350° oven for 45 minutes, until chops are tender. Stir gravy well. Makes 4 servings.

PORK CHOP AND PASTA DINNER
Jama Marvel
X-tra X-amples X-tension Club

1 1/2 c. macaroni twists
6 pork chops, 1/2" thick
2 Tbsp. oil
1-15 oz. can chopped tomatoes
1/4 c. chopped onion
1 tsp. worcestershire sauce
1/2 tsp. crushed basil

1/4 tsp. sugar
1/4 tsp. salt
1/4 tsp. garlic powder
1/4 tsp. oregano
dash of pepper
1/4 c. grated Parmesan cheese

Cook macaroni in boiling salted water according to package directions; drain. Place in 13x9x2 inch baking dish. Brown chops in oil; drain. Season with salt and pepper. Arrange over macaroni. Mix remaining ingredients and pour on top. Sprinkle with Parmesan cheese. Cover and bake at 350° for 1 to 1 1/2 hours or until meat is tender. Serve with additional Parmesan cheese, if desired. Serves 6.

SPICY BARBECUED SPARERIBS
Norma Nab
Pep and Progress

3 lbs. spareribs
salt and pepper
2 Tbsp. butter
1 med. onion, finely chopped
1/2 c. chopped celery

1 c. catsup
2 Tbsp. vinegar
2 Tbsp. lemon juice
2 Tbsp. worcestershire sauce
2 Tbsp. packed brown sugar

Sprinkle spareribs with salt and pepper; place in roasting pan with small amount of water. Bake at 325° for 3 hours. Remove from oven. Drain off excess fat. Cut spareribs into serving pieces and return to roaster pan. Melt butter in saucepan. Brown onion in butter. Combine remaining ingredients with 1 teaspoon salt and 1/2 teaspoon pepper; mix well with onion. Simmer 20 minutes. Pour over spareribs. Return to oven and heat through. Serves 6.

BARBECUE RANCH RIBS
Anne Stieb
Hearth and Home

2/3 c. Karo syrup
1/3 c. soy sauce
1 1/2 tsp. ginger

1/4 c. vinegar
dash pepper
2 Tbsp. cornstarch

| 1 clove garlic | 4 lbs. spareribs |
| 1/4 tsp. salt | 1 c. catsup |

Combine ingredients except ribs in saucepan. Bring to boil. Pour over ribs in a shallow pan. Cover and refrigerate for 4 hours turning occasionally. Grill over a slow fire basting with sauce. Cook until done, 1 to 1 1/2 hours. Makes 4 to 6 servings. May also be baked in oven at 350° for 1 hour.

HAM LOAF

Luella Sonnenberg
Night Owls

3/4 lb. ground ham	2 eggs
1 1/3 lb. ground beef or pork	1 c. milk
1 c. bread crumbs	1/4 tsp. pepper

Crumble the meats. Beat the eggs a bit and add all the ingredients together. Form into a loaf. Bake at 375° for 1 1/2 hours.

Horseradish Sauce:

| 3 Tbsp. whipped cream | 1/4 tsp. salt |
| 1 Tbsp. horseradish | |

Mix just before serving and serve with Ham Loaf.

SWEDISH MEAT BALLS

Eleanor Carlson
Home Hustlers

1 lb. cured ham, ground	1/2 c. vinegar
1 1/2 lbs. fresh pork, ground	1/2 c. water
2 eggs	1/2 c. brown sugar
2 c. bread crumbs	1 tsp. dry mustard
1 c. milk	

Mix meat, eggs, crumbs and milk well. Form into balls and place in shallow baking pan. Make sauce of vinegar, water, brown sugar and mustard. Pour over meat balls and bake 2 hours at 350°. Turn meat balls once at about middle of baking time.

SAUSAGE CUPS

Louise Ebbers
Padroni E.H.

lb. loose pork sausage	2 Tbsp. horseradish
3/4 c. milk	2 tsp. prepared mustard
1/2 c. dry bread crumbs	1 beaten egg
Tbsp. catsup	

Mix ingredients and pack in 12 muffin cups. Bake at 350° for 20 minutes.

ZUCCHINI ITALIAN

Lillian Sitarski
Highland Lassies

1 lb. extra lean ground beef
1 small onion, minced
2 c. tomato sauce
1/2 tsp. oregano, crushed
1/2 tsp. basil, crushed
1/4 tsp. dried rosemary, crushed
4 med. zucchini

salt and pepper to taste
1 c. ricotta cheese
1 c. small curd cottage cheese
2 eggs
4 oz. mozzarella cheese
1/3 c. grated Parmesan cheese

Saute beef and onion. Add sauce and simmer 15 minutes. Layer sauce, zucchini, and cheese like lasagna in a 13x9 inch pan. Bake at 375° for 40 to 50 minutes.

COLD MEAT SALAMI

Minne Korrey
Hearth and Home E.H.

2 lbs. hamburger
2 Tbsp. mustard seed
2 Tbsp. Tender Quick salt
1 Tbsp. liquid smoke

1/2 tsp. onion salt
1/2 tsp. garlic salt
1 tsp. coarse ground pepper
1/4 c. water

Mix all ingredients together. Make into one or two rolls. Wrap in foil and let set in refrigerator 24 hours or longer. Place in pan and bake at 350° for one hour.

DANISH MEATBALLS

Eva Korrey
Rainbows of Happiness

1 env. onion soup mix
2 lbs. ground beef
1/4 c. milk

1 egg, beaten
1/2 c. margarine or butter

In large bowl, combine soup mix with meat, milk and egg. Shape into 1 1/2 inch balls. In large skillet, melt margarine and brown meatballs, turning frequently. Makes 6 servings.

ZUCCHINI MEATBALLS IN SOUR CREAM SAUCE   Iris Lambert

Rainbows of Happiness

1 lb. ground beef
1 chopped onion
1 egg
1 slice bread

3/4 tsp. salt
1 1/2 c. shredded, unpeeled
   zucchini
1/4 tsp. pepper

Sauce:

1 can cream of chicken soup
1/3 c. sour cream

1/4 c. milk
dash of nutmeg

Mix well. Form into 1 1/2 inch meatballs and arrange in 9 inch round glass pan. Cover with paper towel. Microwave on high 6 minutes. Drain fat. Pour sauce over meatballs. Cover with waxed paper and microwave on high 5 mintues. Makes 4 to 6 servings.

MAGGIE AND JIGS

Traci McGeehan
Creative Homemakers

1 lb. hamburger
1-16 oz. can whole kernel
   corn

1 small head cabbage, shredded
1 small onion

Brown hamburger with onion; drain. Add corn with liquid or 8 ounces frozen corn with 1/2 cup water may be substituted. Stir cabbage in and add desired seasonings and cover, cooking over medium heat, until cabbage is tender.

PIZZA BURGERS

Judy Armstrong

1 lb. hamburger
1/2 lb. grated cheddar cheese
1/4 tsp. of the following, oregano,
  garlic salt and pepper

1 med. onion
1 can tomato soup

Brown hamburger and onion; drain. Add rest of ingredients. Refrigerate 4 hours. Put on 1/2 hamburger bun. Bake on cookie sheet at 450° for 9 to 10 minutes.

SNAPPY CHEESE SANDWICHES

Judy Armstrong
Southsiders

1/2 lb. Velveeta cheese
1/2 c. minced, dill pickle
3 Tbsp. mayonnaise

1 c. celery, chopped
2 Tbsp. chili sauce
softened butter

Cut cheese in 3/4 inch cubes. Add celery and pickles. Stir chili sauce in mayonnaise. Mix well and pour over cheese mixture. Toss until all pieces are coated. Scoop out hotdog buns. Spread butter on top crust and fill with mixture; heat in oven.

CALZONE

Norma Penner
Rainbows of Happiness

1 recipe yeast dough
1 lb. hamburger
1 diced bell pepper
1 diced onion

salt and pepper to taste
1 jar Ragu sauce
grated cheese

Brown meat, onion and pepper. Drain fat. Add salt, pepper and sauce. Roll yeast dough into 8 circles. Fill with meat mixture. Add grated cheese to top of meat. Pinch dough closed.
Bake at 375° for 25 minutes.

POOR BOYS

Shirley Herzog
Padroni E.H.

1 lb. hamburger
1 small onion

2 large green peppers
2 loaves frozen bread

Brown hamburger in skillet; add onions and green peppers; drain and cool. Raise frozen bread as for baking; pinch off about a fist full of dough. Flatten dough adding a heaping tablespoon of meat mixture to center. Pinch edges together. Drop into deep fat fryer frying until golden brown. Makes 10 to 12.

SLOPPY JOES

Cleta Carr
Pep and Progress

1 lb. hamburger
1 c. chopped onion
1 1/2 tsp. salt
1/8 tsp. pepper
3 tsp. dry mustard
3 Tbsp. brown sugar
1 1/2 c. catsup

1 Tbsp. worcestershire sauce
1 1/2 c. water
1/4 c. vinegar
1/8 tsp. tabasco sauce (opt.)
1 Tbsp. liquid smoke

Brown hamburger and onion. Add rest of ingredients. Cook 30 minutes or longer. Maybe cooked in crock pot 3 hours on low. Serve on buns.

SLOPPY JOES

Mildred Littler
Night Owls

1 1/2 lbs. ground beef
1 1/2 tsp. salt
1 Tbsp. flour
1 Tbsp. chili powder

1 c. water
1 onion, chopped
1/8 tsp. pepper
1/2 tsp. garlic powder

1 1/2 tsp. paprika   1 c. catsup

Brown onions and meat in skillet. Make a paste of flour and water; add to meat mixture. Then add spices and catsup. Simmer, stirring frequently for 20 minutes or until thick. Serve on warm buns.

WIMPYBURGERS

Rachel Schuppe
Proctor Extension Homemakers

1 onion, chopped
1 1/2 lbs. ground beef
salt and pepper
1/2 c. catsup
1/4 c. vinegar

2 Tbsp. prepared mustard
2 Tbsp. sugar
2 Tbsp. worcestershire sauce
1/4 c. water

Brown the onion in fat. Add the ground beef and season with salt and pepper. After meat is browned, add remaining ingredients. Simmer 20 to 30 minutes. Serve on buns. This makes 12 to 14.

SWEET-SOUR MEATBALLS

Dorothy Smith
Kelly Woman's Improvement Club

2 lbs. hamburger
1 tsp. chili powder

1/2 tsp. garlic salt

Sauce:

2-14 oz. bottles catsup
1/2 box brown sugar

2 Tbsp. vinegar
few drops tabasco sauce

Mix first 3 ingredients together. Form into balls. Drop into boiling water and boil 10 minutes. Simmer balls in sauce for 10 minutes.

DUTCH HASH

Judy Larson

1 1/2 to 2 lbs. lean boneless
   beef, pork or veal
1 tsp. salt
1/4 tsp. black pepper
2 large onions, cut in rings
5 Tbsp. flour

3 c. beef broth
2 bay leaves
2 cloves
1 tsp. sugar
2 Tbsp. vinegar

Toss the diced meat with salt and pepper. Heat the butter and saute the meat and onions over high heat until lightly browned. Add the flour and cook, stirring, 2 minutes. Add the broth

(Cont.)

gradually, stirring up the brown bits clinging to the bottom of the pan. Add the remaining ingredients; cover and simmer slowly 1 1/2 hours.

EASY STEW
Joyce Werner

1 1/2 lbs. lean beef,
  cut in 1 1/2" cubes
2 tsp. salt
1/2 tsp. basil leaves
1/4 tsp. pepper
2 stalks celery, cut in
  diagonal slices

4 carrots, sliced
2 onions, sliced
1-10 1/2 oz. can condensed
  tomato soup
1/2 soup can water
3 potatoes, peeled
  and cubed

Place beef (no need to brown it) in 3 quart casserole. Sprinkle with salt, basil and pepper. Top with celery, carrots and onions. Combine soup and water. Pour over meat and vegetables, coating all pieces. Cover tightly and bake in slow 300° oven for 3 hours. Add potatoes and bake 45 minutes longer. Makes 5 servings.

BEEF CUBES ON RICE OR NOODLES
Ginny Anderson
X-tra X-amples X-tension

2 lbs. lean stewing beef,
  cubed
1/2 pkg. Lipton's onion
  soup (dry)

1 can cream of mushroom soup
  (as is)
1/2 c. water

Place all ingredients in heavy Dutch oven, covered pot. Bake at 275° for 4 to 5 hours. Stir once at about 2 1/2 hours. If too dry, add more water. If desired, add 1 package frozen mushrooms the last 30 minutes. Serve over wild and white rice, or Chinese noodles. Serves 6.

ITALIAN STYLE MEAT LOAF (MICROWAVE)
Sheila Godfrey
Creative Homemakers

1 Tbsp. butter or margarine
3 small onions, finely chopped
  (3/4 c.)
1 lb. ground round
1 lb. bulk pork sausage
1-8 oz. can tomato sauce

2 eggs
3/4 c. pkgd, bread crumbs
1/2 c. grated Asiago Parmesan
  cheese
2 Tbsp. minced fresh Italian parsley
1/2 tsp. ground pepper

Put butter in a 3 quart bowl and cook on high power 45 to 60 seconds, until melted. Add onions and cook 2 minutes, stirring after 1 minute. Add remaining ingredients to onion mixture and mix thoroughly. Divide into 6 even round balls. Put a 5 or 6 ounce glass custard cup upside down in center of a 9 inch glass pie plate. Arrange meatballs around custard cup and press together gently. Place, uncovered, in the center of the microwave oven and cook on high power for 20 minutes, rotating dish every 5 minutes and removing excess pan drippings with a bulb baster, if necessary. (Internal temperature should now register 160°). Remove from oven and cover tightly with aluminum foil; let stand 10 minutes. (Internal temperature should now register 180°. The temperature is important since pork is an ingredient.) If temperature is not designated level, uncover and return to microwave and cook 5 to 10 minutes longer. Conventional cooking: 1 1/4 hours. Makes 6 servings at 87¢ each.

MEXICALI MEAT LOAVES (MICROWAVE)
Sheila Godfrey
Creative Homemakers

1 lb. hamburger
1/2 c. uncooked oatmeal
1 egg
1-8 oz. can tomato sauce
1-4 oz. can diced green chilies

1 Tbsp. plus 1 tsp. instant minced
   onion
1 tsp. chili powder
1/2 tsp. salt
1/8 tsp. garlic powder
1/2 c. shredded cheddar cheese

Combine meat, oatmeal, egg, 1/4 cup tomato sauce, 2 tablespoons chilies, 1 tablespoon onion, chili powder, and salt. Shape to form four loaves. Place in 8 inch square baking dish. Microwave on high for 6 to 7 minutes, rotating 1/4 turn after each 2 minutes of cooking. Combine remaining tomato sauce, chilies, onions and garlic powder. Cook on high about 1 minute, until hot. Spoon over meat and sprinkle with cheese.

MEAT LOAF
Yvonne Davidson
Night Owls

1 egg
1/2 c. water or tomatoes
1 1/2 lbs. chopped beef or
   1 lb. beef and 1/2 lb. pork

1 c. bread crumbs or oatmeal
4 slices bacon
1 tsp. salt
1/8 tsp. pepper

Beat egg in mixing bowl; add water and mix. Add the other ingredients and mix well. Grease baking pan with bacon fat and place the loaf in a pan. Put slices of bacon on top and bake slowly, uncovered for about 1 1/2 hours.

HAWAIIAN BEEF LOAVES

Janice Grauberger
Hearth and Home

1 env. brown gravy mix
1/2 c. milk
1 tsp. instant minced onion
2 beaten eggs
1 Tbsp. snipped parsley

2 tsp. soy sauce
1/2 tsp. salt
dash pepper
1 c. soft bread crumbs
2 lbs. ground beef

In large bowl, blend gravy mix and milk. Stir in minced onion and let stand few minutes. Stir in eggs, parsley, soy sauce, salt and pepper. Mix well. Stir in soft bread crumbs. Add ground beef and mix well. Shape into loaf. Place in shallow pan.

Bake at 350° for 50 minutes. Spoon off excess fat. Pour small amount of sweet-sour sauce over loaf. Bake 15 minutes longer.

LITTLE MEAT LOAVES

Emma Acre
Pep and Progress

2 lbs. hamburger
salt to taste
2 eggs
1 c. bread crumbs
1/2 c. catsup
1/2 c. chopped onion

1/4 tsp. pepper
1/2 tsp. sage
1 c. crushed potato chips
1 c. tomato juice

Mix together hamburger, salt, eggs, bread crumbs, catsup, chopped onion, pepper and sage. Shape into small loaves. Roll in crushed potato chips. Put in pan. Add tomato juice. Bake at 350° for 1 hour.

MINI MEAT LOAVES

Barbara Spelts
Shamrock

1-10 oz. can Campbell's
  tomato soup
2 lbs. ground beef
1/4 c. fine dry bread crumbs
1 egg, slightly beaten
1/4 c. finely chopped onion

1 tsp. salt
1/4 tsp. each pepper, sage,
  crushed thyme
2 Tbsp. shortening
2 to 4 Tbsp. water

Mix thoroughly 1 cup soup, beef, bread crumbs, egg, onion, salt and 1/8 teaspoon each pepper, sage and thyme. Shape firmly into 6 or 8 mini meat loaves.

In skillet brown loaves in shortening. Pour off fat. Stir in remaining soup and seasonings and water. Cover and cook over low heat 20 minutes or until done. Stir liquid occasionally. Serve with parsleyed potatoes and broccoli if desired. Makes 6 to 8 servings.

MEAT LOAF WITH TOMATOES

Marlene Allen
Padroni E.H.

1 1/2 lbs. hamburger
1 onion, chopped
1 tsp. celery salt
2 tsp. dry mustard
1 egg
1/2 tsp. paprika

2 slices bacon, diced
1 1/2 tsp. salt
1/8 tsp. pepper
1 c. canned tomatoes
1 c. cracker crumbs
1 Tbsp. butter

Combine hamburger, bacon, onion, salt, celery salt, pepper, mustard, tomatoes, egg and 3/4 cup cracker crumbs. Pack into greased loaf pan. Cover with remaining cracker crumbs. Sprinkle with paprika and dot with butter.

Bake at 350° for 1 hour. Garnish with parsley and serve with tomato sauce, if desired.

FLUFFY MEAT LOAF

Enid Lindstrom
Kelly Woman's Improvement Club

1 1/2 lbs. ground beef
1/2 c. tomato juice
1 egg

2 slices white bread
1 small potato
1/2 tsp. salt

Preheat oven to 350°. Place ground beef in a bowl; add tomato juice and beaten egg and work through meat. Soak bread with water and tear into bits. Add to meat and work through. Peel and grate potato into meat and add salt; mix well. Pack into loaf pan and bake 1 1/4 to 1 1/2 hours depending on rareness desired.

DEER FILETS IN MUSHROOM SAUCE (CROCK POT)

Janet Kloberdanz
X-tra X-amples X-tension Club

1 lb. deer filets or
  sirloin steak
4 potatoes, peeled and
  quartered

1 small onion, sliced
1 can cream of mushroom soup
salt and pepper to taste

Brown deer or steaks in a little shortening. Put in the bottom of the crock pot. Salt and pepper to taste. Add onions over meat and then add potatoes. Take the drippings off the meat and mix it with the soup plus a little water and pour the soup mixture over

57 (Cont.)

the crock pot mixture. Cover and cook on high for 1 1/2 hours and on low from 6 to 7 hours. Makes 4 servings.

FLANK-STEAK FIX-UP

Debbie Breidenbach
Hearth and Home

2 lbs. flank steak
1 clove garlic
1 tsp. salt
1/4 tsp. pepper
4 to 6 slices bacon
1/2 c. flour

1-8 oz. can tomato sauce
1/2 tsp. salt
1/8 tsp. marjoram leaves
1 Tbsp. parsley
1/2 c. finely chopped onion

Rub steak with garlic; season with 1 teaspoon salt and pepper. Cut meat crosswise into 4 to 6 pieces.

In large skillet, partially cook bacon. Drain bacon and reserve drippings in skillet. Place slice of bacon on each piece of meat. Roll up and secure with wooden picks. Coat the rolls of steak and bacon with flour. Brown this in reserved bacon drippings over medium heat. Stir together tomato sauce, 1/2 teaspoon salt, onion, etc. Pour over meat. Cover tightly and simmer 45 to 60 minutes or until tender. Place on warm platter and remove picks. Heat sauce to boiling, stirring constantly. Pour over rolls. Serves 4 to 6 people.

MUSHROOM CUBE STEAK

Sandy Schneider
Hearth and Home

1/2 lb. fresh mushrooms or 1 can
4 cube steaks, seasoned
3 Tbsp. butter, divided
3/4 Tbsp. mustard

2 tsp. worcestershire sauce
   (divided)
1 Tbsp. finely diced onion

Rinse and pat dry and slice fresh mushrooms or drain canned and set aside.

In skillet, melt 1 1/2 tablespoons butter. Add steak. Brown 1 minute each side; remove to platter. Spread each side with musta and sprinkle with 1 teaspoon worcestershire sauce; set aside.

In same skillet, melt remaining butter. Add onions in mushrooms. Saute 2 minutes. Add remaining worcestershire sauce. Cook and stir until hot. Return steaks to skillet and reheat for 2 minutes.

BAKED STEAK DELUXE

Irene Schneider
Hearth and Home

1-2" thick sirloin top steak
flour
salt and pepper to taste
1 can cream of mushroom soup

1/2 bay leaf
1/2 clove garlic
1 tsp. worcestershire sauce
2/3 c. water
1/2 onion, sliced

Cut steak into serving pieces. Dredge steak in flour and brown on both sides in hot fat in skillet. Place in large casserole or small roaster; season with salt and pepper. Combine remaining ingredients in skillet drippings; bring to boil. Cook for several minutes to blend flavors. Pour over steak. Cover. Place on lowest rack in oven. Bake at 325° for 1 hour and 30 minutes to 2 hours or until tender. Makes 6 servings.

ROUND STEAK MARINADE

Ann Ruf
Pep and Progress

3/4 c. oil
1/4 c. soy sauce
1/4 c. honey
2 Tbsp. cider vinegar

2 Tbsp. onion, chopped or minced
1 clove garlic
1 1/2 tsp. ground ginger
1/2 c. wine

Cut meat into serving steaks. Add marinade. Marinate steak 24 hours in refrigerator and grill.

WINE-SAUCED ROUND STEAK

Jo Ann Rizzolo
Home Hustlers

1 1/2 lbs. beef round steak
2 Tbsp. all purpose flour
1/4 tsp. salt
dash pepper
2 Tbsp. cooking oil
1/2 c. dry red wine
1/4 c. water

1-3 oz. can sliced mushrooms
1/4 c. chopped onion
1 Tbsp. snipped parsley
1/4 tsp. salt
1/4 tsp. dried basil, crushed
1 Tbsp. cornstarch
1/4 c. water

Cut meat into serving size portions. Combine flour, the first 1/4 teaspoon salt and the pepper; coat meat with flour mixture.

In skillet , brown meat in hot oil. Drain off excess fat. Add wine, the first 1/4 cup water, the undrained mushrooms, onion, parsley, the remaining salt and the basil. Simmer, covered, for 1 1/4 hours or till meat is tender. Remove meat to warm platter. Measure pan juices including mushrooms. Add enough additional water to make 1 1/4 cups liquid and return to skillet. Blend cornstarch and the remaining 1/4 cup water. Add to skillet. Cook and stir till mixture thickens and bubbles. Pass sauce with meat. Makes 4 to 5 servings.

BEEF BURGUNDY

Debby Fehringer
Hearth and Home

4 slices bacon
1 1/3 lbs. beef top round
   cut in 1 1/4" cubes
1 can mushroom soup

1/4 c. burgundy
2 Tbsp. chopped parsley
1/8 tsp. pepper
12 small onions
2 c. sliced mushrooms

In large saucepan, cook bacon until crisp; remove and crumble. Brown beef in drippings. Pour off fat. Add soup, wine, parsley and pepper. Cover and cook over low heat for 1 hour and 30 minutes. Add onions and mushrooms. Cover and cook 1 hour longer or until beef is tender. Serve over wide noodles. Garnish with bacon and additional parsley.

EASY LIVER 'N ONIONS

Janet Kloberdanz
X-tra X-amples X-tension Club

4 slices bacon
1 lb. liver, sliced
2 Tbsp. flour

1 can Campbell's onion soup
1/4 c. chili sauce

In a skillet, cook bacon until crisp. Remove from pan and drain; crumble. Dust liver with flour. Brown in bacon drippings. Add bacon and remaining ingredients. Cover; simmer about 30 minutes or until liver is tender. Uncover and cook for a few minutes to thicken sauce. Makes 4 servings.

POT ROAST (MICROWAVE)

Jill Distel
Creative Homemakers

3 lbs. beef chuck roast
1/4 tsp. salt
dash of pepper
1 pkg. dry onion soup mix

1 c. water
3 potatoes, quartered
3 carrots, quartered

Arrange roast in 3 quart casserole. Pour in onion soup mix and water, salt and pepper. Cover with tight fitting lid. Microwave on medium (50°) for 20 minutes. Turn meat and arrange potatoes and carrots around the meat. Cover. Microwave on medium (50°) for 55 to 60 minutes or until meat and vegetables are tender. Makes 6 to 8 servings.

WINE ROAST

Bertha Luft
Pep and Progress

1-5 lb. roast
1 pkg. dry onion soup mix

1 pkg. dry mushroom soup
8 Tbsp. wine

Place on heavy foil the soup mix and 4 tablespoons wine. Place roast on mixture on top of roast. Sprinkle the dry mushroom soup and 4 tablespoons of wine. Close foil loosely around meat, making sure it is well sealed.

Bake as long as you want at 300° (4 hours or longer). Good for inexpensive cuts. If it has not been sealed right, the roast will have a tendency to burn on the bottom.

CHUCK ROAST SUPREME

Rena Morrison
Padroni E.H.

4 Tbsp. seasoned flour
3 Tbsp. shortening
2 c. canned tomatoes
1 green pepper, sliced
3 Tbsp. flour

1-6 lb. chuck roast
1 med. onion, sliced
1/2 c. mushrooms
3 or 4 stalks celery, cut up

Rub meat with seasoned flour. Brown well in hot shortening in a heavy roaster or Dutch oven. Add tomatoes and onion; cover and simmer for 2 1/2 hours. Add mushrooms, green pepper and celery; simmer for 30 minutes longer. Remove vegetables and roast to warm serving platter. Measure broth; add enough water for 2 cups. Make a paste by mixing flour with water or broth. Stir in paste to thicken. Bring mixture to boil, stirring as gravy thickens. Pour gravy over roast and vegetables and serve with rice.

BRAISED BEEF ROAST

Esther Nelson
Sterling Homemakers

4 lbs. beef tip, heel or round
  or rolled rump roast
1 Tbsp. vegetable oil
1 Tbsp. cracked pepper
3 1/4 c. water

2 Tbsp. instant beef bouillon
  or 6 beef bouillon cubes
3/4 c. cold water
1/3 c. all purpose flour

Cook beef roast in oil in Dutch oven over medium to low heat until brown; sprinkle with pepper. Add 3 1/4 cups water and the instant bouillon. Heat to boiling; reduce heat. Cover and simmer on top of range or cook in 325° oven until tender, about 3 hours. Remove beef to warm platter. Reserve 3 cups drippings in Dutch oven; skim excess fat. Shake 3/4 cup cold water and the flour in tightly covered container; stir gradually into broth. Heat to boiling, stirring constantly. Boil and stir 1 minute. Serve gravy with beef. Makes about 14 servings.

Note: To serve au jus, do not thicken beef broth.

PICKLE POT ROAST

Barbara Spelts
Shamrock

4 slices bacon
1 tsp. lemon pepper
   marinade
3 to 4 lb. pot roast

1 can condensed golden
   mushroom soup
1/2 c. chopped dill pickle
2 Tbsp. worcestershire sauce

Fry bacon and drain. Brown roast in 2 tablespoons bacon fat. Combine other ingredients and pour over meat. Top with crumbled bacon. Cover and simmer in oven for 2 1/2 hours or until done at 325 to 350°.

Slow cooker method: Brown as above; put browned meat in slow cooker and top with other ingredients. Cook 4 to 5 hours.

CHILI-BEEF BRISKET OF BEEF OVER WILD RICE ALMANDINE

Alba Desoto
Southsiders

2 1/2 lbs. beef brisket
1 tsp. salt
1/2 c. diced onion
1-12 oz. bottle of beer
2 med. tomatoes, sliced

1/4 tsp. garlic powder
1 tsp. pepper
1-12 oz. bottle of chili sauce
2-2 3/4 oz. pkgs. 5 min. wild rice
several sprigs parsley

Place beef brisket, fat side down, in heavy round 10 inch by at least 2 1/2 inches deep roasting pan. Sprinkle with garlic powder, salt, pepper and onion. Pour the chili sauce on top of the brisket. Roast, covered, for 3 hours at 325°. Remove cover and pour the beer over the brisket. Continue roasting for 30 minute longer. Remove from roasting pan to large serving platter and surround the brisket with the Wild Rice Almandine and garnish with sliced, ripe tomatoes and parsley sprigs. Pour hot sauce into serving dish. Slice the brisket very thin for serving and lay slices on a bed of the wild rice. Spoon hot sauce over each serving. Garnish as with platter.

Wild Rice Almandine:

1/3 c. margarine
1 Tbsp. chopped chives
2 2/3 c. hot water
2-2 3/4 oz. pkgs. 5 minute wild rice

1 Tbsp. chopped onion
1 1/2 tsp. slivered regular almond
1 tsp. instant beef flavored
   bouillon

Melt the margarine over medium heat in a heavy 2 quart skillet. Add the chopped onion, chives, green pepper and slivered almonds. Cook until the almonds begin to turn brown. Do not over Brown. Add the hot water, beef flavored bouillon and the 5 minute wild rice. Bring to a boil. Simmer uncovered for 10 minutes. Let stand covered for 5 minutes longer. Reheat if needed and drain any excess liquid before serving. Serves 8 to 10. Cost of $1.40 per serving. Preparation time, 30 minutes. Cooking time, 3 1/2 hours.

Write your extra recipes here:

Write your extra recipes here:

To preserve leftover egg yolks for future use, place them into a small bowl and add two tablespoons of salad oil. Then put into refrigerator. The egg yolks will remain soft and fresh, and egg yolks kept in this way can be used in many ways.

You may determine the age of an egg by placing it in the bottom of a bowl of cold water. If it lays on its side, it is strictly fresh. If it stands at an angle it is at least three days old and ten days old if it stands on end.

To keep egg yolks from crumbling when slicing hard-cooked eggs, wet the knife before each cut.

Bread crumbs added to scrambled eggs will improve the flavor and make larger helpings possible.

A tablespoon of vinegar added to the water when poaching eggs will help set the whites so they will not spread.

When cooking eggs it helps prevent cracking if you wet the shells in cold water before placing them in boiling water.

Add a little vinegar to the water when an egg cracks during boiling. It will help seal the egg.

Meringue will not shrink if you spread it on the pie so that it touches the crust on each side and bake it in a moderate oven.

When you cook eggs in the shell, put a big teaspoon of salt in the water. Then the shell won't crack.

Set eggs in pan of warm water before using as this releases all white from shells.

Egg whites for meringue should be set out to room temperature before beating, then they can be beaten to greater volume.

If you want to make a pecan pie and haven't any nuts, substitute crushed cornflakes. They will rise to the top the same as nuts and give a delicious flavor and crunchy surface.

To prevent crust from becoming soggy with cream pie, sprinkle crust with powdered sugar.

Cut drinking straws into short lengths and insert through slits in pie crusts to prevent juice from running over in the oven and permit steam to escape.

Put a layer of marshmallows in the bottom of a pumpkin pie, then add the filling. You will have a nice topping as the marshmallow will come to the top.

If the juice from your apple pie runs over in the oven, shake some salt on it, which causes the juice to burn to a crisp so it can be removed.

Use cooking or salad oil in waffles and hot cakes in the place of shortening. No extra pan or bowl to melt the shortening and no waiting.

SOUR CREAM ENCHILADAS

Barb Schaefer
Home Hustlers

12 corn tortillas
1 pt. sour cream
1/4 c. chopped green onion
1 lb. Monterey Jack cheese

1 can cream of chicken soup
1 can chopped green chilies
1/2 tsp. salt

Mix soup, sour cream and chilies and salt in a saucepan and warm. Grate cheese and set aside. Fry tortillas in hot grease just till soft. Drain on paper towel. Put layer of sour cream in bottom of 9x11 inch pan. Sprinkle cheese in the middle of tortilla and roll up. Place on sour cream. Put remaining sour cream over top and sprinkle with remaining cheese. Bake at 375° till bubbles or heat in microwave.

MEXICAN OMELET

Joyce Werner
Home Hustlers

3/4 c. chopped avocado
   or tomato
1/4 c. dairy sour cream
1 Tbsp. chopped green onion
1 tsp. lemon juice
   (for avocado)
2 Tbsp. chopped green chilies

1 corn tortilla
6 beaten eggs
dash hot sauce
1 c. shredded Monterey Jack
   cheese
1 Tbsp. butter
1/4 tsp. salt

Combine ingredients in left column and set aside. Heat oven to 325°.

Melt butter in oven skillet. Add tortilla and cook until soft. Pour in eggs (beaten with hot sauce) , salt and cook in oven for 3 to 5 minutes. Lift and let uncooked mixture flow under. Sprinkle with cheese and return to oven for 3 to 4 minutes or until cheese melts. Spread with avocado or tomato mixture on top half of the omelet. Return to oven 5 to 7 minutes longer. Remove and fold in half and serve.

TWENTY FOUR HOUR OMELET

Dorothy J. Robinson
Home Hustlers

4 slices white sandwich bread,
   trimmed of crusts and
   buttered
3/4 lb. grated cheddar cheese

4 eggs, slightly beaten
2 c. milk
1/2 tsp. salt

(Cont.)

1/2 tsp. dry mustard   dash of cayenne pepper

Butter one side of bread and cut into about 1 inch cubes. Place bread evenly in well greased 9x9 inch pan. Sprinkle bread with cheese. Beat together eggs, milk, salt, mustard and pepper. Pour over bread mixture; refrigerate, covered, overnight. Bake covered in 325° oven about 1 hour, then uncover for last 5 minutes of baking time.

PORK CHOP-RICE CASSEROLE

Sandy Ils
Home Hustlers

4 pork chops
6 Tbsp. raw rice
4 slices onion

4 slices tomato
4 slices green pepper
1 can consomme
marjoram and thyme

Brown pork chops and place on top of rice in fairly deep casserole. Add pork drippings. Put a slice of onion, tomato and green pepper on each chop. Salt and pepper each layer. Pour in 1 can consomme, undiluted. Sprinkle with a couple pinches each of marjoram and thyme. Bake at 350° for 1 hour. Serves 4.

TUNA DINNER DISH

Charlotte Lambrecht
Rainbows of Happiness

1-7 oz. can tuna
2 Tbsp. chopped onion
1 can cream of mushroom
     soup

1 c. milk
2 1/2 c. cooked rice

Drain oil from tuna into saucepan; add onion and cook over 1 heat for 5 minutes, stirring occasionally. Blend in soup, stirring constantly, until smooth. Add milk. Place hot rice in greased 1 1/2 quart casserole. Arrange tuna on rice; cover with sauce. Bake at 350° for 30 to 40 minutes. Serves 6.

CHOP STICK CASSEROLE

Carol Lambrecht
Rainbows of Happiness

1 can mushroom soup
1-3 oz. can chow mein
  noodles
1 can tuna
1/2 c. salted cashew nuts

1/4 c. chopped onion
1/4 c. green pepper, chopped
1 c. celery, chopped

Mix all the ingredients together and bake 15 minutes at 375°.

EASY TUNA CASSEROLE

Yvonne Davidson
Night Owls

1-10 1/2 oz. can condensed
   cream of mushroom soup,
   undiluted
1/2 c. milk
1-7 oz. can tuna, drained

1-8 oz. can peas, drained
2 Tbsp. sliced pimento
   stuffed olives
2 c. corn chips, crushed

Preheat oven to 375°. In 1 1/2 quart casserole, combine soup with milk, mixing until smooth. Add tuna, peas and olives mixing well. Top with corn chips. Bake uncovered for 25 minutes.

TUNA LOAF

Cleta Carr
Pep and Progress

1 1/8 c. evap. milk
3/4 c. water
1 1/2 c. grated cheese
   (American)
2 1/2 Tbsp. margarine
1 1/4 c. soft bread crumbs
1/4 c. finely cut onion

1 small can tuna
1/4 c. pimento (opt.)
1 tsp. salt
1 tsp. pepper
3 eggs, beaten
3 c. cooked macaroni

Combine milk, water and butter. Heat to boiling. Add cheese and stir till cheese melts. Remove from fire. Mix in crumbs, onion, pimento, tuna, salt and pepper; stir. Fold in macaroni and eggs. Pour into greased baking dish. Bake at 350° for 1 1/2 hours.

CHICKEN CASSEROLE

Florence Lindstrom
Kelly Woman's Improvement Club

1 chicken, cooked, boned
   and diced
1 large box Stove Top
   dressing (2 env.)
1 can celery soup

1 can chicken soup
1/2 can water
2 c. crushed potato chips

Prepare dressing as directed on package. Add the celery soup to the dressing mixture and combine with diced chicken. Put into 9x13 inch pan. Dilute the chicken soup with the water and pour over the dressing mix. Top with potato chips and bake 20 to 35 minutes in a 350° oven.

CHICKEN SPECTACULAR

Judy Armstrong
Southsiders

3 c. cooked chicken, bite
   size pieces
1 box long grain and wild rice
   (Uncle Ben's)
1 can cream of celery soup
1 small can water chestnuts, sliced
1 tsp. onion, chopped

1 can French style green beans
chicken broth
1/2 c. mayonnaise
2 tsp. pimento, chopped
salt and pepper to taste

Cook rice in chicken broth as directed on package. Mix together with other ingredients and place in a 2 quart casserole. Bake at 350° for 30 minutes.

CHICKEN DRESSING CASSEROLE

Barbara Wisdom
Home Hustlers

4 c. diced chicken
4 c. chicken broth
1 1/2 c. celery
1 1/2 c. diced cheese
1 can cream of mushroom soup

2 eggs
1/2 tsp. pepper
1 tsp. salt
onion
4 c. soda or Ritz crackers,
   crushed

Combine all ingredients except for 1 cup cracker crumbs for on top. Bake at 350° for 1 hour.
Note: For crock pot use only 3 cups broth.

CHICKEN POT PIE

Jeri Breidenbach
Hearth and Home

Boil chicken and let cool while mixing together (use the water you boiled in for gravy); add 2 chicken bouillon cubes and flour water to thicken.

Add:

2 c. cooked potato cubes
2 c. cooked carrots, sliced
2 c. peas
2 c. corn

2 c. green beans
cubed chicken

Now add to a casserole pie crust with both top and bottom crust. Pour in chicken mix and put top crust on and seal.
Bake at 350° for 20 minutes, till crust is done. With left over chicken mix, it is good as soup or enough to make another pie.

CHICKEN CASSEROLE

Mary May
Hearth and Home

2 c. boned chicken
1 can cream of mushroom soup
1 can chicken with rice soup

1-13 oz. can evap. milk
1 can chow mein noodles

Mix all ingredients. Place in casserole and top with crushed chips. Bake at 325° for 1 hour.

FIVE-CAN CASSEROLE

Eva M. Guenzi
Home Hustlers

1 can Swanson's boned
  chicken
1 can cream of mushroom soup
1 can chicken and rice soup

1 small can condensed milk
1 can chow mein noodles

Mix together and place in greased casserole. Bake at 350° for 45 minutes to 1 hour.

EASIEST CHICKEN CASSEROLE

Doris Harms
Night Owls

1 can cream of chicken soup
1 can mushroom soup
1 1/4 c. Minute Rice
1 can cream of celery soup

1/4 lb. melted butter or margarine
1 cut up chicken
salt, pepper and paprika to
  taste

Blend together soups, butter or margarine and rice in small roaster. Lay chicken over top. Season with salt, pepper and paprika. Cover. Bake 2 1/2 to 3 hours at 275°. Makes 6 large servings.

RICE AND CHICKEN CASSEROLE

Jeri Breidenbach
Hearth and Home

2 c. cubed cooked chicken
2 c. cooked rice
1 c. peas

1 can cream of chicken soup
1 can cream of mushroom soup

Mix together. Add crushed potato chips on top. Bake at 350° for 45 minutes.

CHICKEN CASSEROLE

Esther Schuppe
Pep and Progress

Cream Sauce:

4 Tbsp. flour
4 Tbsp. oleo

1 c. chicken broth

Mix together and cook till thickened.

2 c. chicken
1 c. diced celery
2 tsp. minced onion
2 c. chopped hard boiled
    eggs

1/2 tsp. salt
1/4 tsp. pepper
1/4 tsp. worcestershire sauce
1 Tbsp. lemon juice
3/4 c. mayonnaise
2 c. potato chips

Line dish with half of potato chips. Mix all other ingredients. Pour over potato chips and top with rest of potato chips. Bake, uncovered at 400° until heated. Serves 8 to 10.

CHICKEN RICE CASSEROLE

Ellen Luft
Night Owls

1 fryer, cut
1 1/2 c. Minute Rice
1 pkg. dry onion soup

2 cans cream of chicken soup
1 soup can of water

Place washed rice in bottom of casserole and top with dry onion soup, then place chicken pieces on top. Heat the cream of chicken soup and water. Pour over all and bake uncovered for 2 hours at 350°. Cover and reduce heat to 250° for the last 1/2 hour of baking.

FRIEND OF A FRIEND'S CHICKEN

Clara Werner

1-10 1/2 oz. can cream of celery
    soup
1-10 1/2 oz. can cream of
  mushroom soup
1/2 c. milk

1 1/2 c. instant rice,
  uncooked
1 frying chicken, cut in
    serving pieces
1- 1 3/4 oz. pkg. onion soup

Combine celery soup, mushroom soup and milk. Mix thoroughly and heat. Sprinkle rice in greased shallow casserole. Spoon soup mixture over rice. Arrange chicken pieces on top (remove excess fat from chicken). Shake onion soup in package to mix it. Sprinkle onion soup over and around chicken. Bake covered at 325° for 2 hours.

CHICKEN ENCHILADA CASSEROLE

Diane Freeman
Southsiders of Iliff

1 chicken, cooked and boned
1 large can chopped green chilies
1 can cream of mushroom soup
1 c. chicken broth
1 lb. cheddar cheese, grated
1 large onion, chopped
8 corn tortillas
2 Tbsp. butter
1 can enchilada sauce

Mix all ingredients and bring to simmer. Tear tortillas in pieces and layer in bottom of 9x13 inch pan. Pour simmering mixture over tortillas. Add grated cheese on top. Bake at 350° for 30 minutes.

MEXICAN CHICKEN CASSEROLE

Florence Annan
Home Hustlers

1 fryer chicken, cooked and deboned
Dorito chips
1 can cream of mushroom soup
1 can cream of chicken soup
1-13 oz. can Pet milk
1-7 oz. can chopped green chilies
grated cheddar cheese

Combine both soups with Pet milk and heat slightly. Grease 9x13 inch casserole. Make layers of Dorito chips, chicken, and sauce mix. End with sauce and top with cheese. Bake covered at 350° for 45 minutes to 1 hour. If desired, top with sour cream before serving.

MEXICAN CHICKEN CASSEROLE

Nona Amen
Proctor

1 chicken, cooked, deboned (with broth)
1 med. onion, chopped
1/2 lb. grated cheese
2 cans cream of chicken soup
1 tsp. garlic salt
1 tsp. chili powder
1 can tomato with green chilies
1 pkg. tortilla chips

Soak chips in broth till soft. Line casserole with soft chips. Mix chicken, onion, cheese, spices and tomatoes. Put in casserole. Top with soup mixed with 1/4 cup broth. Bake at 350° for 35 minutes.

MEXICAN CHICKEN CASSEROLE

Catherine Nab
Pep and Progress

1 chicken
1 pkg. corn tortillas
1 bell pepper, chopped
1 c. grated longhorn cheese
1 tsp. chili powder
1 can mushroom soup
1 can cream of chicken soup
1 can dried green chilies

(Cont.)

71

Boil chicken and bone. Reserve broth. In 9x13 inch baking dish, place layer of tortillas that have been dipped in the chicken broth, layer of pepper, onion, chicken and cheese. Sprinkle 1/2 of the chili powder over top. Repeat second layer. Combine soups and chilies. Mix well and pour over layers. Bake at 325° for 1 hour.

CHICKEN TETRAZZINS

Kathy Glassburn
Padroni E.H.

5 lb. hen or turkey
2 c. tomato juice
1 green pepper, chopped
1 small can chopped pimento
1 Tbsp. worcestershire sauce
1 can chow mein noodles

7 oz. pkg. spaghetti
1 c. chopped celery
1 can mushroom pieces and
    liquid
18 sliced stuffed olives
3/4 lb. grated cheese

After cooking chicken, remove broth. Cool and take from bone. Add spaghetti to 3 cups broth, tomato juice and celery and green pepper. Cook until done; add mushrooms and liquid; add pimento stuffed olives, worcestershire sauce, also add salt, celery salt and onion powder to taste. Add cooked chopped chicken (not the small pieces) top with cheese and cover with noodles. Bake at 300.° for 30 minutes. To freeze, omit cheese and noodles until ready to bake. Divide into 2 or 3 casseroles and freeze.

CHICKEN TETRAZZINI

NONA Amen
Proctor

2 c. cooked cubed chicken
  or turkey
1-7 oz. pkg. spaghetti
chicken broth
1 can cream of mushroom soup
1 can sliced mushrooms

2 stalks celery, chopped
pimento, salt and pepper
garlic powder to taste
1/2 c. cheddar cheese

Cook spaghetti in chicken broth till done but firm. Drain and save broth. Combine rest of ingredients with spaghetti. Add 1/4 to 1/2 cup broth if it looks too dry. Bake at 350° for 30 minutes.

BEEF POTATO BOAT

Lillie Manuello
Southsiders

2 large baking potatoes
1-2.5 oz. pkg. dried beef
3 Tbsp. margarine or butter
salt and pepper to taste

4 tsp. diced onion
4 tsp. finely diced green pepper
3 Tbsp. flour
1 1/3 c. milk
4 slices American cheese

Scrub potatoes and dry; grease skin with cooking oil and bake until tender. Meanwhile, about 10 minutes before potatoes are done, cut beef into small pieces. Melt margarine or butter in small saucepan. Add beef, onion and pepper. Cook 3 minutes over medium low heat. Stir in flour and seasonings and cook, stirring often, until thickened.

To serve, cut across, on top of the baked potatoes. Open and fluff potatoes with a fork. Spoon sauce over potatoes and top with cheese. May use ham, chicken, turkey, bacon or whatever meat one desires. Serves 2.

FIONI DI COCUZZI OR STUFFED SPINACH FLOWERS

Margaret Lueck
Hearth and Home

yellow squash flowers
diced thin ham
bread crumbs

grated or finely sliced
mozzarella
2 eggs, beaten

Remove stems and insides of blossoms and wash thoroughly but gently. Soak in salted water about 1 hour, then pat dry in paper towels. Fill each flower with cheese and ham, then dip in egg, then in bread crumbs and fry in olive oil. Drain on paper towels. Different but delicious.

SPRING CASSEROLE

Loretto Lively
Padroni E.H.

6 slices white bread
10 oz. frozen chopped broccoli, cooked and drained
6 eggs, slightly beaten
2 Tbsp. minced onion
1/4 tsp. mustard

8 slices sharp cheddar cheese
1 can cubed Spam or ham may be used
3 1/2 c. milk
1/2 tsp. salt

Fit bread into large buttered pan; put cheese slices over bread. Sprinkle broccoli on top over cheese. Put Spam on top of broccoli. Combine milk, eggs, salt, onion and mustard. Pour on top and cover with a few bread crumbs and some grated cheese. Put in refrigerator overnight. Bake 1 hour and 15 minutes at 325°.

COUNTRY HAM CASSEROLE

Traci McGeehan
Creative Homemakers

1 lb. Velveeta, cubed
1 c. milk
1/2 c. Miracle Whip
2 c. chopped ham

1-10 oz. pkg. frozen chopped broccoli, cooked and well drained

73 (Cont.)

5 oz. spaghetti, cooked   1 Tbsp. chopped chives
  and drained

Heat Velveeta, milk and salad dressing over low heat. Stir
until sauce is smooth. Add remaining ingredients and mix well.
Pour into 2 quart casserole. Bake at 350° for 35 to 40 minutes
or until hot.

HAM AND NOODLE CASSEROLE   Mrs. Walter Marks
Member of former Harding Extension H.C.

8 oz. pkg. med. wide noodles   1 c. milk
2 c. cooked ham   2 Tbsp. butter
1 c. cooked frozen peas   2 Tbsp. flour
1 c. grated cheddar cheese   2 Tbsp. catsup
                                 1 Tbsp. bottled horseradish

  Topping:

1 c. bread crumbs   1 Tbsp. butter

Cook noodles as package directs. Make cream sauce of milk,
butter and flour. Add the cheese to cream sauce and stir until
cheese is melted. Add catsup, horseradish and mix well. Mix all
the ingredients and pour into greased oblong casserole baking
dish, 7 1/2 x 12 inches. Top with bread mixture. Bake at 350°
until crumbs are brown.

QUICK HAM-BROCCOLI TETRAZZINI   Kathy Graham
X-tra X-amples X-tension Club

1-8 oz. pkg. spaghetti   1/2 tsp. salt
4 Tbsp. margarine or butter   1/4 tsp. pepper
1 med. onion, diced   1-10 oz. pkg. frozen chopped
1-4 oz. can sliced mushrooms   broccoli
1/4 c. all purpose flour   2 c. diced cooked ham
3 c. milk   grated parmesan cheese

In 6 quart saucepot, cook spaghetti as label directs; drain
well. Return spaghetti to saucepot; cover and keep warm.
Meanwhile, in 2 quart saucepan over medium heat, melt
butter or margarine; add onion and drained mushrooms; cook until
onions are tender, stirring occasionally. Stir in flour until blended.
Gradually stir in milk, salt and pepper. Cook stirring constantly
until mixture is slightly thickened. Stir in broccoli and ham, separa-
ting broccoli with fork; heat mixture to boiling.
Stir ham mixture into spaghetti. Gently toss to mix well
and heat through. Serve with Parmesan cheese. Makes 6 main
dish servings.

OVERNIGHT CASSEROLE

Esther Schuppe
Pep and Progress

2 c. macaroni, uncooked
1/4 lb. shredded cheese
1/4 lb. ground ham

2 cans mushroom soup
4 hard cooked, diced eggs
1 onion, minced

Combine above ingredients. Let stand overnight. Bake at 350° for 1 hour.

HAM SOUFFLE

Amelia Vendegna
Pep and Progress

1 Tbsp. butter
1 Tbsp. flour
2/3 c. milk

1 1/2 c. chopped ham
salt and pepper
2 eggs, separated

Melt butter in saucepan. Blend in flour and milk, stirring constantly. Add salt and pepper to taste. Cook until thick. Remove from fire and add beaten yolks and ham. Cool. Fold in the stiffly beaten egg whites. Place in greased casserole and bake in moderate 350° oven about 45 minutes.

PINTO BEANS AND FRANKS

Barbara Spelts
Shamrock

2 c. pinto beans
dash of ground cloves
4 Tbsp. butter
2 cloves garlic
1 large onion, chopped

2 c. canned tomatoes
3/4 c. catsup
salt and pepper

Sort and wash beans. Cover cleaned beans with cold water; bring to a boil. Let stand 1 hour. Then cook until tender. Saute onion and garlic in butter until tender. Add cloves, tomatoes, catsup, salt and pepper and cook until thick. Add cooked beans plus 1 cup bean juice (if any), may add water if no bean juice remains. Add sliced hot dogs if desired. Large recipe. Just cook half for small family. Freezes well.

BEANS 'N WIENERS WAIKIKI

Marge Rieke
Pep and Progress

2 Tbsp. butter or margarine
1/4 c. onion, chopped
1/3 c. green pepper, chopped
1-20 oz. can pineapple rings,
 drained (reserve syrup)

1 pkg. wieners, cut in chunks
2 Tbsp. vinegar
1 Tbsp. soy sauce
1/3 c. catsup
1/3 c. firmly packed brown sugar

(Cont.)

1-31 oz. can Van Camp's
 pork and beans

1 can chow mein noodles (opt.)

Cut pineapple into chunks, reserving 3 or 4 rings for garnish. Saute green pepper, onion, pineapple and wiener chunks in margarine. Simmer 5 minutes; add pineapple syrup, vinegar, soy sauce, catsup and brown sugar. Heat until bubbly. Pour pork and beans into baking dish and pineapple mixture. Stir gently to blend. Place halved rings on top of casserole. Bake in moderate 350° oven for 30 minute. Serves 6.

BRUNCH CASSEROLE

Dorothy Bartholomew
Pep and Progress

2 lb. link sausage
 (Swift's Brown and Serve)
 browned and drained
3/4 lb. cheddar cheese, grated

8 slices bread, cubed
 (remove crust)
4 eggs
2 1/4 c. milk
1 can mushroom soup

Use 9x13 inch pan. Slice sausage and put in casserole with bread cubes and cheese. Pour milk, eggs and soup mixture over all. Don't fill to capacity. Refrigerate overnight. Bake at 325° for 1 1/2 hours.

SAUSAGE CASSEROLE

Sadie Slice, Shamrock
Pearly Breidenback, Hearth and Home
Lorraine Johnston, Home Hustlers

8 slices white bread, cubed
2 c. grated sharp cheddar
 cheese
20 link sausages, cut in
 bite size pieces

4 eggs
2 1/2 c. milk
1/4 tsp. dried mustard
1/2 c. milk
1 can cream of mushroom soup

Put cubes of bread in bottom of 9x13 inch baking pan (greased. Add cheese and sausage pieces. Mix eggs and milk and mustard and pour over bread mixture. Cover and refrigerate overnight. Mix other 1/2 cup milk with can of soup and pour over top before baking at 350° for 1 1/2 hours. Let stand 15 minutes before cutting.

ELLENBURG SPECIAL

Millie Boxler
Pep and Progress

2 stalks celery, chopped
1 small onion, chopped
1/3 green pepper, chopped
1 lb. Jimmie Dean pork sausage

1 c. uncooked rice
2 pkgs. Lipton's noodle soup
4 c. hot water

Fry pork sausage, celery, onion and pepper together. Put in 2 quart casserole. Add rice, noodle soup and hot water. Bake covered for 45 minutes at 350°. Stir occasionally.

HAMBURGER MEDLEY

Lillie Manuello
Southsiders

1 lb. ground hamburger
1-8 oz. can tomato sauce

1 can onion soup
1 1/2 c. uncooked noodles

Mix together in a greased 1 1/2 quart casserole. Cover tightly and bake in a 325° oven for 1 hour. Serves 4.

LINDA'S CASSEROLE

Lillie Manuello
Southsiders

1 med. onion, diced
2 Tbsp. butter
1 1/2 lbs. lean ground beef
6 c. or 1 med. head cabbage

2 to 3 slices American cheese
1-10 oz. can tomato soup
1/2 soup can of water

Saute in butter until transparent, the onion. Crumble and add the ground beef. Cook until all redness is gone. Shred cabbage into greased 8x10 inch oblong casserole. Put beef, onion mixture on top of cabbage. Top with slices of cheese, broken up. Pour soup and water on top. DO NOT STIR. Cover and bake at 325° for 1 hour.

CLUB CASSEROLE

Bertha Luft

1 1/2 lbs. hamburger
onion
1 Tbsp. chili powder
1 #2 can chili beans
1 can chili beef soup

1 large can tomato sauce
1 can tomato soup
1 can whole kernel corn
1 c. crushed taco chips

Brown hamburger and onion. Add chili powder, chili beans, chili beef soup, tomato soup, tomato sauce and whole corn. Mix. Put in 9x13 inch greased pan. Put crushed taco chips on top. When almost done, top with grated cheese and cover to melt cheese. Bake about 1 hour at 350°.

MOCK CHICKEN CASSEROLE

Hilda Bredehoft
Pep and Progress

2 lbs. hamburger
1 tsp. salt
1/2 tsp. pepper

1 can cream of celery soup
2 cans chicken soup

77

(Cont.)

3 soup cans milk   1-8 oz. pkg. stuffing mix

Cook hamburger in skillet until brown. Add salt and pepper. Stir in remaining ingredients and blend thoroughly. Place in casserole. Bake in preheated 350° oven for 30 minutes. Serves 12 to 14.

CARPET BAGGERS
Shirley Herzog
Padroni E.H.

2 lbs. hamburger   2 eggs
1/2 c. milk   1/2 c. bread crumbs
1/4 c. onion   2 boxes Stove Top stuffing
                               mix (chicken)

Mix first 5 ingredients in bowl; form round balls, about 2 inches, and place between 2 pieces of waxed paper. Flatten until thin. Mix Stove Top mix; place 2 tablespoons in center and bring meat pattie to center and close. Place in casserole dish. Cover with 3 cans mushroom soup and 1/2 cup catsup. Bake uncovered about 1 1/2 hours at 325°, top will open.

COUSIN JACKS
Bette McBride
Proctor

Crust:

3 c. sifted flour   1 tsp. salt
1 c. shortening   1/2 c. water

Filling:

2 1/4 c. round or sirloin tips   3/4 c. chopped onion
1/2 c. finely chopped   1 1/2 Tbsp. butter
   potatoes   salt and pepper to taste

Cut crust ingredients   together like cornmeal. Roll and cut into 6 inch squares. In the center of each pastry square, layer meat, potatoes, onion and season with salt and pepper. Sprinkle 1 tablespoon bouillon or water over mix. Fold pastry over in center and crimp edges together to seal. Bake at 350° for 45 minutes to 1 hour.

ZUCCHINI MEAT CASSEROLE
Kathy Glassburn
Padroni E.H.

1 lb. sausage or hamburger   1 1/2 c. zucchini, shredded
1 1/2 c. Minute Rice   1/2 onion, chopped

1 c. grated cheese
1 c. tomatoes
1 c. hot water

1 tsp. mustard
1 tsp. garlic salt and pepper

Brown meat in electric skillet; add all other ingredients but the cheese. Simmer on low heat until zucchini are tender. Sprinkle with cheese before serving.

BEEF NOODLE BAKE

Marlene Allen
Padroni E.H.

2 lbs. ground beef
2 tsp. salt
1/4 tsp. pepper
1 Tbsp. sugar
2 large cans tomato paste

1 onion or 1 bunch green onions
1-8 oz. pkg. cream cheese
1 c. sour cream
1 c. cheddar cheese, grated
   (for topping)
1-12 oz. pkg. noodles

Brown beef and add salt, pepper, tomato sauce and sugar. Cook noodles. Mix cream cheese and onions and sour cream. Put a layer of noodles, then meat, then half of cream mixture and repeat twice. Top with cheese. Bake 30 minutes at 350°.

HAMBURGER CASSEROLE

Phyllis Moore
Pep and Progress

1 lb. hamburger
2 c. sliced potatoes
1 c. whole kernel corn

1 can tomato soup
sliced onion to taste
1 c. diced cheese

Place hamburger in skillet; cook until light gray in color, stirring constantly. Add soup, potatoes, onion, corn and cheese. Place in casserole. Bake at 325° for 1 hour.

FRICCADILLIES

Louise Ebbers
Padroni E.H.

1 1/2 lbs. ground beef
2 slices bread (may use more)
1 tsp. salt
1/2 soup can water
dash of pepper

2 eggs, beaten
1 c. milk
1 can mushroom soup
3/4 c. flour

Combine beef, beaten eggs, bread, milk and salt. Spoon meat mixture about size of large egg into small bowl containing flour. Shape meat into patties and roll in flour. Put into lightly greased skillet; brown on both sides. Place meat balls in 8x12 inch baking

79   (Cont.)

dish; add mushroom soup diluted with 1/2 can water and stir to make a gravy. Add dash of pepper. Pour gravy around and over meatballs. Bake at 350° for about 25 minutes. I have baked in microwave oven.

CRESCENT ITALIANO BAKE

Earline Schuppe
Proctor

1 lb. ground beef
1 c. mushrooms
1/2 c. chopped onion
1/2 tsp. salt
1/2 tsp. pepper
8 oz. can tomato sauce

1 c. shredded cheddar cheese
8 oz. can crescent rolls
1/2 c. sour cream
1/4 tsp. oregano
1/4 tsp. basil or rosemary

Preheat oven to 375°. In frying pan, brown ground beef, mushrooms and onion. Add salt, pepper and tomato sauce. Place in an ungreased 8x12 inch baking pan. Sprinkle with cheese. Separate dough into 8 triangles. Combine sour cream and herbs. Sprinkle 1 tablespoon of this mixture on each triangle. Roll up starting on the wide end. Arrange on top of casserole. Bake at 375° for 25 to 30 minutes or until golden brown. Serves 4 to 6.

COUNTRY PIE

Cheryl Monheiser
X-tra X-amples X-tension Club

Crust:

1/2 of 8 oz. can tomato sauce
1/2 c. bread crumbs
1 lb. ground beef

1/4 c. chopped onion
1/4 c. chopped green pepper
1/8 tsp. pepper and oregano

Filling:

1 1/3 c. Minute Rice
1 1/2 cans tomato sauce
1/2 tsp. salt

1/2 c. water
1 c. grated cheddar cheese

Crust: Combine ingredients in a bowl and mix well with a fork. Then pat the mixture into the bottom and sides of a 9 inch pie plate.

Filling: Combine rice, sauce, salt, water and 2/3 cup cheese. Spoon into meat shell. Cover with foil and bake at 350° for 25 minutes. Top with remaining cheese. Bake uncovered 10 to 15 minutes. Spoon off grease. Makes 5 to 6 servings.

HAMBURGER PIE

Debby Fehringer
Hearth and Home

1 lb. ground beef
Potato Buds instant
  puffs (enough for 8
    servings)
1 egg
1 tsp. salt
1/8 tsp. pepper

1 Tbsp. instant minced onion
1/4 c. catsup
1 c. milk
1/2 c. shredded sharp cheddar
  cheese

Heat oven to 350°. Mix meat, 1 1/3 cups of the instant puffs (dry), the egg, salt, pepper, onion, catsup and milk. Spread in un-greased pie pan. Bake uncovered 35 to 45 minutes. Prepare remaining instant puffs as directed on package for 4 servings. Top baked meat loaf with mashed potatoes. Sprinkle with cheese. Bake 3 to 4 minutes longer or until cheese melts. Makes 4 to 5 servings.

MAZETTI

Marlene Allen
Padroni E.H.

1 1/2 c. chopped onions
1 c. chopped celery
1 1/2 lbs. ground beef
1 can tomato sauce
1-12 oz. pkg. wide noodles,
  cooked
salt and pepper to taste
1/2 c. sliced olives

1/4 c. chopped green pepper
2 Tbsp. salad oil
1 1/2 c. tomatoes
2/3 c. tomato paste
1 can sliced mushrooms, drained
1/4 lb. cheddar cheese, shredded

Cook onions, green pepper and celery in salad oil until tender but not brown. Add beef and cook until lightly browned. Remove excess fat. Add tomatoes, tomato sauce and tomato paste. Add cooked noodles and mushrooms; mix well. Season to taste with salt and pepper. Pour into greased 3 quart casserole. Bake at 350° for 30 minutes. Garnish with the cheese and olives while hot.

GROUND BEEF AND RICE CASSEROLE

Carrie Terrell
Creative Homemakers

1 lb. hamburger
2 small onions
1 can cream of chicken soup

1 can cream of mushroom soup
1 soup can water
1/2 c. uncooked rice

Brown meat and onions. Add soups, water, rice. Mix well. Pour in greased casserole. Bake 1 1/2 hours at 350°.

LINGUINI

Janice Grauberger
Hearth and Home

8 oz. linguini
4 oz. Italian sausage
1 small onion, chopped
6 oz. tomato paste
1 tsp. oregano
3/4 c. tomato juice
1/4 c. Parmesan cheese

1 tsp. leaf oregano
1 tsp. parsley flakes
1/4 tsp. salt
1-6 1/2 oz. can minced
  clams, undrained
1-4 oz. can mushroom pieces,
  undrained

Crumble sausage into 1 quart casserole. Add onion and garlic. Heat medium high, uncovered, for 2 1/2 to 3 minutes, until no longer pink. Stir meat into small pieces; drain. Stir in tomato paste, oregano, parsley, salt, thyme, pepper, clams, mushrooms, and juice; mix well. Cover on medium to high, for 8 to 9 minutes, stirring twice. Cook linguini and place on a serving plate. Spoon hot sauce over and sprinkle with cheese. Can use ground beef in place of sausage.

MANICOTTI

Marilyn Gerk
X-tra X-amples X-tension Club

1/2 lb. ground beef
1 clove garlic
1 c. creamed cottage cheese
4 oz. shredded mozzarella
1/2 tsp. salt

1/2 c. real mayonnaise
8 manicotti noodles (cooked, drained
1 (16 oz.) can spaghetti sauce
1/2 tsp. dried oregano leaves
Parmesan cheese

Brown beef and garlic; drain fat. Mix cottage cheese, mozzarella cheese, salt and mayonnaise in a bowl. Stir in beef. Stuff each manicotti with about 1/4 cup of cheese and beef mixture. Place in baking dish. Cover with sauce. Sprinkle with Parmesan cheese and oregano. Cover with foil and bake 15 minutes at 350°. Remove foil and bake 10 minutes longer.

WESTERN CASSEROLE

Loretto Lively
Padroni E.H.

1 lb. ground beef
1 1/2 tsp. salt
3/4 c. cooked rice
1 can condensed tomato soup
1/2 tsp. oregano
1-1 lb. can (approx.) cut
  green beans, drained

1-12 to 16 oz. can whole kernel
  corn, drained
1/2 c. grated American cheese
1 Tbsp. salad oil
1/2 c. chopped onion
1 soup can water
1/4 tsp. dry mustard

Mix ground beef lightly with cheese and 1 teaspoon salt until well blended; shape into 12 balls. Brown in salad oil in a large frying pan; remove with slotted spoon and place in ungreased 8 cup baking dish. Sprinkle with uncooked rice and onion. Stir soup, water, oregano, mustard and remaining 1/2 teaspoon salt into drippings in pan; heat slowly, stirring several times to boiling. Pour over meat mixture, cover. Bake in moderate 350° oven for 45 minutes, stirring with fork to mix well. Spoon drained green beans on corn in a double ring on top, then cover again. Bake 30 minutes longer, or until rice is tender and vegetables are heated through. Serves 4 to 6 people.

HAMBURGER CASSEROLE

Lorene Freeman
Southsiders

2 lbs. hamburger meat
small chopped onion
1 can tomato soup

1 can chow mein noodles
salt
1 can cream of mushroom soup

Cook hamburger meat and onions; drain off grease. Add tomato soup, cream of mushroom soup, and 1/2 can of chow mein noodles. Mix well. Put in 9x13 inch baking dish. Put the remaining half of chow mein noodles on top. Bake for 30 minutes at 350°.

TATER TOT CASSEROLE

Patty Craven
Creative homemakers

1 lb. hamburger
1 can cream of mushroom soup

1-16 oz. can green beans,
    drained
1 bag Tater Tots

Pat uncooked hamburger in bottom of casserole dish, then mushroom soup and green beans. Top with Tater Tots. Bake at 350° for 1 hour.

HAMBURGER HOT DISH

Bonnie Janda
X-tra X-amples X-tension Club

1 1/2 lbs. hamburger
1 1/2 c. diced celery
1 small onion
1 1/4 c. raw rice, cooked
  or same amt. instant rice

1 can mushroom soup
1 can cream of chicken soup
2 Tbsp. soy sauce
1 can Chinese noodles

After cooking first 3 ingredients (brown together cooking 10 minutes; drain fat); mix all ingredients together and sprinkle Chinese noodles over the top after putting in casserole dish. Bake for 30 minutes at 350°.

TATER TOT CASSEROLE

Florence Lindstrom
Kelly Woman's Improvement Club

2 lbs. ground beef
salt and pepper to taste
1 c. chopped onion
2 tsp. green pepper, chopped

2 cans mushroom soup
1/2 c. cheese, grated
1 large pkg. Tater Tots
  (frozen)

Salt and pepper beef to taste; add onion and green pepper. Press mixture into bottom of 9x13 inch pan. Cover with mushroom soup. Spread grated cheese on top. Place Tater Tots over cheese and bake in 350° oven for 1 hour. (This may be put in two smaller pans.) Freezes well.

TATER TOT CASSEROLE

Hilda Bredehoft
Pep and Progress

1 lb. ground beef, lean
1 can cream of chicken soup
1/2 can milk
1 can green beans
salt, as desired

1 small box frozen onion rings
1-16 oz. box frozen Tater Tots

Brown beef; pour off fat. Mix soup, milk and beans. Add to meat. Put mixture in ungreased casserole. Press onion rings on top and put Tater Tots on top of all. Bake at 350° for 1 hour. Salt as desired.

CALICO BEANS

Mrs. R. Burkholder
Kelly Woman's Improvement Club

1 large can pork and beans
1 can kidney beans
1 can butter beans
1/4 lb. bacon, diced
1 lb. ground beef

1 med. onion, diced
1/2 c. brown sugar
1/2 c. catsup
2 Tbsp. vinegar
1/2 tsp. salt

Drain kidney and butter beans; save the liquid. Brown bacon and ground beef and chopped onion. Combine all 3 cans of beans with ground beef and bacon and onion. Put in a greased 9x12 inch baking dish. Combine brown sugar, catsup, vinegar and salt into a sauce. Pour over the beans. If it is too dry, add some of the bean liquid. Bake at 350° for at least 1 hour.

HARLEQUIN BEANS (CROCK POT) Florence Mette, Southsiders
Dorothy Bartholomew, Pep and Progress

1/2 lb. hamburger
1/2 lb. bacon, coarsely
   chopped
1 med. onion, minced
1/2 c. catsup
1 tsp. salt
1/2 c. brown sugar

1 tsp. mustard
2 tsp. vinegar
1 #2 can pork and beans
1 #2 can lima or butter beans
1 #2 can kidney beans

    Brown hamburger, bacon and onion. Pour off fat and combine with remaining ingredients. Bake at 350° for 40 minutes or put in a crock pot for 2 to 3 hours on low.

BEEF AND VEGETABLE CASSEROLE
Gail Wagner
Pep and Progress

1 1/2 lbs. ground beef
1/2 tsp. onion powder
1/2 tsp. garlic powder
2 c. green beans, drained

1 lb. pkg. frozen Tater Tots
1 can cream of mushroom soup
1/2 to 2/3 c. milk

    Brown ground beef, onion and garlic powder. Drain off fat. Add rest of ingredients. Place all in 2 1/2 quart casserole dish. Bake at 325° for 1 hour. Add one 6 ounce can French fried onions during last 15 minutes.

MICROWAVE GOULASH (MICROWAVE)
Sheila Godfrey
Creative Homemakers

1 lb. lean ground beef
1/3 c. chopped onion
1 c. uncooked macaroni

1-16 oz. can Spanish style
   or regular tomato sauce
1/4 c. water
season to taste with garlic
   powder, salt, pepper and chili
     powder

    Mix all ingredients in 2 quart casserole, covered. Microwave 18 minutes. Let rest at least 5 minutes.

SPANISH RICE SKILLET
Dorothy Bartholomew
Pep and Progress

1 lb. ground beef
2 slices bacon, chopped
1 med. onion, chopped

1/4 c. chopped green pepper
1-16 oz. can tomatoes,
   cut up

(Cont.)

2 c. water
1 c. long grain rice
1/2 c. chili sauce

1 tsp. salt
1 tsp. worcestershire sauce
1/8 tsp. pepper

In skillet, cook beef, bacon, onion and green pepper until meat is browned and vegetables are tender. Drain off excess fat. Stir in undrained tomatoes, water, uncooked rice, chili sauce, salt, worcestershire and pepper. Bring to boil; reduce heat. Simmer covered 25 to 30 minutes or until liquid is absorbed and rice is tender. Makes 6 servings.

TORTILLA ROLL-UPS

Sharon Roberts
Creative Homemakers

1 1/2 lbs. Italian sausage,
  cooked and drained
2 c. cream style cottage
  cheese
2 Tbsp. flour
1 tsp. oregano, crushed
1 tsp. dried basil, crushed

1/4 tsp. garlic powder
3 c. bottled spaghetti sauce
10 tortillas
1 1/2 c. shredded mozzarella
  cheese

Stir into meat the cottage cheese and flour. Add spices to spaghetti sauce. Stir 1/2 cup sauce into sausage. Spoon 1/3 cup meat onto tortilla. Roll up. Place seam side down in 9x13 inch pan. Pour sauce over tortillas. Bake, covered in 375° oven for 35 to 40 minutes. Uncover. Sprinkle cheese on top. Bake 3 minutes for cheese to melt. Serves 8 to 10.

TACO CASSEROLE

Vickie Lehmkuhl
X-tra X-amples X-tension Club

1 lb. hamburger
1/2 c. chopped onion
1/4 c. taco sauce
1 can mushroom soup

6 corn taco shells
1 c. shredded cheddar cheese
1 can green whole chilies

Brown hamburger and onion. Drain off grease. Stir in taco sauce and soup (undiluted). Simmer for 15 minutes. Layer in a greased 9x9 inch casserole dish, 3 of the taco shells. Spoon on half meat mixture, half of the chilies and 1/2 cup shredded cheese Use remaining 3 taco shells, meat mixture, chilies and cheese. Bake at 350° for 30 minutes. Makes 4 to 6 servings.

ENCHILADA CASSEROLE

Cecilia Pyle
Padroni E.H.

1 onion, chopped
1 can cream of mushroom soup
1 green chilie
salt
longhorn cheese

2 lbs. ground beef
1 small can tomato sauce
1 can tomato paste
tortilla chips

Brown meat and onion; stir in soup, sauce, tomato paste, chilies and salt. Cook until mixture begins to boil. Place half of tortilla chips in bottom of pan. Pour meat mixture over chips and add cheese, then rest of chips. Bake at 375° for 25 to 30 minutes.

ENCHILADA PIE

Connie Lechman
Proctor E.H. Club

2 lbs. ground beef
cumin
1 can cream of chicken soup
1-4 oz. can green chilies,
    chopped
1 can pinto beans
garlic powder

1 can cream of mushroom soup
1 can enchilada sauce (mild)
1/2 pkg. plain tortilla chips
1 c. grated cheddar cheese

Brown the ground beef and sprinkle with garlic powder and the cumin. Drain off the grease. Place in a 9x13 inch pan; add the remaining ingredients with the exception of the cheddar cheese. Be sure to carefully fold in the tortilla chips. Bake at 350° for 30 minutes or until bubbly. Sprinkle with the grated cheddar cheese and return to oven until melted, about 5 minutes.

ROCKO'S SPAGHETTI

Carole Quint
Pep and Progress

Sauce:

3/4 c. chopped onion
1 clove garlic, minced
3 Tbsp. olive oil
2-1 lb. cans tomatoes
2-6 oz. cans tomato paste
1 bay leaf

1 c. water
1 Tbsp. sugar
1 1/2 tsp. salt
1/2 tsp. pepper
1 1/2 tsp. crushed oregano

Cook onion and garlic in hot oil until tender but not brown. Stir in remaining ingredients. Simmer uncovered 30 minutes. Remove bay leaf. Add meatballs. Cook 30 minutes longer. Makes 6 servings.

(Cont.)

Meatballs:

4 slices dry bread
1 lb. ground beef
2 eggs
1/2 c. grated parmesan cheese
2 Tbsp. chopped parsley

1 clove garlic, minced
1 tsp. oregano
1 tsp. salt
dash pepper
2 Tbsp. olive oil

Soak bread in water 2 to 3 minutes. Squeeze out moisture. Combine bread with remaining ingredients, except oil; mix well. Form in small balls, then brown slowly in hot oil. Add to sauce and cook 30 minutes. Serve over spaghetti.

IMPOSSIBLE TAMALE PIE

Zelma Stunkard
Shamrock

1 lb. ground beef
1/2 c. chopped onion
1-1 1/4 oz. env. taco
 seasoning mix
1-8 oz. can stewed tomatoes,
 drained and chopped

1 c. frozen corn, thawed
 and drained
3 eggs
1 1/2 c. milk
2/3 c. baking mix
1/2 c. yellow cornmeal

Heat oven to 400°. Grease pie plate, 10 x 1 1/2 inches. Cook and stir ground beef in 10 inch skillet until brown; drain. Stir in onion and seasoning mix; spread in plate. Sprinkle with tomatoes and corn. Beat remaining ingredients until smooth, 15 seconds in blender on high or 1 minute with hand beater. Pour into plate. Bake until knife inserted in center comes out clean, 30 minutes to 35 minutes. Cool 5 minutes.

IMPOSSIBLE TACO PIE

Catherine Nab
Pep and Progress

1 lb. ground beef
1/2 c. chopped onion
1-1 1/4 oz. env. taco
 seasoning mix
1-4 oz. can chopped green
 chilies, drained
2 c. milk

1 1/2 c. Bisquick baking mix
4 eggs
2 tomatoes, sliced
1 c. shredded Monterey Jack
 or shredded cheese

Lightly grease pie plate, 10x1/2 inch. Cook and stir ground beef and onion in skillet until beef is brown; drain. Stir in taco seasoning mix. Spread in plate and sprinkle with chilies. Beat milk, baking mix and eggs until smooth, 15 seconds in blender on high or 1 minute with hand beater. Pour into plate. Bake at 400° for 35 minutes.

Top with tomatoes and sprinkle with cheese. Bake until cheese
is golden brown and knife inserted in center comes out clean.
Bake 8 to 10 minutes longer. Cool 5 minutes. Serve with dairy
sour cream, chopped tomatoes and chopped lettuce if desired
Makes 6 to 8 servings.

MACARONI STROGANOFF

Doris Seghi
Night Owls

1-7 oz. pkg. or 2 c.
 uncooked elbow macaroni
1 lb. ground beef
1/2 c. finely chopped onion
1 tsp. salt
1 tsp. pepper
1 Tbsp. vegetable oil

1 can cream of mushroom soup
1 pkg. frozen peas, drained
1-8 oz. sour cream, at
 room temp.
2 Tbsp. dry or Cocktain sherry(opt.)

Preheat oven to 350°. In medium bowl, combine meat, onion,
salt and pepper; mix well. Shape into 18 meatballs. In large skillet,
brown meatballs in oil. Pour off fat. In large bowl, combine cooked
macaroni, meatballs, soup, peas, sour cream and sherry. Turn
into greased 2 1/2 quart baking dish. Bake covered 35 to 40 minutes
or until hot. Makes 6 servings.

CHILI RELLENO BAKE

Carol Atkin
Home Hustlers

1 lb. hamburger
1 onion
2 cloves garlic, chopped
2 flat cans green chilies
2 c. grated sharp cheese

4 eggs
1/4 c. flour
1 1/4 c. milk
1 tsp. salt
dash tabasco or chili
    powder

Brown meat, onion and garlic; place one can green chilies
on bottom of greased square baking pan. Top with 1 1/2 cups of
the grated cheese; add meat mixture and top with second can
of chilies. Beat eggs and flour together; add milk and seasonings.
Pour over top of mixture. Sprinkle with remaining 1/2 cup cheese.
Bake at 350° for about 45 minutes.

BURRITO CASSEROLE

Philomena Sewald
Pep and Progress

1 1/2 lbs. hamburger
2 cans Ranch Style beans
1 small onion, chopped
2 c. grated cheese

1 tsp. chili powder
1 Tbsp. garlic salt
1 can tomatoes
1 small can green chilies

89   (Cont.)

1 can cream of mushroom soup   6 floured tortilla shells

Brown hamburger; drain. Mix in 1 teaspoon chili powder, 1 tablespoon garlic salt. Grease 13x9 inch pan. Line bottom of pan with 3 of the tortilla shells. Make alternate layers of meat mixture and beans. Then add grated cheese. Cover with remaining tortilla shells. Mix tomatoes, green chili and mushroom soup together. Pour on top. Bake at 350° for 1 hour. Cover with foil before baking.

LAYERED BURRITO CASSEROLE

Vicki Gertner
X-tra X-amples X-tension Club

4 to 6 flour tortillas
1 can refried beans

1 can Verde green chile
  sauce
2 or 3 c. grated Colby cheese

Pour 1/2 cup chile verde in bottom of casserole dish. Place tortilla on top. Put a layer of refried beans, sauce and cheese on top of tortilla. Repeat on each layer. Sprinkle remaining cheese on top. Bake at 350° for 15 to 20 minutes.
Variation: Add hamburger to mix, onions, olives, and green peppers Microwave 6 to 8 minutes on high.

HAMBURGER-NOODLE CASSEROLE

Marilyn Crane
Creative Homemakers

1 1/2 lbs. hamburger
1 Tbsp. minced onion
1 can cream of chicken soup
1 can cream of mushroom soup
1 c. sour cream

3 c. noodles
3/4 tsp. salt
1/4 tsp. pepper
1/2 Tbsp. Accent
1 can whole kernel corn

Brown hamburger and drain. Cook noodles and then add all ingredients in greased casserole. Top with buttered bread pieces. Bake for 30 minutes at 350°.

HAMBURGER CASSEROLE

Barbara Wisdom
Home Hustlers E.H.

2 Tbsp. butter
1/2 c. chopped onion
1 can cream of mushroom soup
1 pkg. thin noodles

1/2 c. buttered crumbs
1 lb. ground beef
1-8 oz. pkg. Velveeta

Melt butter over low heat; add ground beef and onions; brown and simmer. Cook noodles in salted water; drain. Put noodles in

90

buttered baking dish and pour ground beef (mixed with the soup and cheese) over top. Top with crumbs. Bake at 350° for 30 minutes.

BEEF AND CABBAGE CASSEROLE

Barbara Wisdom
Home Hustlers E.H.

1 Tbsp. salad oil
1 lb. ground beef
1 onion, chopped
4 Tbsp. rice

1 can tomato soup
1 soup can water
4 c. chopped cabbage
salt and pepper

Brown beef and onion in salad oil. Add soup, water, salt, pepper and rice. Bring to boil. Reduce heat and simmer 3 minutes. Put in oblong 3 quart casserole. Put meat mixture on top; cover. Bake at 350° for 1 hour.

SATURDAY NIGHT CASSEROLE

Rachel Schuppe
Proctor

1 lb. ground beef, browned
1 c. pork and beans
1 #303 can tomatoes, drained
1 tsp. salt

1 large onion, thinly sliced
2 slices bacon
1/4 c. brown sugar

Add beans, tomatoes and salt to browned beef. Pour half of mixture into a baking dish. Layer the onion mixture in the casserole and add the rest of the beef mixture. Top with bacon and sprinkle with brown sugar. Bake about 40 minutes or until heated through.

CHUNKY CHOW MEIN

Opal Vance
Sterling Homemakers

1 lb. hamburger
1/2 c. chopped onion
10 3/4 oz. can condensed
   cream of mushroom soup

1 lb. can Chinese vegetables,
   drained
1 tsp. soy sauce

Brown hamburger and chopped onion. Stir in soup, Chinese vegetables and soy sauce. Heat and serve over chow mein noodles. Serves 4 to 6.

AMERICAN CHOP SUEY CASSEROLE

Nona Amen
Proctor

1 lb. ground beef
1 large onion, chopped
1 tsp. salt
4 oz. can mushrooms

1/2 of 8 oz. can water chestnuts
1 green pepper, chopped
3/4 c. rice, uncooked

1 c. chopped celery   4 c. canned tomatoes

Cook meat, onion and green pepepr till meat loses pink color, breaking it up with a fork. Add rice, celery, tomatoes, salt, mushroo and liquid and water chestnuts. Stir to blend. Cover casserole. Bake at 350° for 1 hour. Makes 6 to 8 servings.

CHINESE EGG ROLLS

Darlene Denton
X-tra X-amples X-tension Club

soy sauce
1 lb. ground pork
1 bunch green onions
1 small can bamboo shoots
1 small can water chestnuts

1 head of Japanese cabbage
2 carrots
1-1 lb. pkg. egg roll wraps
1 egg

(Makes 32 egg rolls.)

Sprinkle the ground pork generously with soy sauce. Work it into the meat, and refrigerate the meat so it can "cure" for about 8 hours in a covered bowl. The onions, bamboo shoots, and water chestnuts must all be diced, sliced or chopped in small pieces. The cabbage and carrots must be shredded . After all the above is done, cook your meat and drain off the fat, then add your onions and cabbage in the already hot skillet, and turn them occasionally, (and just leave them in there long enough to become limp, or wilted) not brown. Then combine the cooked meat, wilted cabbage and onions, carrots, bamboo shoots and water chestnuts into a large mixing bowl. Mix together well.

To fill the egg rolls, place egg roll wrap, with one corner pointing towards you. Place 2 to 3 tablespoons of filling near center of skin (closer to you). Fold bottom corner (closest to you) over filling. Then fold left and right corners toward the center. Roll egg roll away from you. Press tightly so filling is secure, not loose (if it is loose, when you are frying oil will get inside, and become trapped, making them greasy). Brush inside of corner furthest away from you with the sealer (one beaten egg), and seal egg roll like an envelope. Repeat until all egg rolls are filled . If the skin should break on one, go ahead and fry it anyway; don't let it go to waste, just fry it last.

To cook, submerge in hot oil (either deep fat fryer, or oil in pan on stove) until golden brown. They need to be turned and rotated so they don't float on one side all the time. One side will burn, while the other won't cook. Drain on paper towels.

These may be cooked just slightly then frozen and cooked fully later. They can also be fully cooked, and warmed later in an oven.

92

They may be served with hot mustard, sweet and sour sauce, or soy sauce.

You may use a variety of fillings; any of the items may be deleted or increased. You can make all vegetable egg rolls by deleting the meat.

All of the items needed (soy sauce, wrappers, in produce section, bamboo shoots, water chestnuts, Japanese cabbage, etc, may be purchased at Safeway. Usave has some, but not all items.
Note: This is a Chinese dish.

MEAT-ZA PIZZA

Debbie Garcia
Creative Homemakers

1 can tomato or cheddar
  cheese soup
1 1/2 lbs. ground beef
1/2 c. fine dry bread crumbs
1/4 c. finely chopped onion
1 egg, slightly beaten

1 tsp. salt
1 med. clove garlic, minced
1/8 tsp. oregano, crushed
3 oz. mozzarella or mild process
  cheese, shredded

Mix thoroughly 1/2 cup soup with all ingredients except cheese; pat meat evenly on baking sheet into 10 inch circle with 1 inch stand up rim. Bake at 450° for 10 minutes. Spoon off fat. Spread rest of soup on meat and top with cheese. Sprinkle with more oregano. Top with mushrooms, anchovies, olives or sausage, if desired. Bake 10 minutes longer.
Note: If using cheddar cheese soup, substitute 4 slices tomato, cut in quarters for sliced cheese.

LITTLE PIZZAS (MICROWAVE)

Sheila Godfrey
Creative Homemakers

1-8 oz. can tomato sauce
1/2 tsp. garlic salt
1/2 tsp. dried basil
2 tsp. oregano

1 lb. ground beef, browned
shredded mozzarella cheese
grated Parmesan cheese
English muffins

Mix first 5 ingredients together. Put mixture on half of muffins. Top with mozzarella and Parmesan cheese. Bake in microwave 30 seconds each or until cheese melts.

BREAKFAST PIZZA

Sharon Roberts
Creative Homemakers

5 eggs
1/4 c. milk
1/2 tsp. salt

1/8 tsp. pepper
2 Tbsp. Parmesan cheese

1 lb. sausage, cooked,
 drained
1 pkg. of 8 crescent
 rolls (refrigerated)
1 c. frozen loose-pack
 hash browns, thawed

1 c. shredded sharp cheddar,
 Swiss or Monterey Jack
 cheese

Mix together first 4 ingredients. Separate rolls into 8 triangles. Place in ungreased pizza pan, points toward center. Press into pan. Seal perforations. Spoon sausage over crust. Sprinkle with potatoes. Top with cheese. Pour egg-milk mixture into crust. Sprinkle with Parmesan cheese. Bake in 375° oven for 25 to 30 minutes. Serves 6 to 8.

PIZZA CRUST

Barb Korrey
X-tra X-amples X-tension Club

1 pkg . yeast
1 c. lukewarm water
1 Tbsp. oil

1 tsp. salt
1 tsp. sugar
3 c. flour

Dissolve yeast in water. Add rest of ingredients and press out 1/2 onto greased pizza pan. Top with sauce, cheese, meat, etc. Makes two pizzas. Bake at 450° for 25 minutes.

BASIC QUICHE

Julie Schaefer
X-tra X-amples X-tension Club

1 c. cheese
5 eggs, whipped
1 c. milk
1/4 tsp. salt

Ham Quiche:
 1 c. cubed ham, 1 can sliced
  olives
Corn Quiche:
1 can creamed corn
1/4 c. onions (cooked tender
  in margarine)

Spray 9 inch pie pan with Pam. Coat with corn meal. Beat eggs and add milk and salt. Put meat in pie pan along with grated cheese. Pour eggs over the meat. Sprinkle with paprika and bake at 350° for 30 minutes.

LASAGNA

Carole Quint

1 box lasagna noodles
1 1/2 lbs. hamburger
1-1 lb. 12 oz. can tomato sauce

1 tsp. salt
1/4 tsp. pepper
3/4 tsp. oregano

| 1 Tbsp. chili powder | 1 Tbsp. brown sugar |
| 1 tsp. garlic | 1 small diced onion |

Simmer everything down from hamburger for 45 minutes. Brown hamburger and cook lasagna noodles until tender. Add hamburger and sauce together; spread sauce mixture in 9x13 inch baking dish then top with lasagna noodles. Sprinkle your favorite cheese either sliced or grated on top of this and repeat until meat mixture is used. Bake in moderate oven until cheese is melted. Serves 6.

EASY LASAGNA (MICROWAVE)

Pam Fey
X-tra X-amples X-tension Club

1/2 lb. ground beef	1 egg
1-32 oz. jar spahgetti sauce	1/2 tsp. pepper
1/2 c. water	8 lasagna noodles, uncooked
1 1/2 c. ricotta or cottage cheese	1/2 lb. mozzarella cheese (thinly sliced)
	1/2 c. grated Parmesan cheese

Set power select at High.

In a large glass bowl, crumble ground beef. Heat 2 to 3 minutes until beef is browned, stirring once; drain. Stir in spaghetti sauce and water.

Meanwhile, combine cottage cheese, egg and pepper. In oblong baking dish, spoon 1/2 sauce, alternately layer of noodles, egg mixture, mozzarella cheese, and sauce, forming two layers. Heat, covered, for 8 minutes at High. Set Power Select at medium-low. Heat covered 30 to 32 mintues or until noodles are tender. Top with Parmesan cheese and let stand, covered, 15 minutes before serving.

LAZY DAY LASAGNA

Ardis Bazata
Highland Lassies

1 lb. ground beef	1/2 c. water
1-14 1/2 oz. can tomatoes, undrained	2 c. cottage cheese
1-6 oz. can tomato paste	1/4 c. Parmesan cheese
1 1/2 tsp. salt	1 egg
1 1/2 tsp. basil leaves	1 Tbsp. parsley flakes
1/2 tsp. oregano leaves	8 uncooked lasagna noodles
1/8 tsp. garlic powder	2 c. shredded mozzarella cheese

Crumble ground beef into 1 1/2 quart glass casserole.

Microwave (high) 5 to 6 minutes, or until no longer pink, stirring once. Stir to break meat into pieces; drain. Stir in tomatoes, tomato paste, salt, basil, oregano, garlic powder and water. Cover with casserole lid and microwave (high) 4 to 5 minutes or until mixture boils. Combine cottage cheese, Parmesan cheese, egg and parsley; mix well. Pour 1 1/2 cups tomato sauce mixture into 12x8 inch glass baking dish; spread evenly in dish. Place 4 uncooked noodles evenly over sauce. Top with half the cottage cheese mixture, spreading evenly. Sprinkle with half the mozzarella cheese. Spoon 1 cup sauce evenly over cheese. Place 4 or more noodles on sauce. Top with layer of remaining cottage cheese, mozzarella cheese and tomato sauce. Cover tightly with plastic wrap. Microwave (high) 15 minutes. Rotate dish and microwave (medium 50% power) 15 to 20 minutes. Remove plastic wrap. Sprinkle with 2 tablespoons parmesan cheese. Microwave (high), uncovered 1 1/2 to 2 minutes. Let stand about 10 minutes before cutting into squares.

LASAGNA

Nona Amen
Proctor

1-8 oz. pkg. lasagna noodles
 (I use crinkled wide noodles)
1 c. creamed cottage cheese
1 c. dairy sour cream
1 lb. ground beef
1/2 c. chopped onion

2 c. tomato sauce
1 tsp. garlic salt
1/2 tsp. oregano
dash of pepper
3/4 c. shredded cheddar cheese

Cook noodles in salted boiling water according to directions; drain. Mix sour cream and cottage cheese with noodles. Brown ground beef and onion. Stir in tomato sauce, garlic salt and oregano and pepper. Simmer 5 minutes.
 In casserole, arrange alternate layers of noodle mixture and meat sauce starting with noodles. Top with cheddar cheese. Bake at 350° about 45 minutes. Makes 8 servings.

SKILLET LASAGNA

Zelma Stunkard
Shamrock

1 lb. ground beef
1 env. spahgetti sauce mix
1 lb. creamed cottage cheese
1-8 oz. pkg. lasagna noodles
2 tsp. basil
1 Tbsp. parsley flakes

1 tsp. salt
1-16 oz. can tomatoes, broken
 up in pieces
1-16 oz. can tomato sauce
1 c. water
8 oz. mozzarella cheese, shredded

Cook meat in a 10 inch skillet over medium heat until browned drain off fat. Sprinkle meat with half of the spaghetti sauce mix, then spread cottage cheese over meat. Break noodles in half

lengthwise; layer on top of cottage cheese. Sprinkle with remaining spaghetti sauce mix, basil, parsley, and salt. Pour tomatoes,
tomato sauce and water over mixture. Cover and simmer over
low heat for 35 minutes or until noodles are tender. Sprinkle shredded
cheese over top. Cover and let stand 5 minutes. Serve.

LASAGNA

Florence Mette
Southsiders

Sauce:

3 Tbsp. olive oil
1 c. finely chopped onions
1 Tbsp. finely chopped garlic
4 c. whole packed tomatoes,
   coarsely chopped
1-6 oz. can tomato paste

1 Tbsp. finely cut basil
1 bay leaf
1 tsp. salt
pepper to taste
1 1/2 lbs. ground beef

Simmer 1 hour. May add sauted mushrooms. Brown ground
beef and add to sauce while simmering.

1 lb. ricotta cheese
mozzarella cheese, sliced thin
parmesan cheese
1 tsp. salt

1 Tbsp. oil
1-10 oz. pkg. frozen spinach
   (thawed)
1 box lasagna noodles

Prepare ricotta mixture by adding 1 teaspoon salt and 1
tablespoon oil to the thawed spinach, stirring in the ricotta cheese.
Keep in the refrigerator until ready to layer the lasagna. Boil
the noodles in water with 1 teaspoon salt and 1 tablespoon oil
added. Cook about 15 minutes. Drain noodles.
Alternate sauce, lasagna noodles, mozzarella cheese slices
and ricotta mixture until pan is full. Top with Parmesan cheese.
Bake at 350° for 30 minutes.

Write your extra recipes here:

Write your extra recipes here:

VEGETABLES

BUYING GUIDE
Fresh vegetables and fruits

Experience is the best teacher in choosing quality but here are a few pointers on buying some of the fruits and vegetables.

ASPARAGUS—Stalks should be tender and firm, tips should be close and compact. Choose the stalks with very little white—they are more tender. Use asparagus soon—it toughens rapidly.

BEANS, SNAP—Those with small seeds inside the pods are best. Avoid beans with dry-looking pods.

BERRIES—Select plump, solid berries with good color. Avoid stained containers, indicating wet or leaky berries. Berries such as blackberries and raspberries with clinging caps may be underripe. Strawberries without caps may be too ripe.

BROCCOLI, BRUSSELS SPROUTS, AND CAULIFLOWER—Flower clusters on broccoli and cauliflower should be tight and close together. Brussels sprouts should be firm and compact. Smudgy, dirty spots may indicate insects.

CABBAGE AND HEAD LETTUCE—Choose heads heavy for size. Avoid cabbage with worm holes, lettuce with discoloration or soft rot.

CUCUMBERS—Choose long, slender cucumbers for best quality. May be dark or medium green but yellowed ones are undesirable.

MELONS—In cantaloupes, thick close netting on the rind indicates best quality. Cantaloupes are ripe when the stem scar is smooth and space between the netting is yellow or yellow-green. They are best to eat when fully ripe with fruity odor.

Honeydews are ripe when rind has creamy to yellowish color and velvety texture. Immature honeydews are whitish-green.

Ripe watermelons have some yellow color on one side. If melons are white or pale green on one side, they are not ripe.

ORANGES, GRAPEFRUIT, AND LEMONS—Choose those heavy for their size. Smoother, thinner skins usually indicate more juice. Most skin markings do not affect quality. Oranges with a slight greenish tinge may be just as ripe as fully colored ones. Light or greenish-yellow lemons are more tart than deep yellow ones. Avoid citrus fruits showing withered, sunken, or soft areas.

PEAS AND LIMA BEANS—Select pods that are well-filled but not bulging. Avoid dried, spotted, yellowed, or flabby pods.

ROOT VEGETABLES—Should be smooth and firm. Very large carrots may have woody cores, oversized radishes may be pithy, oversized turnips, beets, and parsnips may be woody. Fresh carrot tops usually mean fresh carrots, but condition of leaves on most other root vegetables does not indicate degree of freshness.

SWEET POTATOES—Porto Rico and Nancy Hall varieties—with bronze to rosy skins—are soft and sweet when cooked. Yellow to light-brown ones of the Jersey types are firmer and less moist.

VEGETABLES

STEAMED WHEAT

Patty Ament
Proctor E.H. Club

1 c. cleaned wheat
2 1/2 c. cold water

1 1/2 tsp. salt, or to taste

Place ingredients in top of double boiler. Bring to a rolling boil and set into bottom of double boiler. Set steam on low heat for 3 or 4 hours or overnight. Delicious with milk and sugar for breakfast and with butter as a dinner vegetable.

SIMMERED SOY BEANS

Patty Ament
Proctor E.H. Club

Soak 1 pound soy beans overnight in water to more than cover. Partially cook 6 to 8 slices of bacon. Add bacon and grease to beans. Bring to a boil in same water, and skim off foam.

Add 1 tablespoon oil to prevent boiling over. Add 1 to 2 tablespoons salt or to taste. Add pepper to taste and 1 chopped onion. Lower heat and simmer 2 or 3 hours.

Add 1 quart canned tomatoes and 1 tablespoon basil. Bring to boil again and lower heat and simmer until done. Can be simmered indefinitely and frozen and reheated.

SCALLOPED POTATOES SUPREME

Hazel Pyle
Proctor E.H. Club

2 qts. thinly sliced
  pared potatoes (8)
1/4 c. minced onion
1 c. milk

1/4 c. chopped green pepper (opt.)
1 can cream of mushroom soup
salt to taste

In greased 11x7x 1 1/2 inch baking dish or 2 quart casserole, alternate layers of potatoes, green peppers, and onions. Combine remaining ingredients, dash of pepper and pour over. Cover. Bake at 350° for 45 minutes. Uncover and bake 20 to 30 minutes longer or until potatoes are tender. Makes 8 servings.

WESTERN BAKED POTATOES

Philomena Sewald
Pep and Progress

10 large potatoes
1 cube butter
salt to taste

1/2 c. sour cream with chives
1 1/2 c. shredded cheese

(Cont.)

few finely chopped green onion tops   1/2 c. Baco's

Bake 10 large potatoes until done. Cut lengthwise. Scoop out insides being careful not to ruin skin. Mash potatoes. Add butter, salt, sour cream, cheese, onion, and Baco's. Mix well. Put back into skins. Sprinkle with paprika. Line back into baking dish. Bake at 350° for about 20 minutes.

POTATO BOAT CRUNCH

Carole Quint
Pep and Progress

6 potatoes, cut in wedges
1 c. melted butter

1 Tbsp. paprika
1 1/2 c. corn flake crumbs

Leave peelings on your potatoes and slice lengthwise into wedges. Dip each wedge in melted butter and place in a 9x13 inch pan. Dribble remaining butter over potatoes. Mix paprika with corn flake crumbs. Coat each wedge generously with crumbs and sprinkle with salt to taste. Bake at 350° for 40 to 50 mintues or until tender. Serves 6.

MICRO POTATOES PARMESAN

Jan Nixon
Extension Home Economist

2 Tbsp. butter
2 med. potatoes, unpeeled
  and sliced 1/4" thick
1/3 c. chopped onion
1 clove garlic, minced

1/2 c. 1" green pepper
1/4 tsp. salt
1/8 tsp. pepper
1/4 c. grated Parmesan cheese
paprika

Melt butter in shallow 9 inch dish. Add potatoes, onion, garlic and toss. Cover loosely with plastic wrap and place in microwave oven. Cook on High for 5 minutes. Stir in green pepper, salt and pepper; toss. Cover and microwave on High for 3 minutes. Gently mix in cheese. Toss gently and dust with paprika. Microwave on full power, uncovered, for 3 minutes. Let rest 2 minutes. Sprinkle with parsley. Makes 2 to 3 servings.

MAKE AHEAD POTATO CASSEROLE

Mrs. Joe Gerk
Hearth and Home

Boil 6 to 8 large potatoes in jackets. Cool, peel and slice. Put half in bottom of 9x13 inch pan.

1 can cream of mushroom
    soup
1/2 c. milk
1/2 lb. cheddar cheese

1 cube melted margarine
1/2 small onion, chopped
1 slice bread, broken in
    small pieces

Mix together. Pour half over potatoes; add rest of potatoes and pour remaining sauce over top. Put shredded cheddar cheese over all. Bake in 350° oven until bubbly. May be made ahead and refrigerated until ready to use.

QUICK POTATO CASSEROLE

Margaret Ann Stieb
Hearth and Home

8 med. potatoes, wash and
    cut up
1 c. hot water
1 pkg. dry onion soup mix

1/2 c. margarine
1/4 tsp. pepper

Combine hot water, soup mix, margarine and pepper. Mix. Pour over potatoes in greased baking dish. Bake at 350°, covered, and uncovered the last 10 minutes.

PARTY POTATOES

Hazel Korrey
Hearth and Home

8 to 10 potatoes, boiled
    and whipped
1-8 oz. pkg. cream cheese

1/4 c. dairy sour cream
butter or oleo
salt
paprika

Mix cheese and cream together until smooth. Fold together with potatoes and salt; mix well. Spoon into buttered 2 quart casserole. Brush top with soft oleo or butter. Sprinkle with paprika. Bake in 350° oven for 30 minutes. (Can be prepared ahead of time and heat 30 minutes before serving.)

HOLIDAY POTATO DISH

Irene Schneider
Hearth and Home

4 lbs. potatoes, cooked
    and drained
1 c. chopped onion
1/4 c. butter
3 Tbsp. melted butter
pimento strips
chopped fresh parsley

1-10 3/4 oz. can condensed cream
    of celery soup
1 pt. dairy sour cream
1 1/2 c. crushed corn flakes
1 1/2 c. shredded cheddar cheese

Remove skins from potatoes; shred into bowl. Saute onion in 1/4 cup melted butter until tender. Remove from heat. Stir

(Cont.)

in soup and sour cream. Pour over potatoes and cheese. Mix well. Turn into greased 13x9 inch baking dish. Cover and refrigerate overnight. Sprinkle with corn flakes. Drizzle with 3 tablespoons butter. Bake in a 350° oven for 1 hour. Garnish with pimento and parsley. Makes 12 servings.

JIFFY POTATO CASSEROLE

Alba Desoto
Southsiders

1-10 3/4 oz. can cream of
  potato soup
1 c. milk
1-2 lb. pkg. hash browns,
  thawed
cheddar cheese

1-10 3/4 oz. can cream of
  celery soup
1-8 oz. carton sour cream
salt and pepper

Combine soups, milk and sour cream. Mix until smooth. Add potatoes and seasonings. Put mixture in 9x13 inch pan. Bake casserole covered in preheated 350° oven about 1 1/2 hours. Top with cheese the last 30 minutes. Serves 12.

COMPANY POTATOES

Thelma Davis
Sterling Homemakers

2 boxes frozen hash browns
2-4 oz. pkgs. shredded
  cheddar cheese
2 cans cream of mushroom soup

2 containers sour cream
  with chives
1 tsp. salt
1/2 tsp. pepper

Combine all ingredients and bake in a 9x13 inch pan for one hour at 350°. This makes a large dish. Good for reunions and large groups but can be cut in half for the family.

CHEESE POTATOES

Barbara Wisdom
Home Hustlers E.H. Club

1-2 lb. bag frozen hash
  browns
1 can cream of chicken soup
1 carton sour cream

salt and pepper
2 c. cheddar cheese , grated
onion

Thaw hash browns slightly; mix all ingredients together. Put in 9x12 inch buttered baking dish. Cover for first 30 minutes. Bake at 350° for 1 hour.

SWEET POTATO BALLS

Esther Schuppe
Pep and Progress

3 c. mashed sweet potatoes
1/4 c. butter or oleo
3/4 c. brown sugar
2 Tbsp. milk

1/4 tsp. salt
1/2 tsp. grated lemon rind
8 large marshmallows
1/2 c. crushed corn flakes

Combine potatoes, salt, butter, brown sugar, milk and lemon rind. Take 1/4 cup of mixture at a time and form into balls with a marshmallow in center of each ball. Roll in corn flakes and place in a buttered baking dish. Bake at 350° for 20 minutes. Serves 8. (May be frozen.)

SWEET POTATOES WITH ORANGE SAUCE

Ruth Reed
Padroni E.H.

1/3 c. brown sugar
1 Tbsp. cornstarch
1 c. orange juice
canned sweet potatoes

1/3 c. white sugar
pinch of salt
3 Tbsp. butter, melted

Mix sugar, cornstarch and salt; stir in orange juice and butter. Cook until thickened. Pour over sweet potatoes. Bake at 350° for 15 to 20 minutes.

RICE CASSEROLE

Connie Lechman
Proctor E.H. Club

1 can onion soup
1 c. uncooked rice

1 can chicken broth
1/2 stick oleo

Melt butter and mix all ingredients in casserole dish. Bake 1/2 hour at 350°. Stir well and bake 1/2 hour longer.

RICE AND MUSHROOM CASSEROLE

Hazel Korrey
Hearth and Home

1 c. raw regular rice
1 can onion soup
3/4 can water

1 stick (1/2 c.) margarine
1-2 1/2 oz. jar sliced
  mushrooms

Put above ingredients in a 2 quart greased casserole with lid. Do not stir. Bake in 325° oven for 1 1/2 hours.

CABBAGE CASSEROLE

Rena Morrison
Padroni E.H.

1 small head cabbage
  or 1/2 large head

1/2 c. milk
bread or cracker crumbs

(Cont.)

1 can cream of mushroom or   1/2 c. cheese
   cream of chicken soup

Chop up cabbage; boil in salted water 10 minutes. Drain carefully; rinse with cold water twice. Mix soup and milk; add to cabbage. Shred cheese over top. Sprinkle with crumbs. Bake at 350° for 30 minutes.

ORIENTAL GREEN BEANS

Annie Neff
Southsiders E.H. Club

3 c. fresh green beans   3 Tbsp. oil
  (1" pieces)   1 Tbsp. cornstarch
1 tsp. salt   1 beef bouillon cube
1 1/2 c. sliced celery   1 Tbsp. soy sauce
4 oz. can mushroom pieces   1/2 c. slivered almonds
  and stems, drained

In medium saucepan, combine beans, salt and enough water to cover. Bring to boil. Cook until tender. Drain, reserving 1 cup liquid.

In large skillet, cook celery and mushrooms in oil until celery is crisp-tender. Combine reserved liquid with cornstarch, bouillon cube and soy sauce. Stir into celery till mixture thickens and boils. Stir in almonds. Makes ten 1/2 cup servings.

STRING BEAN CASSEROLE

Sadie Slice

1 large can green beans   frozen onion rings
1 can mushroom soup

Drain beans but save liquid. Mix beans and soup in baking dish, if needed, add more bean juice. Bake until flavors mix. Cover with layer of onion rings and return to oven for 10 mintues.

SCALLOPED CORN

Carole Quint

1 can creamed style corn   1 1/2 c. cracker crumbs
1 can whole kernel corn   1/4 c. diced onion
2 eggs, well beaten   salt and pepper to taste
1/2 green pepper, chopped   small amount of cream or
                    milk

Mix all together and place in a buttered casserole dish. Sprinkle some cracker crumbs on top and drizzle some cream on top. Bake at 325° for 1 hour. Serves 6 to 8.

EASY CORN PUDDING

Kathy Graham
X-tra X-amples X-tension Club

1-16 oz. can corn, well drained
2 Tbsp. flour
1/4 c. sugar
1 egg

1/4 c. milk
2 Tbsp. butter
salt to taste
pepper to taste

Grease 1 1/2 quart casserole. Drop egg in and beat with fork. Add to casserole and mix together the flour, sugar, milk, salt, and pepper. Fold in corn. Cut 2 tablespoons butter into small pieces and push into top of mixture in several places. Bake 1 hour in preheated 325° oven.

CORN PUDDING

Amelia Vandegna
Pep and Progress

1 can corn
1 Tbsp. flour
1 Tbsp. sugar
salt and pepper

3 eggs, separated
1/2 c. milk
1 Tbsp. melted butter
1 tsp. baking powder

Put corn into bowl; add all other ingredients except whites of eggs. Beat whites stiff and fold into corn mixture. Butter casserole. Pour in pudding. Bake at 350° for 45 minutes.

SCALLOPED CORN

Hazel Pyle
Proctor E.H. Club

2 1/2 c. corn
1/2 to 3/4 c. milk
1 c. dry bread or cracker
    crumbs
2 Tbsp. butter or margarine

1/2 small onion, chopped
3 Tbsp. chopped green pepper
salt and pepper to taste

Combine corn and 1/2 cup milk. Add crumbs, onions, green peppers, and seasonings. Pour into greased casserole; dot with butter. Bake at 350° for 30 minutes or until slightly brown on top.

CRISPY SCALLOPED CORN

Clara Werner
Pep and Progress

2 eggs, slightly beaten
1/2 c. milk
1 tsp. sugar
1 tsp. salt
1/8 tsp. pepper
1/3 c. diced onion

2 c. cubed bread
1-1 lb. 1 oz. can cream style
    corn
1 c. slightly crushed Rice Krispies
3 Tbsp. butter

(Cont.)

Combine eggs with milk; add remaining ingredients except cereal and butter. Pour into 10x6x2 inch baking dish. Combine cereal and butter; sprinkle over top. Bake at 350° about 50 minutes.

SWISS SCALLOPED CORN (MICROWAVE)
Pam Fey
X-tra X-amples X-tension Club

3 slices bacon, crisp
  cooked and crumbled
2-16 oz. cans whole kernel
  corn, drained
1 c. shredded Swiss cheese
1 egg
1-5 1/3 oz. can evap. milk

1 1/2 tsp. onion powder
1/8 tsp. pepper
1 1/2 tsp. flour
1/4 c. dry bread crumbs
1 Tbsp. butter or margarine,
  melted

In 2 quart oblong baking dish, combine bacon, corn and cheese. Blend in egg, milk, onion powder, pepper and flour. Top with bread crumbs blended with butter. Sprinkle with paprika. Cover with plastic wrap. Set power at medium for 9 minutes; rotate dish once.

ZUCCHINI CASSEROLE
Minnie Korrey
Hearth and Home E.H.

4 or 5 small zucchini
1/2 c. chopped onions
3/4 c. grated carrot
6 Tbsp. butter
1 can cream of chicken soup

1/2 c. sour cream
2 1/2 c. plain croutons
1 c. Velveeta cheese
  chunks

Slice and pan boil zucchini. Saute onions, carrots and butter. Mix soup, sour cream, croutons and cheese. Mix together and bake in buttered casserole at 350° for 40 mintues, uncovered.

ZUCCHINI SQUASH
Anne Stieb
Hearth and Home

5 med. zucchini
1/2 lb. grated longhorn
  cheese

1 can tomatoes and green chilies
1/2 c. butter, melted
crushed Ritz crackers

Wash and slice squash, adding salt. Cook until tender; drain. In 9x13 inch pan, lay as follows, the squash, butter, cheese, tomatoes then top with crackers. Bake at 350° for 20 minutes.

ZUCCHINI AND CAULIFLOWER SKILLET

Jo Ann Rizzolo
Home Hustlers

1/4 c. chopped onion
1 clove garlic, minced
2 Tbsp. cooking oil
1-7 1/2 oz. can tomatoes,
   cut up
1 Tbsp. snipped parsley
1 Tbsp. tomato paste
1/2 tsp. salt

1/2 tsp. dried oregano, crushed
1/4 tsp. pepper
2 med. zucchini, bias sliced
   1/2" thick
2 c. cauliflowerettes
1/2 c. water
1 c. shredded mozzarella cheese
   (4 oz.)

In saucepan, cook onion and garlic in oil till onion is tender. Stir in undrained tomatoes, parsley, tomato paste, salt, oregano and pepper. Boil gently uncovered, for 10 to 15 minutes or till slightly thickened, stirring occasionally.

Meanwhile, in 10 inch covered skillet, cook zucchini and cauliflowerettes in water over medium heat about 5 minutes or till crisp-tender; drain. Pour tomato mixture over vegetables. Cover and cook for 4 or 5 minutes, or till heated through. Sprinkle with mozzarella cheese. Cook, uncovered, about 3 minutes longer or till cheese is melted. Sprinkle with additional snipped parsley, if desired. Makes 4 to 6 servings.

FRIED TOMATOES

Amelia Vendegna
Pep and Progress

6 med. tomatoes
4 Tbsp. sugar
4 Tbsp. flour
milk

salt
pepper
oleo or butter

Pare tomatoes; cut in halves. Roll pieces of tomatoes in sugar, flour, salt and pepper mixture. Fry slowly in plenty of butter for about 1/2 hour. Put what is left of sugar and flour mixture on top of the tomatoes while frying. When cooked, remove the tomatoes. Stir milk into the flour which is left in the pan and cook well until thickened a little. Pour over the tomatoes. (Do not cover tomatoes while frying.)

FROZEN VEGETABLE CASSEROLE

Marge Rieke
Pep and Progress

1-20 oz. pkg. California
   blend vegetables
1 can green beans
1 cube margarine

1 can cream of mushroom soup
1 lb. Velveeta cheese
1 can French canned onion
   rings

(Cont.)

Grease 9x13 inch baking pan. Put frozen vegetables in baking pan. Top with green beans. Melt margarine, cheese and mushroom soup together. Pour over vegetables. Top with French onion rings. Bake at 350° for 30 minutes.

SPINACH CASSEROLE
Kathy Martinez

2-10 oz. pkgs. frozen chopped
    spinach, thawed
2 c. cottage cheese
1/4 c. butter, in pieces
1 1/2 c. cheddar cheese,
    cubed

3 eggs, beaten
1/4 c. flour
1 tsp. salt

Combine all ingredients in slow cooker. Cook on high for 1 hour. Reduce heat to low and cook an additional 4 to 5 hours.

CANDY APPLES AND CARROTS
Mrs. Joe Gerk
Hearth and Home

Slice 8 large carrots and boil until tender; drain. Layer carrots in buttered 1 quart casserole with 2 cooking apples, peeled, cored and sliced. Sprinkle with mixture of 1/4 cup each of brown sugar and granulated sugar and 1 teaspoon cinnamon. Dot with 2 table-spoons margarine. Bake at 325° for about 45 minutes. Makes 4 servings.

CARROTS MARINADE
Mary May
Hearth and Home

2 lbs. carrots, sliced and
    cooled
1 sliced onion
1 sliced pepper
1 can tomato soup

1 tsp. dry mustard
1/2 c. vinegar
3/4 c. sugar
1/2 c. oil

Mix tomato soup, dry mustard, vinegar, sugar and oil. Pour the hot marinade over the cooked carrots, onion and sliced pepper. Serve hot or cold.

CARROT CASSEROLE
Luella Sonnenberg
Night Owls

1 1/2 lbs. carrots
1 c. orange concentrate
1/4 c. butter

2 Tbsp. cornstarch
1 c. coconut
2 Tbsp. sugar

Pare, slice and cook the carrots until tender; drain. Make a sauce with the orange juice, sugar, butter and cornstarch. Put carrots in a buttered casserole. Pour the sauce over this. Top with grated coconut and bake in 375° oven until bubbly and browned a little.

CARROT CASSEROLE

Julie Sonnenberg
Southsiders

2 lbs. carrots
2 Tbsp. onions, diced
8 to 10 soda crackers
2 Tbsp. canned milk
1 c. sharp cheese, grated
salt and pepper to taste
1 c. liquid from carrots

Peel and cut carrots in small pieces. Cook till tender; drain (save liquid) and mash. Add salt, pepper, cracker and cheese, then milk and carrot juice. Mix well and put into greased dish and bake for 30 minutes at 350°.

MARINATED MUSHROOMS

Darlene Denton
X-tra X-amples X-tension Club

2/3 c. olive oil
1/2 c. water
1/4 c. lemon juice
2 garlic cloves, halved
5 whole peppercorns
1/2 tsp. salt
1 lb. fresh or canned
   (drained) button mushrooms

Combine all ingredients except mushrooms in a glass or stainless steel saucepan and bring to a boil. Lower heat; cover and simmer 10 minutes. Remove garlic and peppercorns; add mushrooms and simmer 5 minutes. Allow mushrooms to cool in the marinade. Drain before serving, at room temperature or chilled. Serves 6 as an appetizer, more in an antipasto spread. This is an Italian dish.

STUFFED MUSHROOMS PARMEGIANA

Lillian Sitarski
Highland Lassies

24 large fresh mushrooms
2 Tbsp. butter
1 med. onion, finely chopped
2 oz. diced pepperoni
1/4 c. finely chopped green
   pepper
small garlic clove, minced
1/2 c. seasoned bread crumbs
3 Tbsp. Parmesan cheese
1 Tbsp. parsley
1/2 tsp. seasoned salt
1/4 tsp. dried oregano
dash of pepper
1/3 c. chicken broth or
   bouillon

Wash mushrooms; remove stems. Finely chop stems and

109   (Cont.)

reserve. Saute onion, pepperoni, green pepper, garlic and mushroom stems in the butter. Cook until vegetables are tender, but not brown. Add bread crumbs, cheese, parsley, and seasonings. Mix well. Stir in chicken broth. Spoon stuffing into mushroom caps, rounding the tops. Place caps in shallow pan with 1/4 inch of water covering the bottom of the pan. Bake uncovered in 325° oven for 25 minutes.

THE EGGONY AND THE EGGSTASY

Hazel Korrey
Hearth and Home

1 med. sized eggplant	salt and pepper
2 eggs (naturally)	1 1/2 c. grated cheese
1/2 c. bread crumbs	2 tomatoes
2 cloves	dashes of oregano, thyme, basil and sage

Wash but do not peel eggplant. Slice into 1 inch thick slices. Place in 3 inches boiling salted water and cook 10 minutes or until very soft; drain .

Mash the eggplant, then add the eggs, bread crumbs, garlic and salt and pepper to taste. Let this mixture cool, then add 1/2 cup of the grated cheese (mozzarella, Parmesan or cheddar).

Next wash and slice tomatoes and arrange them in a layer in a greased casserole dish. Dash a selection of the above spices. Spoon eggplant goop on top of the tomatoes and sprinkle with remaining cup of grated cheese. Cover with foil. Bake at 350° for 45 minutes or until bubbly.

BAKED CUCUMBERS

Amelia Vendegna
Pep and Progress

goodsize cucumbers	green pepper
salt	fresh tomatoes
pepper	butter
bread crumbs	cracker crumbs

Take cucumbers of fairly good size; cut them in half lengthwise and scoop out the inside, leaving enough shell to be firm. Put the seeds and pulp into a chopping bowl and add salt, pepper, bits of green pepper, fresh tomatoes, and bread crumbs. Chop all fine and mix well. Fill each half shell and put plenty of butter in the stuffing and on top to make it brown well. Put cracker crumb on top of the cucumbers. Bake in moderate 350° oven for about 1 hour.

ASPARAGUS WITH WINE SAUCE

Florence Mette
Southsiders

Wine Sauce:

2 egg yolks
1 Tbsp. water
1 c. dry white wine

2 Tbsp. butter, softened
1/4 c. heavy cream
1/4 tsp. freshly ground white
pepper

Asparagus:

3 lbs. asparagus
1 qt. boiling water

1/2 tsp. salt

Make the sauce first. Combine the egg yolks, water and
wine in the top of double boiler. Place over warm water and beat
with a wire whisk, increasing the heat of the water and continuing
to beat until the mixture is thick and creamy. Do not allow to
boil. Beat in the butter. Remove from the hot water and mix in
the cream and pepper. Keep the sauce warm.
Wash the asparagus, cut off the hard ends, pare the stems
and steam over boiling salted water until tender-crisp (7 minutes).
Remove from the steamer and arrange in a single layer on a platter.
Cover with wine sauce and serve at once.

ASPARAGUS CASSEROLE

Irene Schneider
Hearth and Home

1 large can asparagus
3 sliced hard cooked eggs
butter

1/4 lb. grated cheese
1 can mushroom soup
2 crackers, crumbled

Drain asparagus. Place asparagus in greased baking dish;
add layer of eggs, layer of grated cheese and layer of soup.
Sprinkle with crumbs, and dot with butter. Bake at 350° for 25
minutes. Makes 4 servings.

BROCCOLI CASSEROLE

Marilyn Crane
Creative Homemakers

1 c. cooked rice
1 c. chopped celery
1 chopped onion
1 box frozen broccoli
(cook in 1 c. water till
thawed; drain)

1 can cream of chicken soup
1/2 c. evap. milk
2 Tbsp. oleo
8 oz. jar Cheez Whiz
salt and pepper to taste

Mix together and bake in greased casserole at 350° for 45 minutes.

RICE–BROCCOLI–CHEESE BAKE

Lorraine Johnston
Home Hustlers

1 pkg. frozen chopped
  broccoli
1 1/2 c. cooked rice
1-8 oz. jar Cheez Whiz

1/2 onion, chopped
2 stalks celery, chopped
1 can cream of mushroom soup
2 Tbsp. butter

Cook broccoli to thaw. Cook rice. Saute celery and onion in butter. Mix all ingredients in casserole and bake at 350° for 30 minutes.

BROCCOLI BAKE

Carol Atkin
Home Hustlers

1 1/2 c. Minute Rice, cooked
2 Tbsp. butter
1 c. chopped celery
1/2 c. onions

1/2 c. bell peppers
1/2 c. chopped mushrooms
2 boxes frozen, chopped
  broccoli, cooked and drained
1-8 oz. jar Cheez Whiz
1 can mushroom soup

Saute celery, onions, bell peppers and mushrooms in 2 table-spoons butter. Mix cooked broccoli, Cheez Whiz, mushroom soup, cooked rice and vegetables together. Put in baking dish.
Bake 20 minutes or until mixture bubbles on top at 350°.

BROCCOLI–CHEESE CASSEROLE

Dorothy Miller
Highland Lassies

1 c. onion, chopped
1/3 c. celery, chopped
3 Tbsp. margarine
3 c. cooked rice
1 can cream of chicken soup

1 tall can evap. milk
1-10 oz. pkg. chopped
  broccoli, thawed
1-8 oz. jar cheese sauce
  (Cheez Whiz)

Saute onion and celery in margarine. Add remaining ingredient except Cheez Whiz. Pour into casserole. Spoon cheese sauce on top and bake at 350° for 30 to 45 minutes.

BROCCOLI AND RICE CASSEROLE

Philomena Sewall
Pep and Progress

2 cans cream of chicken soup
or 1 can cream of chicken
soup and 1 can cream of
mushroom soup
2 pkgs. frozen broccoli

1 c. Minute Rice
2/3 c. milk
3/4 c. grated cheese
1 tsp. onion flakes
1 small jar mushrooms

Cook broccoli; drain well. Add rest of ingredients and mix well. Put in buttered casserole baking dish. Bake at 325° for 45 minutes.

BROCCOLI AND RICE CASSEROLE

Ann Ruf, Pep and Progress
Carol Atkin., Home Hustlers
Philomena Sewald, Pep and Progress

2-10 oz. pkgs. chopped
broccoli, cooked and drained
1 c. rice, cooked
1/2 c. onion
1/2 c. chopped celery

1 can cream of chicken soup
1 can cream of mushroom soup
1/4 can water
1-8 oz. jar Cheez Whiz

Saute onion and celery in 2 tablespoons butter, then combine all the ingredients in a casserole dish. Bake 45 minutes in a 300° oven. Serves 10 to 12.

PEAS AND RICE PROVENCALE

Jan Nixon
Extension Home Economist

2 c. cooked rice, salted
and buttered
2 c. peas, heated and
drained
1/4 c. chopped onion
1/2 clove garlic, finely
chopped

1/2 c. sliced green olives
1 Tbsp. salad oil
1/4 c. chopped parsley
pimento strips

Gently combine rice and peas. Saute onion, garlic and olives in oil until onion is tender. Mix with peas and rice; toss gently. Garnish with thin pimento strips. Serves 6.

RICE DISH

Dorothy Miller, Highland Lassies
Norma Ruf, Home Hustlers

1 c. chopped onion
1/3 c. celery
1 can chicken soup
1-8 oz. can milk

1-8 oz. jar Cheez Whiz
1 pkg. chopped broccoli
3 c. cooked rice

(Cont.)

Mix ingredients in casserole. Bake 1 1/2 hours at 350°.

BROCCOLI-RICE CASSEROLE

Werdna Montgomery
Shamrock

2 pkgs. frozen broccoli,
  chopped
1 small pkg. (1 1/3 c.)
  Minute Rice

8 oz. jar Cheez Whiz
1 can cream of chicken soup

Cook broccoli and rice separately as package directs. While ;
rice is still hot, stir in Cheez Whiz and chicken soup. Combine
rice mixture and broccoli. Put in baking dish. Top with crumbs
and bake until hot. (Celery or mushroom soup may be used.)

BROCCOLI CASSEROLE

Rosalie Wolfe, Home Hustlers
Mrs. Frank Green
Member of former Mount Hope Extension H.C.

1 box chopped broccoli
1 c. uncooked Minute Rice
3/4 c. milk
1/2 c. diced celery
1/2 c. diced onion

1 can cream of chicken soup
1-8 oz. jar Cheez Whiz
  (plain or with jalapeno)
1 can water chestnuts (opt.)
1 1/2 c. chopped ham (opt.)

Heat soup and Cheez Whiz together until Cheez Whiz melts.
Add other ingredients. Bake in an oiled 2 quart baking dish, uncovered for 45 minutes at 350°.

BROCCOLI-CORN BAKE

Katherine Kalinowski
Sterling Homemakers

1-1 lb. can cream style
  corn
1-10 oz. pkg. frozen chopped
  broccoli, cooked and
  drained
1 egg, beaten
1/2 c. coarse saltine cracker
  crumbs

1/4 c. chopped onion
1/2 tsp. salt
dash pepper
5 Tbsp. melted butter or
  margarine, divided
1 c. bread cubes

In mixing bowl, combine corn, cooked broccoli, egg, cracker
crumbs, onions, salt, pepper and 3 tablespoons butter (melted).
Pour into 1 quart casserole. Combine bread cubes and remaining
2 tablespoons melted butter. Sprinkle over top of corn mixture.
Bake uncovered in 350° oven for 35 to 40 minutes. Makes 6 to
8 servings.

BROCCOLI SUPREME

Ginny Anderson
X-tra X-amples X-tension

1 slightly beaten egg
1-10 oz. pkg. chopped,
 partly thawed broccoli
1 can cream style corn
1 Tbsp. grated onion

1/4 tsp. salt and pepper
3 Tbsp. butter
1 c. herb stuffing

Combine egg, broccoli, corn, onion, salt and pepper. Melt butter; add herb stuffing and toss to coat. Stir 3/4 cup buttered stuffing into vegetable mixture. Turn into quart casserole and sprinkle with remaining stuffing. Bake uncovered at 350° for 35 to 40 minutes.

BROCCOLI EGG BAKE

Janet Weingardt
Rainbows of Happiness

1 pkg. frozen broccoli
 (10 oz.)
2 Tbsp. margarine
2 Tbsp. flour
1/2 tsp. salt
1 c. milk

1/8 tsp. pepper
1/2 c. grated cheese
6 hard cooked eggs

Cook broccoli according to package directions. Drain and set aside. Melt margarine in small saucepan; remove from heat. Blend in flour, salt and pepper and slowly stir in milk. Cook over low heat, stirring constantly until sauce thickens and boils for 1 minute. Add grated cheese; stir until melted. Arrange 2 layers each of broccoli and sliced eggs in a shallow 1 1/2 quart casserole dish. Pour cheese sauce over. Bake in 350° oven about 30 minutes or until bubbly hot.

BROCCOLI AND PEAS

Helen Davis
Highland Lassies

1-10 oz. box frozen cut
 broccoli
1-10 oz. box frozen peas
1 can mushroom soup

1-8 oz. jar Cheez Whiz
frozen onion rings

Break up vegetables, the broccoli and peas and put in the bottom of a greased baking dish. Spread the soup and Cheez Whiz on top of the frozen vegetables and cover with the frozen onion rings. Bake at 350° for 45 minutes if vegetables are frozen, 20 minutes if thawed.

BROCCOLI CASSEROLE

Joyce Werner
Home Hustlers

1/4 c. finely chopped onion
8 Tbsp. butter
2 Tbsp. flour
1/4 c. water

1-8 oz. jar Cheez Whiz
1/4 c. cracker crumbs
2 pkgs. thawed broccoli
3 eggs, well beaten

Brown onions in 6 tablespoons butter. Add flour and water (mixed). Cook until thick. Add Cheez Whiz. Melt 2 tablespoons butter and combine with 1/4 cup cracker crumbs. Add broccoli to onion and Cheez Whiz. Put in a 2 quart buttered casserole. Add eggs. Top with buttered crumbs. Bake at 325° for 30 minutes.

BROCCOLI CASSEROLE

Ruth Reed, Padroni
Nell Berdine Druyff, Sterling Homemakers
Alba DeSoto, Southsiders

1-10 oz. pkg. frozen broccoli
1/2 c. shredded sharp cheese
1/4 c. milk
1/4 c. fine bread crumbs

1 can cream of mushroom soup
1/4 c. mayonnaise
1 egg, slightly beaten
1 Tbsp. melted butter

Bread up the chopped broccoli in a baking dish. Mix soup, shredded cheese and mayonnaise and stir in with the broccoli. Add milk and beaten egg; stir thoroughly. Combine bread crumbs and melted butter and spread over top. Bake 45 minutes at 350°.

BROCCOLI MUSHROOM SCALLOP

Elma Dickinson
Sterling Homemakers

1 Tbsp. oil
1 c. sliced mushrooms
1 tsp. grated onion
2 Tbsp. flour
1/4 tsp. salt
1/8 tsp. pepper

1 c. skim milk
1/2 lb. fresh broccoli or
    10 oz. pkg frozen broccoli,
    cooked and cut in 2" pieces
1/2 c. shredded mozzarella cheese
1/4 c. dried bread crumbs
1/8 tsp. paprika

Heat oil in a medium skillet over moderate heat. Add mushroom and onion. Cook until onions are soft. Sift in flour, salt and pepper. Cook a few minutes over moderate heat, stirring. Gradually add milk, stirring until mixture is smooth and thickened. Spread broccoli in casserole, 1 quart size. Pour mushroom sauce over broccoli. Sprinkle with cheese, bread crumbs and paprika. Bake uncovered in preheated 350° oven about 20 minutes or golden brown. Makes 4 servings.

Potatoes soaked in salt water for 20 minutes before baking will bake more rapidly.

Sweet potatoes will not turn dark if put in salted water (five teaspoons to one quart of water) immediately after peeling.

Let raw potatoes stand in cold water for at least half an hour before frying to improve the crispness of french fried potatoes.

Use a strawberry huller to peel potatoes which have been boiled in their 'jackets'.

Use greased muffin tins as molds when baking stuffed green peppers.

A few drops of lemon juice in the water will whiten boiled potatoes.

The skins will remain tender if you wrap potatoes in aluminum foil to bake them. They are attractively served in the foil, too.

If you add a little milk to water in which cauliflower is cooking, the cauliflower will remain attractively white.

When cooking cabbage, place a small tin cup or can half full of vinegar on the stove near the cabbage, and it will absorb all odor from it.

It is important when and how you add salt in cooking. To blend with soups and sauces, put it in early, but add it to meats just before taking from the stove. In cake ingredients, salt can be mixed with the eggs. When cooking vegetables always salt the water in which they are cooked. Put salt in the pan when frying fish.

It is easy to remove the white membrane from oranges—for fancy desserts or salads—by soaking them in boiling water for five minutes before you peel them.

You can get more juice from a dried up lemon if you heat it for five minutes in boiling water before you squeeze it.

If it's important to you to get walnut meats out whole, soak the nuts overnight in salt water before you crack them.

If the whipping cream looks as though it's not going to whip, add three or four drops of lemon juice or a bit of plain gelatin powder to it and it probably will.

For quick and handy seasoning while cooking, keep on hand a large shaker containing six parts of salt and one of pepper.

Dip your bananas in lemon juice right after they are peeled. They will not turn dark and the faint flavor of lemon really adds quite a bit. The same may be done with apples.

BREAD, ROLLS, PIES, PASTRY

FLAT BREAD
Marilyn Brehe
Padroni E.H.

1 pkg. dry yeast
1 3/4 c. warm water
4 Tbsp. oil

2 tsp. salt
1 tsp. sugar
4 c. whole wheat flour

Mix first 5 ingredients and half the flour. Beat well with wooden spoon; add the rest of the flour and knead for 5 mintues, adding more flour if needed. Put dough in oiled bowl and turn over; cover and let rise till doubled, then punch down. Cut into 4 equal parts. On floured surface, roll each to a 10x14 inch rectangle or a 15 inch circle about 1/16 thick. Place on ungreased baking sheet. Prick all over with fork. Put into 400° oven and bake until surface is bubbly and is arched somewhat in the middle, about 15 minutes. If bottom is not browned, turn over and return to oven for a few minutes, but watch carefully. Repeat with all the dough. Break up if necessary and store in air tight container. Keeps a long time.

WHOLE WHEAT BREAD
Esther Pace
Night Owls

2 pkgs. yeast
2 c. warm water
2 Tbsp. sugar or honey
2 tsp. salt
3 1/2 c. enriched white
    flour

1/2 c. hot water
1/2 c. brown sugar
3 Tbsp. shortening
3 1/2 c. whole wheat flour

Soften yeast in warm water until dissolved. Add sugar, salt and white flour. Beat until smooth. Keep in warm place until light and bubbly. Combine hot water, brown sugar and shortening. Stir until lukewarm. Add to yeast mixture. Add whole wheat flour and mix until smooth. Knead down. Cut in half and shape each half into ball. Cover and let rise 10 minutes. Shape into loaves and place in lightly greased loaf pan. Cover and let rise till double in size. Bake 50 minutes at 375°.
Variation: Use 1/2 cup cracked wheat, 1 cup raisins and 1 cup peeled, chopped apples.

MIX TOGETHER QUICK BREAD

Jill Distel
Creative Homemakers

2 eggs, beaten
6 Tbsp. melted oleo
1 tsp. salt
2 Tbsp. sugar

2 pkgs. yeast
1 1/2 c. warm milk
4 c. flour

Mix yeast with warm milk. Add rest of ingredients with flour. Mix, knead and let rise 15 minutes. Shape and let rise 15 minutes. Bake at 425° for 15 minutes.

BEDOUIN BREAD

Ginny Anderson
X-tra X-amples X-tension

1 oz. fresh yeast cake
1 1/2 c. water (hot from tap)
3 1/2 c. flour

1 Tbsp. honey
1 tsp. salt

Dissolve the yeast and honey in the water. Stir in the flour and salt. Mix well, and knead on lightly floured board. Cut the dough in eight pieces and shape it into rounds. Roll or flatten the bread with the hands until the cakes are about 5 inches across and 1/4 inch thick. Place them on a lightly greased cookie sheet. Cover with a clean towel and let rise an hour or two. When over 1/2 inch thick, bake the bread at 500° for 7 minutes. Serve with honey and butter when bread is still hot.

GRANDMA'S OVERNIGHT BREAD

Earline Schuppe
Proctor

1 pkg. dry yeast
1 qt. milk, scalded
1 scant c. sugar
13 to 14 c. flour

1/2 c. warm water
1 c. melted shortening
3 tsp. salt

Dissolve yeast in warm water. Let stand until bubbly. Add cooled milk. (You can substitute 1 quart water mixed with 2 cups dry milk powder then no scalding is necessary.) Add melted shortening, sugar, and salt. Stir real well. Gradually add about 12 cups of flour, kneading with your hands. Cover with plastic wrap and let it stand in a cool, draft-free place overnight or 8 to 14 hours.

In the morning, sprinkle 1/2 cup or more of flour on dough and turn out onto floured board. Knead for at least 8 minutes, adding flour to prevent sticking, until dough is smooth and satiny. Divide into 4 pieces and shape into loaves and put in greased bread pans. Cover and let rise until doubled in bulk, an hour or so.

Bake at 400° for about 25 minutes. Remove from pans and cool. (This dough is also good for cinnamon rolls or dinner rolls.)

OLD FASHIONED HONEY WHEAT BREAD   Annie Neff
Southsiders E.H. Club

1 1/2 c. water	1 c. whole wheat flour
1 c. cottage cheese	2 Tbsp. sugar
1/2 c. honey	3 tsp. salt
1/4 c. margarine	2 pkgs. active dry yeast
5 1/2 to 6 c. unbleached flour	1 egg

In medium saucepan, heat water, cottage cheese, honey and margarine until very warm (120°). Lightly spoon flour into measuring cup; level off. In large bowl, combine warm liquid, 2 cups flour and remaining ingredients; beat 2 minutes at medium speed. By hand, stir in remaining flour. On wellfloured surface, knead dough until smooth and elastic, about 2 minutes. Place in greased bowl. Cover and let rise in warm place until light and doubled in size, 45 to 60 minutes. Grease two 9x5 inch loaf pans. Punch down dough and divide and shape into two loaves. Place in greased pans. Cover and let rise in warm place until light and doubled in size. Heat oven to 375°.

Bake 35 to 40 mintues or until deep golden brown and loaf sounds hollow when lightly tapped. If loaf becomes too brown, loosely cover with foil the last 10 minutes of baking. Immediately remove from pans. If desired, brush with butter. Makes 2 loaves.

TUPPERWARE BREAD   Mrs. Helen Koester
Padroni E.H.

1 1/2 c. scalded milk	1 1/2 c. cold water
2 eggs, beaten	1 tsp. salt
2 pkgs. dry yeast	9 c. flour
3/4 c. sugar	

In a Mix and Fix bowl, put in 9 cups flour. Make a well in the center. In a 2 quart Mix 'n Stor bowl, mix well the above ingredients. Add to flour; do not mix. Seal and burp. Store in warm place till seal pops, 15 to 20 mintues. Melt one cup margarine and pour over flour mixture, then knead a little; leave very sticky. Seal and burp and store in warm place till seal pops off, 20 to 30 minutes. Makes 4 loaves or one loaf and 2 pans of rolls. Can be used for cinnamon rolls (rise again). Bake at 375° for 25 to 30 minutes or until done.

SUNFLOWER SEED SQUARES

Margaret Lueck
Hearth and Home

2 c. all purpose flour
1 pkg. active dry yeast
3 tsp. wheat germ
1/2 c. butter
1/2 c. chopped walnuts

1 tsp. honey
1 tsp. salt
1 egg
1 c. whole wheat flour
1/2 c. shelled sunflower seeds

In large mixer bowl combine 1 1/2 cup of all purpose flour, the yeast and wheat germ. In saucepan, heat 1 1/4 cups water, butter, honey and salt just till warm. Stir until butter almost melts. Add to dry ingredients; add egg. Beat at low speed 1/2 minute, scraping sides of bowl constantly. Beat 3 minutes at high speed. By hand, stir in remaining white flour, whole wheat flour, and half of sunflower seeds and nuts. Cover and let rise in warm place for 30 to 45 minutes, or until double. Stir batter down. Spread evenly in greased 15x10 inch pan. Sprinkle with remaining seeds and nuts. Press into batter lightly with hands. Cover and let rise in warm place until doubled. Bake in 400° oven for 30 minutes. Cool in wire rack. Cut in squares. Makes 36 squares.

OLIEBOLLEN

Janet Kloberdanz
X-tra X-amples X-tension Club

3 1/4 c. flour
2 pkgs. yeast (dry)
1 c. milk
1/3 c. sugar
1/4 c. butter
1 tsp. salt
1 tsp. vanilla

2 eggs
3 egg yolks
1/2 c. raisins
1/2 c. chopped mixed candied
    fruit
fat for frying
1/2 c. sugar
1 tsp. cinnamon

Combine 2 cups of the flour and yeast. In a saucepan, heat milk, the 1/3 cup sugar, butter and salt just until warm, stirring constantly. Stir in vanilla. Add to dry ingredients; add eggs and egg yolks. Beat at low speed of electric mixer for 1/2 minute, scraping bowl. Beat 3 minutes at high speed. Stir in the remaining flour, raisins and candied fruits and peels. Cover; let rise until doubled (about 30 minutes.) Carefully drop batter by tablespoonfuls into hot 375° fat. Cook 3 mintues, turning to brown. Drain well on paper towel. While warm, dust with sugar-cinnamon mixture.

TEA RING

Marilyn Brehe
Padroni E.H.

1/2 c. warm water	2 pkgs. active dry yeast
1 1/2 c. lukewarm milk	1/4 c. sugar
1 Tbsp. salt	3 eggs
1/4 c. soft shortening	7 1/4 to 7 1/2 c. flour

Dissolve yeast in water. Stir milk, sugar, salt, eggs and short-ening and half the flour into yeast. Mix until smooth; add enough remaining flour to handle. Turn onto floured board and knead; let rise till doubled.

Melt 4 tablespoons butter. Divide dough in half; roll to 15x9 inch oblong. Spread 2 tablespoons butter on dough. Sprinkle with 1/2 cup brown sugar, 2 teaspoons cinnamon and 1/4 cup chopped nuts. Roll jelly roll style and shape into a circle, seam side down on a lightly greased cookie sheet. Repeat with other half of dough. Let rise till double.

Bake at 375° for 20 minutes. Cool and frost with powdered sugar icing. Decorate with chopped nuts and candied fruit. Makes two rings. Can be frozen before frosted.

CINNAMON-NUT COFFEE RING

Joyce Jones
Sterling Homemakers

1-1 lb. loaf frozen plain dough	1/2 c. chopped walnuts
1/2 c. (1 stick) butter, softened	1/2 c. sugar
	2 tsp. ground cinnamon

Thaw dough overnight in the refrigerator. Allow dough to stand at room temperature on a lightly floured surface, 1 hour. Roll and push dough to a 14x8 inch rectangle. Spread 2/3 of the dough with all but 2 tablespoons of the butter; fold entire rectangle in thirds. Tap gently with rolling pin. Turn dough so open edge faces you and roll out again. Fold in thirds again. Let rest 15 minutes while making filling.

Combine nuts, sugar and cinnamon. Roll dough to 14x8 inch rectangle. Spread remaining 2 tablespoons butter over surface. Sprinkle with sugar mixture almost to edges. Roll jelly roll fashion from long side. Place seam side down on greased jelly roll pan. Shape into a circle, pinching seam well to seal. Using scissors, make deep cuts from outside almost to center, 1 inch apart. Turn each section, cut side up. Cover; let rise 1 hour. Bake at 350° for 25 minutes. Cool and drizzle with icing.

CARAWAY PUFFS

Bonnie Amen
Proctor

2 1/3 c. sifted all purpose flour
1/4 tsp. baking soda
1 c. cream style cottage
   cheese
1/4 c. water
2 Tbsp. sugar

1 Tbsp. butter
1 tsp. salt
1 egg
2 tsp. caraway seeds
2 tsp. grated onion
1 pkg. active dry yeast

In bowl, combine 1 package active dry yeast, 1 1/3 cups sifted all purpose flour, and 1/4 teaspoon baking soda. Heat together 1 cup cream style cottage cheese, 1/4 cup water, 2 tablespoons sugar, 1 tablespoon butter and 1 teaspoon salt till butter melts. Add to dry ingredients. Add 1 egg, 2 teaspoons caraway seeds and 2 teaspoons grated onion. Beat at low speed for 1/2 minute. Beat 3 minutes at high speed. Stir in 1 cup additional flour. Place in greased bowl, turning once. Cover and let rise till double, about 1 1/2 hours. Divide among 12 well greased muffin pans. Cover and let rise, about 40 minutes. Bake at 400° for 12 to 15 minutes.

CHRISTMAS MORNING ROLLS

Betty Ballinger
Hearth and Home

1 bag frozen dinner rolls
1-3 3/4 oz. pkg. butterscotch
   pudding (not instant)
1/2 c. butter

3/4 c. brown sugar
3/4 tsp. cinnamon
1/2 c. nuts

Place rolls in Bundt pan. Sprinkle pudding over rolls. Cook butter, sugar, cinnamon over low heat until mixture bubbles. Pour over rolls. Cover with foil and let stand all night. Bake at 350° for 30 minutes. Let stand 5 minutes inverted on dish.

OVERNIGHT COFFEE CAKE

Norma Nab
Pep and Progress

1 pkg. frozen cloverleaf
   roll dough (25 rolls)
4 oz. pkg. vanilla pudding
   mix (not instant)

1/2 c. brown sugar
1/2 c. chopped nuts
1 stick butter or margarine,
   melted

Separate frozen roll dough into pieces (each cloverleaf makes 3 pieces). Other rolls will work but with larger pieces of dough use only 2 (more maybe too many for your pan).

Combine dry pudding mix with brown sugar and nuts. Melt butter. Place pieces of frozen dough in a well buttered Bundt pan. Pour melted butter over frozen dough and sprinkle with pudding mixture. Leave cake pan at room temperature overnight. The dough rises beautifully by morning.

Bake at 350° for 30 minutes. Invert on serving plate to serve. Sticky but good.

TIRZA CAMPBELL DINNER ROLLS

Diane Freeman
Southsiders of Iliff

2 pkgs. yeast	2 tsp. salt
1/4 c. warm water	1/2 c. shortening
1 3/4 c. milk	2 eggs
1/2 c. sugar	6 c. flour

Dissolve yeast in warm water. Scald milk. Add sugar and salt; let cool. Melt shortening. Let cool. Add eggs, yeast and 2 cups of the flour to milk; beat well. Add shortening and 2 more cups flour. Mix in last 2 cups flour and knead well till smooth. Let rise 1 hour. Punch down and knead well again. Let double, about 1 hour. Shape into dinner or cinnamon rolls. Let rise about 30 minutes. Bake at 325° for 20 minutes.
Note: Tirza Campbell was a long time resident of Iliff and was well known for her delicious baked goods. I submit this recipe in her memory.

60 MINUTE ROLLS

Sammy Shaw
Sterling Homemakers

2 pkgs. yeast	3 Tbsp. sugar
1/2 c. warm water	2 tsp. salt
1 tsp. sugar	1 egg
1 c. milk	4 1/2 c. flour
4 Tbsp. shortening	

Dissolve yeast in warm water and 1 teaspoon sugar. Heat 1 cup milk, shortening, sugar, salt and cool to lukewarm. Add to the yeast mixture. Beat in the egg and add the flour. Turn on a lightly floured board and knead lightly. Let stand 15 minutes; form into rolls. Place in well oiled pans and let rise for 60 minutes.
Bake at 425° for 12 to 15 minutes.

WHOLE WHEAT CROISSANTS

Ardis Bazata
Highland Lassies

1 pkg. yeast
1 c. warm water
3/4 c. undiluted evap. milk
1 1/2 tsp. salt
1/3 c. honey
1 egg

2 c. whole wheat flour
1/4 c. melted butter, cooled
1 c. whole wheat flour
3 c. all purpose flour
1 c. firm butter

In a large bowl, dissolve yeast in warm water (110°). Add evaporated milk, salt, honey, 1 egg and 2 cups whole wheat flour. Beat on medium speed until smooth. Stir in the cooled melted butter and set aside.

In another large bowl, stir together the 1 cup whole wheat flour and the all purpose flour and cut in the 1 cup firm butter until the particles are about "pea" size. Pour the yeast mixture into the flour, butter mixture and stir until all the flour is evenly moistened. Cover with plastic wrap and refrigerate at least 4 hours or up until 4 days. Turn dough out onto a well floured board and knead for about 5 minutes. Divide dough into 4 equal parts. Working with one part of the dough at a time, roll into a 17 inch circle, using a sharp knife, cut into 8 equal wedges. Loosely roll each wedge toward the center point. Shape each roll into a crescent and place point side down on an ungreased baking sheet about 1 1/2 inches apart. Cover until almost doubled in bulk, about 2 hours. Brush rolls with 1 egg, beaten with 1 tablespoon water. Bake in a 325° oven for 25 minutes or until lightly browned. Remove from baking sheet and cool on racks. Makes about 32 croissants.

PIZZA DOUGH

Rosie Nicholas
Creative Homemakers

3 c. flour
3/4 tsp. garlic salt
1/4 tsp. pepper
1 small pkg. yeast

3/4 c. lukewarm water
1/2 c. warm milk
1 Tbsp. oil or melted shortening

Mix flour, salt and pepper. Dissolve yeast in water in another bowl. Add milk and shortening. Combine flour and liquid gradually. Knead dough about 2 minutes. Grease bowl; place dough in it and let rise for 20 minutes. Punch dough down and allow to rise 10 minutes longer. Do not punch down or knead again. Divide dough in half. Roll each half on a lightly greased pan. Put on topping, sauce and cheese. Bake 15 to 20 minutes at 425°. Our favorite pizza is Canadian bacon, pepperoni, and hamburger. Makes two.

BRAN ROLLS

Nona Amen
Proctor

1 c. boiling water
1 c. All Bran
1/2 c. sugar
1 1/2 tsp. salt
2 eggs

1/2 c. shortening
2 pkgs. yeast
1 c. warm water
1 Tbsp. sugar
5 1/2 c. flour

Mix boiling water, All Bran, sugar, salt and shortening together until shortening is melted and let cool. Combine yeast, warm water and 1 tablespoon sugar and let sit for 5 minutes. Then add 2 eggs and 5 1/2 cups flour. Knead. Put in well greased bowl. Let rise and punch down. Let rise again. Make out into rolls. Let rise and bake at 375° for 20 to 25 minutes.

MEXICAN CORNBREAD

Shirley Herzog
Padroni E.H.

1 c. cornmeal
1 c. milk
1 can cream style corn
1/2 tsp. soda
3/4 tsp. salt

1/2 c. bacon drippings
2 eggs
1/2 lb. grated cheese
1 c. chopped onion
4 to 6 chopped jalapeno peppers

Mix first 7 ingredients in bowl; pour 1/2 of mixture in pans. Top with cheese, onion, pepper mixture. Pour remaining batter over that. Bake 45 minutes. Goes well with sausage and eggs, or with a cool summer salad. Bake at 375° in two 9x9 inch pans. Serves 12 to 15.

SOPAPILLAS

Rosie Nicholas
Creative Homemakers

1 3/4 c. flour
2 tsp. baking powder
1 tsp. salt

2 Tbsp. shortening
2/3 c. cold water

Combine flour, baking powder and salt. Cut in shortening with pastry blender. Add enough water to make dough stiff. Turn dough onto lightly floured board and knead lightly until smooth. Cover with clean towel and let rest 10 minutes. Roll dough very thin into a 15x12 inch rectangle. Cut in 3 inch squares. Fry in very hot fat (Fry Daddy). Turn. Remove with slotted spoon. Drain. Serve with honey.

HOBO BREAD

Carrie Terrell
Creative Homemakers

2 c. raisins
2 1/2 c. boiling water

4 tsp. soda

The night before, mix above ingredients together. Let stand overnight.

The next morning:

3/4 c. brown sugar
1 c. white sugar
1 tsp. salt

4 Tbsp. cooking oil
4 c. flour

Add above ingredients and mix well. Stir and divide in three one pound coffee cans that have been oiled and floured.

Bake 1 hour at 350° or until done. Let stand 1/2 hour before removing.

COFFEE CAKE

Bonnie Amen

1 c. brown sugar
3/4 c. sugar
2 1/2 c. flour
1 tsp. nutmeg
1 tsp. salt
3/4 c. salad oil

2 tsp. cinnamon
1/2 c. nuts
1 egg
1 c. buttermilk
1 tsp. soda

Mix sugars, flour, nutmeg and salt and oil. Take out 1/4 to 1/3 of mixture for topping. Add nuts and cinnamon plus remaining ingredients with soda dissolved in buttermilk. Sprinkle topping over batter in 9x13 inch pan. Bake 45 minutes at 350°.

CHERRY COFFEECAKE

Nell Berdine Druyff
Sterling Homemakers

2 sticks oleo
1 3/4 c. sugar
4 eggs, add one at a time
1 1/2 tsp. vanilla
3 c. flour
1/2 tsp. vanilla
powdered sugar

1/2 tsp. salt
1 1/2 tsp. baking powder
1 can cherry pie mix
1 tsp. almond extract
2 Tbsp. oleo
2 Tbsp. milk

Cream oleo, sugar. Add eggs one at a time and vanilla. Add flour, salt and baking powder. Spread 3/4 batter in greased 12x15 inch pan (jelly roll size). Spread over this 1 can cherry pie mix. Add almond extract to cherries.

Drop remaining batter hit and miss, over cherries. Bake at 350° for 30 to 45 minutes.

Making icing: Warm oleo and milk until oleo melts. Add vanilla; stir in powdered sugar to make a thin icing and drizzle over coffee cake.

BREAKFAST CAKE
Mrs. R. Burkholder
Kelly Woman's Improvement Extension H.C.

1 pkg. yellow cake mix
3/4 c. water
4 eggs
1 tsp. butter flavoring

1 pkg. instant vanilla pudding
  mix
3/4 c. cooking oil
1 tsp. vanilla
1/2 c. nuts

To be added between layers:

1/4 c. sugar

2 tsp. cinnamon

Grease tube or Bundt pan and sprinkle part of nuts on greased bottom (use rest of nuts to sprinkle over the last layer of batter).

Beat all ingredients (except cinnamon and sugar mixture and nuts) 8 minutes at high speed. Sprinkle 1/4 cup chopped nuts in bottom of greased and floured tube or Bundt pan. Layer batter in 3 layers. Between each layer, sprinkle sugar and cinnamon mixture. Sprinkle 1/4 cup nuts on the top of last layer.

Bake in 350° oven for 50 to 55 minutes. When partially cooled, pour glaze made of:

1 c. powdered sugar
2 to 3 Tbsp. milk

3 drops butter extract

QUICK COFFEE CAKE
Mrs. Lorin Lindstrom
Kelly Woman's Improvement Extension H.C.

This recipe is from Edna Stack, Home Agent of Logan County 1937 for 6 1/2 years.

2 c. sifted flour
3 Tbsp. baking powder
2 Tbsp. sugar
1/2 tsp. salt
4 Tbsp. butter or other fat
1/2 c. milk

1 c. chopped raisins
1/4 c. chopped nuts (opt.)
1 tsp. cinnamon
2 Tbsp. sugar
2 Tbsp. flour (from the 2 c. flour
  for batter)

Sift dry ingredients (less 2 tablespoons flour to be used in the topping). Cut the fat in with a biscuit cutter. Add the milk. Pour batter into greased 9 inch square pan. Cover batter with raisins, nuts, cinnamon, sugar and flour mixture. Bake 30 minutes in 375° oven.

CINNAMON TWISTS

Mrs. Joe Gerk
Hearth and Home

1 c. sour cream
3 Tbsp. sugar
1/8 tsp. soda
1 tsp. salt
1 pkg. yeast

1 large egg
2 Tbsp. soft oleo
3 c. sifted flour
2 Tbsp. soft oleo
1/3 c. brown sugar
1 tsp. cinnamon

Heat to lukewarm in saucepan the sour cream, 3 tablespoons sugar; remove from heat and stir in soda and salt. Add to mixture the yeast and stir until dissolved; add egg, soft oleo and 3 cups sifted flour.

Roll into oblong shape and spread on half this mixture of 2 tablespoons soft oleo, 1/3 cup brown sugar and 1 teaspoon cinnamon. Fold over other half and cut into 1 inch strips. Twist and bake on cookie sheet 12 to 15 minutes at 375°. Frost if desired.

HAWAIIAN COFFEE CAKE

Mrs. Joe Gerk
Hearth and Home

1 1/2 c. sifted flour
2 1/2 tsp. baking powder

1/2 tsp. salt
1/2 c. sugar

Combine 1 beaten egg, 1 cup crushed pineapple, 1/4 cup melted oleo. Add pineapple mixture to flour mixture and stir until flour is moistened. Pour in greased 8 inch pan. Top with 1/2 cup brown sugar, 1/2 cup coconut, 2 tablespoons flour and 2 tablespoons butter. Bake at 400° for 25 minutes.

SOUR CREAM TWISTS

Anne Stieb
Hearth and Home

1 c. sour cream
1 pkg. yeast
1/4 c. warm water
2 Tbsp. butter softened
3 Tbsp. sugar

1 tsp. salt
1 egg
3 c. flour
Creamy Glaze

Filling:

2 Tbsp. butter
1/3 c. brown sugar

1 tsp. cinnamon

Heat sour cream to lukewarm. Dissolve yeast in water. Stir in sour cream, butter, sugar, salt, egg, 1 cup flour. Beat. Mix in remaining flour. Turn on floured board. Knead until smooth. Place

128

in bowl. Cover and let rise about 1 hour. Punch down; roll out in rectangle. Brush with butter. Mix brown sugar and cinnamon and sprinkle over. Fold other half sugared half. Cut in strips; twist on opposite ends. Place 2 inches apart on cookie sheet (greased). Cover and let rise 1 hour.

Bake at 375° for 12 to 15 minutes, until golden brown. Spread with a sugar glaze while still warm.

CHERRY KUCHEN

Rosalie Wolfe
Home Hustlers

1 box Pillsbury hot roll
   mix
1 egg
1 Tbsp. sugar
1 Tbsp. cooking oil
1 large can cherry pie filling

Topping:
6 Tbsp. melted butter or margarine
3/4 c. sugar
3/4 c. flour

Dissolve yeast in 3/4 cup warm water; add egg, sugar, flour and mix well. Let rise 60 minutes. Then place dough in large jelly roll pan. Pat and roll out to edges making a small ridge. Spread cherries on dough. Combine topping ingredients and crumble over filling. Let rise 15 minutes.

Bake 15 to 20 minutes at 350° or until edges are light brown. Cut into squares and serve warm.

MAMMOTH PECAN BRAID

Barb Schaefer
Home Hustlers

1 pkg. yeast
1/4 c. water
1/2 c. oleo
1 c. scalded milk

1/2 tsp. salt
1/2 c. sugar
1 egg, beaten
4 to 5 c. flour
1 c. chopped pecans
Orange Snow Icing

Orange Snow Icing:

2 tsp. orange juice
1/2 tsp. vanilla

1 c. powdered sugar

Vanilla Butter Filling:

3/4 c. oleo

1 1/2 c. powdered sugar

Soften yeast in water. Mix sugar, butter and salt in bowl. Pour scalded milk over and dissolve. Cool to lukewarm and add 1 cup flour. Stir in yeast and mix; add 2 cups flour and mix. Add egg and remaining flour to make soft dough. Knead lightly. Let rise about 2 hours. Punch down and let rest 5 to 10 minutes. Roll into 9x18 inch rectangle. Cut in thirds and spread on Vanilla Butter Filling and sprinkle with chopped nuts. Roll each strip lengthwise and seal tightly. Braid the 3 rolled strips and place on cookie sheet or use pizza pan to make wreath. Let rise 1 to 1 1/2 hours.

Bake at 350° for 20 to 25 minutes or till golden brown. Cool partially. While still warm, drizzle with Orange Snow Icing.

POTATO REFRIGERATOR ROLLS
Jo Ann Rizzolo
Home Hustlers

1 1/2 c. warm water
 (110 to 115°)
1 pkg. active dry yeast
2/3 c. sugar
1 1/2 tsp. salt
2/3 c. soft shortening

2 eggs
1 c. lukewarm mashed
 potatoes (can use instant)
7 to 7 1/2 c. flour

In bowl, dissolve yeast in water. Stir in sugar, salt, shortening, eggs and potatoes. Measure flour; mix with hand until dough is easy to handle. Turn onto lightly floured board. Knead until smooth and elastic. Place greased side up in greased bowl. Cover with damp cloth and let rise till double . Work into rolls or place in refrigerator to bake later. About 2 hours before baking (when kept in refrigerator, shape into rolls, coffee cakes, etc. Cover and let rise until double, 1 1/2 to 2 hours. Heat oven to 325°.

Bake 12 to 15 minutes. Makes 4 dozen medium rolls.
Note: Dough may be kept in refrigerator about 5 days. Punch down occasionally as it rises. Keep covered with damp cloth.

RICH REFRIGERATOR ROLLS
Pearly Breidenbach
Hearth and Home

2 pkgs. yeast
1/2 c. warm water
6 well beaten eggs
1 c. sugar
1 c. butter (soft)

4 tsp. salt
1 1/2 c. instant potatoes
2 1/2 c. water
10 c. flour

May be left in refrigerator overnight. Punch down after they rise. Mold into shape. Bake at 350° for 35 minutes.

ROLLS
Mildred Littler
Night Owls

1/2 c. sugar
2 pkgs. yeast

1/4 c. soft shortening
1 1/2 tsp. salt

1 egg   6 1/2 to 7 c. flour

Mix together 2 cups warm water or potato water, sugar, salt and yeast. Stir until dissolved. Stir in 1 egg and soft shortening. Mix with spoon. Add 6 1/2 to 7 cups sifted flour. Round up dough. Place in bowl and rub with butter. Cover with waxed paper or put in Tupperware. Let rise and make into rolls. Makes 3 1/2 dozen.

SOUTHERN SPOON BREAD

Mrs. Lorin Lindstrom
(from Mrs. Albert Lindstrom)
Kelly Woman's Improvement Extension H.C.

2 c. milk	4 Tbsp. sugar
1 c. yellow corn meal	2 Tbsp. fat
4 eggs, well beaten	2 tsp. baking powder
	1/2 tsp. salt

Scald milk and stir in corn meal. When slightly cooled, stir the beaten eggs and fat. Sift baking powder, salt and sugar into the batter. Pour into oiled baking dish. Bake in 350° oven for 45 minutes. Serve hot using a spoon.

CORN MEAL GRIDDLE CAKES

Sammy Shaw
Sterling Homemakers

1 c. boiling water	3 tsp. baking powder
3/4 c. yellow corn meal	1 tsp. salt
1 c. buttermilk or sour milk	1/4 tsp. soda
2 eggs	1/4 c. salad oil
1 c. flour	

Pour boiling water over corn meal; stir until thick. Add milk; beat in eggs. Sift flour, baking powder, salt and soda. Add to corn meal. Stir in salad oil. Bake on hot ungreased griddle.

LUCKY BUCKS

Katherine Kalinowski
Sterling Homemakers

1 c. milk	1 pkg. yeast
2 Tbsp. sugar	1/4 c. warm water
3/4 tsp. salt	1 egg, beaten
1/4 c. shortening	1 c. sifted flour

Scald milk; stir in sugar, salt and shortening. Cool to lukewarm. Sprinkle yeast in warm water. Stir until dissolved. Stir in warm milk mixture. Add egg and flour. Beat until smooth. Cover and let rise in warm place free from draft until doubled in bulk. Stir down batter. For each pancake pour one tablespoon batter on greased griddle and bake.

DILLY BREAD

Annie Neff
Southsiders E.H. Club

1 pkg. dry yeast
1/4 c. warm water
1 c. creamed cottage cheese
2 Tbsp. sugar
1 Tbsp. instant minced onion
1 Tbsp. butter

2 tsp. dill seed
1 tsp. salt
1/4 tsp. baking soda
1 egg
2 1/4 to 2 1/2 c. flour

Sprinkle yeast over warm water (110°). Heat cottage cheese to lukewarm. Combine in mixing bowl with sugar, onion, butter, dill, salt, soda, beaten egg and yeast mixture. Add flour to form a stiff dough, beating well after each addition. Cover and let rise in warm place until double, about 1 hour. Stir down dough. Turn into well greased 1 1/2 quart casserole. Let rise in warm place until light, 30 to 40 minutes. Bake at 300° about 45 minutes. Brush with melted butter and sprinkle with salt.

MOM'S WAFFLES

Nell Berdine Druyff
Sterling Homemakers

2 egg whites
2 egg yolks
1 2/3 c. milk
2 c. flour

1 tsp. salt
3 tsp. baking powder
1 Tbsp. sugar
6 Tbsp. melted Crisco

Beat egg whites until stiff; set aside. Beat egg yolks and milk. Sift and add flour, salt, baking powder and sugar. Quickly stir in melted Crisco and fold in the egg whites. Bake

ANGEL BISCUITS

Helen Vaughn
Padroni E.H.

2 1/2 c. flour
1 tsp. baking powder
1 tsp. salt
1/8 tsp. sugar

1/2 c. shortening
1/4 c. warm water
1 pkg. dry yeast
1 c. buttermilk

Dissolve yeast in 1/4 cup warm water and set aside. Mix dry ingredients in order given. Cut in the shortening. Stir in buttermilk, also the water-yeast mixture. Blend thoroughly. (The dough may be refrigerated at this stage for use later) or roll out and cut with biscuit cutter and place in a greased pan. Let biscuits rise slightly. Allow additional time if dough is cold.

Bake in 400° oven until lightly browned. Use 1/2 whole wheat flour if desired.

OATMEAL PANCAKES

Mrs. Helen Koester
Padroni Extension Homemakers

1 1/2 c. quick oatmeal
1 tsp. soda
2 c. buttermilk

1/2 c. flour
1 tsp. salt
2 eggs, beaten

Mix rolled oats and buttermilk. Beat in rest of ingredients. Fry in very little greased hot skillet. Flip pancakes over when bubbles form on one side. Makes 12 four inch pancakes.

EGG BISCUITS

Fran Hofmann
Hearth and Home

1/2 tsp. cream of tartar
2 c. flour
4 tsp. baking powder
2 tsp. sugar

1/2 tsp. salt
1 egg
2/3 c. milk
1/2 c. shortening

Sift dry ingredients. Cut in shortening. Blend in milk and egg. Knead. Roll or pat out to 1/2 inch thick. Cut and bake at 450° for 10 to 15 minutes.

CARAMEL BUBBLE RING – A QUICK COFFEE CAKE

Mary Ellen Breidenbach
Hearth and Home

1 1/4 pkgs. brown sugar
1/2 c. chopped nuts
1/2 c. butter or margarine

3 tsp. water
2-8 oz. cans buttermilk
  or plain biscuits

Generously grease 9 to 10 inch Bundt pan. In medium saucepan, combine all ingredients except biscuits. Stir over low heat until margarine melts; set aside. Separate biscuits and cut into quarters. Shake in a small paper sack with sugar and cinnamon mixture. Shake sack to coat. Remove quarters and put into sugar mixture. Stir lightly until all are coated. Spread into pan.

Bake 20 to 30 minutes. Let stand 3 minutes after removing from oven. Invert pan on plate to remove ring. Serve warm with coffee or whatever.

MONKEY BREAD

Florence Annan
Home Hustlers

3 cans biscuits
1 cube oleo

1/2 c. brown sugar
1/2 c. chopped nuts

(Cont.)

133

Cut each biscuit into quarters and roll each piece in a little ball. Roll each ball in cinnamon and sugar mixture. Arrange in layers in Bundt pan.

Topping: Melt oleo and then add brown sugar. Bring to a boil. Take from heat and add 1/2 to 1 cup chopped nuts. Pour over top of layered biscuits.

Bake at 350° for 30 minutes. Cool 10 to 20 minutes before turning out of pan.

NUT BREAD

Olive Myers
Sterling Homemakers

1 c. sugar	2 tsp. baking powder
1 egg	1/2 tsp. salt
1 c. milk	1/2 c. nuts
2 c. flour	3 Tbsp. soft margarine

Mix all together. Put in 9x5x3 inch greased pan. Bake at 350° for 40 to 50 minutes or till a toothpick comes out clean.

APPLE BREAD

Betty Robinett
Highland Lassies

1 c. sugar	1 tsp. baking soda
1/2 c. shortening	1/2 tsp. salt
2 eggs	2 c. chopped pared apple
1 tsp. vanilla	(about 4 med.)
2 c. Gold Medal all	1 Tbsp. sugar
purpose flour	1/4 tsp. ground cinnamon
1 tsp. baking powder	

Heat oven to 350°. Grease and flour loaf pan, 9x5x3 inches. Mix 1 cup sugar, the shortening, eggs and vanilla. Stir in flour, baking powder, baking soda and salt until smooth. Stir in apples and nuts. Spread in pan. Mix 1 tablespoon sugar and the cinnamon; sprinkle over batter. Bake until wooden pick inserted in center comes out clean, 50 to 60 minutes. Immediately remove from pan. Cool bread completely before slicing. Store tightly covered.

If using self rising flour, omit baking powder, baking soda and salt.

RHUBARB NUT BREAD

Vicki Gertner
X-tra X-amples X-tension Club

1 1/2 c. packed brown sugar	1 tsp. salt
1 egg	1 tsp. vanilla
1 c. buttermilk	1 1/2 c. diced rhubarb

2/3 c. oil
1 tsp. soda

2 1/2 c. flour
1/2 c. nuts (opt.)

In a large bowl, mix sugar, oil, eggs, buttermilk, salt, soda, vanilla, flour, then add rhubarb and nuts. Pour into two 9x5 inch greased and floured loaf pans.

Topping:

1/2 c. sugar
1/2 tsp. cinnamon

1 Tbsp. margarine

Blend together and sprinkle on top. Bake at 325° for 1 hour.

ZUCCHINI MUFFINS

Cecilia Pyle
Padroni E.H.

1 1/2 c. brown sugar
1 egg
1 1/2 c. shredded raw zucchini
1 c. sour cream
2/3 c. shortening

1 tsp. vanilla
1 tsp. soda
1 tsp. salt
1/2 c. nuts
2 1/2 c. flour

Mix all. Bake in muffin tins that are greased. Bake at 350° for 25 minutes or until done. You may add 2 tablespoons wheat germ, 1/2 cup raisins. These keep well and can be frozen.

REFRIGERATOR BRAN MUFFINS

Ellen Luft
Night Owls

1 1/2 c. sugar
1/2 c. solid shortening
2 eggs
2 1/2 c. unsifted flour
2 1/2 tsp. soda
1/2 tsp. salt

2 c. buttermilk
1 c. boiling water
1 c. 100% Bran
 (Nabisco ready to eat cereal)
3/4 c. seedless raisins
2 c. All Bran (ready to eat
 cereal, Kellogg's)

Thoroughly cream together sugar and shortening. Add eggs, one at a time , mixing well after each addition. Add flour, soda, salt and buttermilk, mixing until smooth. Meanwhile, pour boiling water over 100% Bran and let stand until cereal has absorbed water and has cooled slightly. Blend this mixture into batter. Add raisins and All Bran mixing thoroughly. Refrigerate batter, covered, up to 5 weeks. When ready to use, dip batter from container (without stirring) into greased muffin tins.

Bake in oven (preheated to 400°) about 20 minutes or until done. Recipe may be doubled if desired.

BRAN MUFFINS

Julie Sonnenberg
Southsiders

1 1/8 c. sugar
1/4 c. plus 1 tsp. shortening
1 egg
1 pt. buttermilk
1 c. Bran Buds

1 1/2 c. flour
1 1/4 tsp. soda
1/2 tsp. salt
1/4 c. boiling water*
1/2 c. 100% Bran*

*Pour boiling water over 100% Bran and let soak while mixing other ingredients.

Mix in order given; add 100% Bran mixture at end. Bake at 400° for 12 minutes in greased muffin tins. Mixture can be stored uncovered in the refrigerator for up to 2 weeks and baked as needed.

For "muffins by the pail" for large crews or for sharing, multiply this recipe by four.

ZUCCHINI BREAD

Irene Golgart
Kelly Woman's Improvement Club

3 eggs
1 1/4 c. oil
3 1/4 c. flour
1/2 tsp. salt
1/4 tsp. baking powder
1 tsp. soda

3 tsp. cinnamon
3 tsp. allspice
2 tsp. nutmeg
3 c. grated zucchini
3 tsp. vanilla

Combine eggs, oil, sugar and squash. Add dry ingredients and mix well. Bake in two bread pans at 375° for 1 hour.

BANANA WHEAT BREAD

Cecilia Pyle
Padroni E.H.

1 1/4 c. flour
1/2 c. whole wheat flour
1 c. sugar
1 tsp. soda
1 tsp. salt
2 1/4 Tbsp. orange juice

1 1/2 c. bananas (3)
1/4 c. margarine
1 egg
1/4 c. nuts or raisins
1/2 orange, rind and all
  (put in food processor)

Heat oven to 325°. Grease and flour bottom of 9x5   inch or 8x4 inch pans.

In large bowl, mix all ingredients. Beat 3 minutes at medium speed. Pour batter into pan. Bake at 325° for 50 to 60 minutes. Let cool 5 minutes and remove from pan. If you don't want to mess with your own juice, frozen will work.

BANANA PUMPKIN BREAD

Bonnie Amen
Proctor

1/2 c. margarine
1/2 c. sugar
1/2 c. brown sugar
2 c. flour
1 1/4 tsp. soda
1 1/2 tsp. pumpkin spice

2 eggs
1/2 c. pumpkin
1/2 c. bananas (2)
1 tsp. vanilla
1/4 tsp. salt
1/2 c. nuts (opt.)

Mix margarine and sugar together. Add eggs, pumpkin, bananas and spices. Mix thoroughly. Add flour, soda, salt and nuts. Bake at 350° for about 1 hour.

BANANA BREAD

Marge Rieke
Pep and Progress

1/2 c. shortening
1 c. sugar
2 eggs, beaten
3 Tbsp. buttermilk
3 med. bananas, mashed

2 c. flour
1 tsp. soda
1/4 tsp. salt
1/2 c. chopped nuts

Mix well in order given. Pour batter in greased 5x9x3 inch loaf pan. Bake at 350° 1 hour or longer. When a toothpick comes out clean, bread is done.

BANANA NUT BREAD

Hazel Pyle
Proctor E.H. Club

3 bananas
1 c. sugar
2 c. sifted flour
1 tsp. baking powder
1/2 c. nut meats

1 tsp. salt
2 eggs
1 tsp. soda
1/2 c. shortening

Mash bananas and add sugar. Let stand about 15 minutes. Sift flour before measuring; add baking powder and salt. Beat eggs. Dissolve soda in a little water (about 1 tablespoon). Add shortening to banana and sugar mixture and beat thoroughly. Add dry ingredients, soda, beaten eggs and nut meats. Stir only until mixed. Bake in greased loaf pan at 350° for 50 to 60 minutes.

CORN BREAD

Bonnie Janda
X-tra X-amples X-tension Club

1/2 c. corn meal
1/2 c. flour

1/2 c. cooking oil
1/4 to 1/2 c. sugar

137   (Cont.)

1/2 c. milk
1 egg
1 Tbsp. baking powder
1 tsp. salt

Optional, choose one:
2 Tbsp. Parmesan cheese
1 tsp. cinnamon
1/2 c. raisins

Mix all ingredients on high speed for 4 minutes. Pour into greased pan and bake for 30 minutes at 375°.

MILE HIGH FROZEN BISCUITS

Jan Nixon
Extension Home Economist

3 c. flour
1/4 c. sugar
4 tsp. baking powder
1/2 tsp. cream of tartar

3/4 tsp. salt
1/2 c. shortening
1 egg, beaten
1 c. milk

Combine dry ingredients in mixing bowl. Cut in shortening until mixture resembles coarse crumbs. Add egg and milk all at once. Mix until dough forms a ball. Turn dough onto lightly floured surface and knead 10 to 12 times. Roll out 3/4 inch thick. Cut with floured biscuit cutter. Place on ungreased baking sheet and freeze. When frozen, store in freezer container until needed.

Bake on lightly greased baking sheet at 475° for 10 to 12 minutes.

CREAM PUFFS

Millie Boxler
Pep and Progress

1/2 c. margarine or butter
1 c. boiling water
1 c. sifted all purpose flour

1/4 tsp. salt
4 eggs

Melt butter in boiling water. Add flour and salt all at once. Stir vigorously. Cook stirring constantly until mixture forms a ball that doesn't separate. Remove from heat and cool slightly. Add eggs one at a time, beating vigorously after each until smooth. Drop dough by heaping tablespoonfuls 3 inches apart on a greased cookie sheet.

Bake at 450° for 15 minutes, then bake at 325° for 25 minutes. Remove cream puffs from oven. Split and turn oven off and put cream puffs back in to dry out, about 20 minutes. Cool on rack. Fill with cream. Makes 10 puffs.

DANISH PASTRY APPLE BARS

Irene Schneider
Hearth and Home

2 1/2 c. sifted flour	1 egg yolk
1 tsp. salt	1 c. cornflakes
1/2 c. shortening	8 to 10 apples, pared and
1/2 c. margarine	sliced
1 egg white	1 c. sugar
1 c. sifted powdered sugar	3 or 4 tsp. milk

Combine flour and salt. Cut in shortening and margarine. Beat egg yolk in measuring cup; add enough milk to make 2/3 cup liquid. Mix well and stir into flour mixture. Roll half of the dough into a 17x12 inch rectangle. Fit into and up side of a 1x 15 1/2 x 10 1/2 inch baking pan. Sprinkle corn flakes on dough. Top with apples. Combine sugar and cinnamon and sprinkle on top. Roll out remaining dough and place over top. Seal edges and cut slits in dough. Beat egg white until frothy. Brush on top of crust. Bake in 375° oven for 50 minutes. Combine powdered sugar and milk. Drizzle on warm pastry.

OUT OF THE WORLD PIE

Ireme Schneider
Hearth and Home

This makes two pies.

3/4 c. sugar	1 tsp. red food coloring
1 can cherry pie filling	1-3 oz. pkg. raspberry gelatin
1 large can crushed pineapple	6 bananas, sliced
and juice	1 c. chopped pecans
1 Tbsp. cornstarch	2 baked 10" pie shells
whipped topping	

In a saucepan, combine cherry pie filling, sugar, pineapple and juice, cornstarch and food coloring. Cook until thick. Remove from heat and add gelatin. Allow to cool. Add bananas and pecans. pour into two baked pie shells and top with chilled topping. Chill.

CREAM PEACH PIE

Florence Annan
Home Hustlers

5 med. peaches	1 c. half and half
1 c. sugar	dash of nutmeg
3 Tbsp. flour	1/2 tsp. vanilla
pinch of salt	

Peel peaches and slice. Mix together with sugar, flour, salt and nutmeg. Stir into cream. Pour all ingredients into an unbaked pastry shell. This is just a one crust pie. Bake at 425° for 15 minutes. Reduce heat to 350° and continue baking for 30 minutes or until filling is set. Center area will be soft.

PEANUT BUTTER CREAM PIE
Kathy Graham
X-tra X-amples X-tension Club

1-8 oz. pkg. cream cheese,
  softened
1 lb. powdered sugar
  (2 1/2 c.)
1 c. peanut butter

1-13 oz. tub Cool Whip
2 graham cracker crusts
crushed peanuts

Cream together cream cheese, powdered sugar and peanut butter. Add Cool Whip and beat/whip thoroughly together (use mixer of food processor). Put into the two graham cracker pie crusts. Top with crushed peanuts. Store in refrigerator.

COCONUT MACAROON PIE
Sandy Ils
Home Hustlers

1 1/2 c. sugar
2 eggs
1/2 tsp. salt
1/2 c. soft butter or margarine
1/4 c. flour

1/2 c. milk
1 1/2 c. shredded coconut
1-9" pie shell, unbaked

Beat sugar, salt, eggs until well mixed and lemon colored. Add butter and flour and blend well. Add milk. Fold in 1 cup coconut. Pour into pie shell and top with remaining coconut. Bake in slow 325° oven about 60 minutes.

IMPOSSIBLE COCONUT PIE
Dorothy Bartholomew
Pep and Progress

4 eggs
1/4 c. oleo
1 c. sugar
1/2 c. flour
1 tsp. vanilla

1/4 tsp. salt
1/2 tsp. baking powder
2 c. milk
1 c. coconut

Combine ingredients and mix well or blend in blender. Pour into a greased 10 inch pie pan. Bake at 350° for 1 hour.

ALMOND BAR PIE

Mary May
Hearth and Home

16 marshmallows
5 chocolate almond bars
1/2 c. milk
1 1/2 c. graham cracker
    crumbs

3 Tbsp. sugar
1/3 c. margarine
1 c. whipping cream

Place marshmallows, bars, and milk in double boiler. Cook until marshmallows and bars melt. Cool. Combine graham crumbs, sugar and margarine. Press in pie pan and bake 10 minutes at 325°; cool. Whip cream; add to chocolate mixture and pour into crust. Refrigerate.

KENTUCKY PECAN PIE

Lorene Freeman
Southsiders

1 c. white corn syrup
1 c. dark brown sugar
1/3 tsp. salt
1/3 c. melted oleo

1 tsp. vanilla
3 whole eggs, slightly beaten
1 c. whole pecans

Combine syrup, sugar, salt, oleo and vanilla; mix well. Add slightly beaten eggs. Pour over 9 inch unbaked pie shell. Sprinkle pecans over all. Bake in preheated oven for 45 minutes.

ICE CREAM PUMPKIN PIE

Ruth Reed
Padroni E.H.

1 baked pie shell
1/2 c. packed brown sugar
1/4 c. milk
1 tsp. cinnamon
1 env. unflavored gelatin
1/2 c. cream
1/4 c. sugar

3 egg yolks, beaten
1 1/2 c. pumpkin
1/2 tsp. salt
1/2 tsp. nutmeg
1/4 c. cold water
1 c. vanilla ice cream

Blend egg yolks, brown sugar, pumpkin, milk, salt and spcies. Cook in double boiler until thick, stirring constantly. Soak gelatin in cold water and stir into hot mixture. Chill the above mixture, then whip the cream and add sugar. Combine with ice cream. Fold into gelatin mixture. Then pour all into baked pie shell.

PUMPKIN PECAN PIE

Connie Lechman
Proctor E.H. Club

3 eggs, slightly beaten
1 c. pumpkin
1 c. sugar
1 c. dark syrup
1 tsp. vanilla

1 tsp. cinnamon
1/2 tsp. salt
2 Tbsp. melted margarine
1 c. pecans

Mix all ingredients but nuts and pour into 9 or 10 inch pastry lined pie pan. Sprinkle or arrange nuts on top. Bake 40 minutes at 350°.

SPRING DAFFODIL PIE

Dorothy Smith
Kelly Woman's Improvement Club

1 env. unflavored gelatin
1/4 c. cold water
1/2 c. milk
1 c. sugar
1/4 tsp. salt
3 egg yolks

3/4 c. orange juice
1/4 c. lemon juice
1 tsp. grated orange rind
1/2 tsp. grated lemon rind
1 c. whipped topping
1-9" baked pie shell

Soften gelatin in cold water. Combine milk, sugar, salt and egg yolks in small saucepan. Cook over medium heat, stirring constantly until mixture thickens. Add gelatin; stir until dissolved. Stir in orange and lemon juices and orange and lemon rinds. Chill mixture until slightly thickened. Fold whipped topping into mixture and turn into pie shell. Chill several hours or until set. Garnish with puffs of whipped topping.

SURPRISE PIE

Loretto Lively
Padroni E.H.

1 c. sugar
1/4 tsp. salt
1/2 c. butter or margarine

1/2 c. dark Karo syrup
1 tsp. vanilla
2 eggs

Blend until creamy; add 1 cup cooked, mashed pinto beans and blend well. Stir in 1/2 to 1 cup chopped pecans. Pour into a 9 inch unbaked pie shell. Start at 375° oven for 15 minutes. Reduce to 325° for 15 minutes. Turn off heat and leave in oven for another 15 minutes.

PINTO BEAN PIE (MOCK PECAN PIE)

Iris Lambert
Rainbows of Happiness

1 c. cooked pinto beans
  (no seasoning)
4 eggs
1 c. dark Karo syrup

1 1/2 c. sugar
1/2 stick butter
2 tsp. vanilla

Mix all the above ingredients well and pour into unbaked pie shell. Bake at 375° for 1 hour and 15 minutes or until done.

VINEGAR PIE

Mrs. Ben Benson (deceased)
Kelly Woman's Improvement Club

1 c. sugar
2 egg yolks
1 Tbsp. vinegar
1 tsp. lemon extract

1 Tbsp. butter
2 Tbsp. flour
1 c. hot water

Combine sugar and flour. Slowly add water, then add remaining ingredients and cook until it thickens. It is best to add the lemon extract after cooking. Pour into pie shell and cover with meringue made from the two egg whites. Brown in oven.

O-SO-GOOD-PIE

Hazel Korrey
Hearth and Home

1 unbaked pie shell
4 whole eggs
2 tsp. butter
2 c. sugar

1 tsp. each cinnamon, allspice
  and cloves
1 c. raisins

Cream butter and sugar until light. Add beaten yolks and vinegar. Then spices and raisins; beat well. Fold in beaten egg whites. Pour into pie shell. (It forms it's own meringue while cooking.) Bake slowly until thoroughly set at 325° for 25 to 35 minutes.

SOUR CREAM RAISIN PIE

Ginny Anderson
X-tra X-amples X-tension

2 Tbsp. cornstarch
1 c. sugar, divided
1/4 tsp. salt
1/2 tsp. cinnamon
1/4 tsp. nutmeg
1/4 tsp. cloves, ground

2 eggs, separated
1 c. sour cream
3/4 to 1 c. raisins
1 1/2 tsp. lemon juice
1-9" baked pie shell

In the top of a double boiler mix together cornstarch, 3/4 cup sugar, salt, cinnamon, nutmeg, and cloves. Add egg yolks and mix well. Add sour cream. Cook over hot water until thick, stirring constantly. Stir in raisins and lemon juice. Cool. Pour into baked pie shell. Beat egg whites until stiff. Gradually beat in the remaining 1/4 cup sugar. Spread over filling. Bake in a hot 425° oven for 5 to 10 minutes or until delicately browned.

SOUR CREAM RAISIN PIE

Lakie Taylor (Deceased)
Kelly Woman's Improvement Club

1/2 c. cooked raisins
1/2 c. sugar
1 Tbsp. flour
1 Tbsp. lemon juice

1 c. sour cream
2 egg yolks, beaten
1/4 tsp. cinnamon

Meringue:

2 egg whites, at room temp.
1/4 tsp. salt

1/2 tsp. cream of tartar
4 Tbsp. sugar

Meringue: Beat egg whites with salt and cream of tartar. When foamy, add sugar slowly. Beat until sugar is completely dissolved.

Filling: Combine all filling ingredients and cook slowly, stirring constantly until thick. Pour into a baked pie shell and cover with meringue. Bake in a 350° oven till lightly browned.

FRESH HARVEST PIE

Norma Penner
Rainbows of Happiness

3 large apples, pared,
  cored and sliced
2 large pears, pared, cored
  and sliced
1 1/2 c. seedless grapes
1/2 tsp. grated lemon rind
1 Tbsp. lemon juice

1/2 c. sugar
2 Tbsp. flour
1/2 tsp. cinnamon
1/4 tsp. nutmeg
pastry for 2 crust pie

Combine fruit, rind, juice, sugar, flour, cinnamon, and nutmeg. Mix well. Spoon mixture into pastry lined 9 inch pie plate. Top with upper crust. Bake in a 350° oven for 50 to 60 minutes.

STRAWBERRY PIE GLAZE

Earline Schuppe
Proctor

1 c. water
1/2 c. sugar

2 Tbsp. cornstarch
3 Tbsp. strawberry jello powder

Mix together sugar and cornstarch. Add water and cook until

thick and clear. Remove from heat. Add jello powder and stir to dissolve. Cool to room temperature. Pour over 1 1/2 to 2 cups of strawberries for fresh strawberry pie or other desserts. Keep refrigerated.

SPRING FRUIT PIE

Irene Schneider
Hearth and Home

2 c. sliced strawberries
2 c. 1" pieces of rhubarb
1/2 c. drained, crushed
  pineapple
2 Tbsp. lemon juice

1 c. sugar
1/4 c. cornstarch
dash of salt
2 Tbsp. margarine
1 double crust pastry

Stir together strawberries, rhubarb, pineapple and lemon juice. Add sugar, cornstarch and salt. Toss well. Fill a 9 inch plate with 1/2 the pastry rolled 1/8 inch thick. Turn fruit mixture into pastry lined plate. Dot with margarine. Roll out remaining pastry for top crust. Cut slits to permit steam to escape during baking and place over filling. Seal and flute edges. Bake in 425° oven for 40 to 45 minutes or until lightly browned. Makes one 9 inch pie.

RHUBARB STRAWBERRY PIE

Clara Werner
Pep and Progress

1-9" unbaked pie shell
1 1/2 c. sugar
1/4 c. flour
1/4 tsp. salt
1/4 tsp. nutmeg

2 c. cut up rhubarb
2 c. sliced strawberries
1 Tbsp. butter, softened

Mix sugar, flour, salt and nutmeg then add rhubarb and strawberries. Let stand 20 minutes. Mix with butter and pour into unbaked pie shell. Bake at 400° for 45 minutes.

RHUBARB CUSTARD PIE

Bette McBride
Proctor

Filling:

2 c. diced rhubarb
2 egg yolks
1 c. sweet cream
1 1/3 c. sugar

1/8 tsp. salt
2 Tbsp. cornstarch
1 unbaked pie shell

Meringue:

1 Tbsp. cornstarch (and
  enough water to moisten)
1/2 c. boiling water

3 egg whites
6 Tbsp. sugar
dash salt

Cover rhubarb with boiling water and let stand until ready
to use. Mix beaten egg yolks, sugar, salt and cream in which cornstarch has been dissolved. Drain rhubarb; mix with cream mixture.
Pour in pie shell. Bake at 350° until firm and set. Cover with meringue
and brown at 375°.

Meringue: Moisten cornstarch in water. Stir in boiling water.
Cook until thick and clear. Cool. Beat the egg whites until stiff.
Add salt and sugar gradually. Beat in cornstarch mixture until
it stands in peaks. Spread on cooked pie and brown at 375°.

EASY PIE CRUST

Zelma Stunkard
Shamrock

1/2 c. butter or margarine
2 Tbsp. granulated sugar

1/2 tsp. almond extract

Cream these three ingredients thoroughly and blend in one cup
flour. Now press this mixture evenly into a 9 inch pie pan. Do
not try to roll the dough. It won't work. Bake at 375° for 12 to
15 minutes.

VINEGAR PIE PASTRY

Nora Karg
Shamrock

4 c. flour
1 Tbsp. sugar
2 tsp. salt
1 3/4 c. shortening

1/2 c. water
2 Tbsp. cider vinegar
1 egg

Combine flour, sugar and salt. Cut in shortening. Mix water,
vinegar and egg and add to flour mixture. Dough will be sticky.
Cover and chill at least 2 hours. Can be refrigerated up to 2 weeks
or freeze up to 2 months. If frozen thaw in refrigerator about
2 hours. Makes two big pies or 4 to 5 single crusts.

MILKY WAY PIE CRUST

Dorothy Smith
Kelly Woman's Improvement Club

1 c. flour
1/2 tsp. salt

1/4 lb. butter or margarine
   (1 stick)
1/4 c. milk

Stir together the flour and salt; add butter or margarine (melted); add 1/4 cup milk, stirring until the dough leaves the sides of the bowl. Press dough into a ball and roll out. Ease into pie pan and bake at 450° for 15 minutes. Using milk instead of water makes it easier to roll out. Makes one 8 inch crust.

Write your extra recipes here:

Write your extra recipes here:

Worth Remembering

★ A pie crust will be more easily made and better if all the ingredients are cool.

★ The lower crust should be placed in the pan so that it covers the surface smoothly. And be sure no air lurks beneath the surface, for it will push the crust out of shape in baking.

★ Folding the top crust over the lower crust before crimping will keep the juices in the pie.

★ In making custard type pies, bake at a high temperature for about ten minutes to prevent a soggy crust. Then finish baking at a low temperature.

★ Fill cake pans about two-thirds full and spread batter well into corners and to the sides, leaving a slight hollow in the center.

★ The cake is done when it shrinks slightly from the sides of the pan or if it springs back when touched lightly with the finger.

★ After a cake comes from the oven, it should be placed on a rack for about five minutes. Then the sides should be loosened and the cake turned out on rack to finish cooling.

★ Cakes should not be frosted until thoroughly cool.

★ Kneading the dough for a half minute after mixing improves the texture of baking powder biscuits.

Candy & Frosting Chart

230 degrees - 234 degrees	Thread
234 degrees - 240 degrees	Soft Ball
244 degrees - 248 degrees	Firm Ball
250 degrees - 266 degrees	Hard Ball
270 degrees - 290 degrees	Soft Crack
300 degrees - 310 degrees	Hard Crack

SNICKER CAKE

Doris Harms , Mary Ellen Breidenbach
Hearth and Home

1 box German chocolate
   cake mix
1 pkg. Kraft caramels
1/3 c. milk

1/2 c. margarine
1-6 oz. pkg. chocolate chips
1 c. chopped nuts

Grease and flour 9x13 inch pan. Prepare cake mix as directed.
Pour 1/2 batter into pan and bake 20 minutes. Melt caramels,
milk and margarine. Pour over cake; sprinkle chips and nuts on
top of caramel. Pour rest of batter on top.
    Bake for 10 minutes at 350°, then 20 minutes at 250°. May
be served with whipped cream or topping.

CHOCOLATE ROLL

Bertha Luft
Pep and Progress

5 egg yolks
1 c. powdered sugar
1/4 c. flour
1/2 tsp. salt

3 Tbsp. cocoa
1 tsp. vanilla
5 egg whites, stiffly beaten

Beat egg yolks till lemon colored; add sifted dry ingredients
and beat till blended. Add vanilla and fold in egg whites. Spread
in greased pan (waxed paper lined 10 1/2 x 15 inch).
    Bake at 375° for 15 to 20 minutes.
    Turn out on towel; sprinkle with powdered sugar; remove
waxed paper from cake and cut off crisp edges. Roll up and cool.
When cool, unroll and spread with Cool Whip or whipped cream.
Roll like jelly roll and dust with powdered sugar. Keep in refrigerator.

POOR MAN'S CAKE

Zelma Stunkard
Shamrock

2 c. brown sugar
2 c. hot water
2 tsp. lard or margarine
1 c. raisins
1 tsp. each, salt, cinnamon,
  and ground cloves

3 c. flour
1 tsp. soda dissolved in
  2 tsp. hot water

Mix together brown sugar, hot water, lard, raisins, salt and

149   (Cont.)

spices and boil for 5 minutes after mixture begins to bubble. Remov
from heat. When mixture is cold, add flour and soda mixture.

Bake in a greased tube pan at 350° to 375° for 30 to 40 minut
until it tests done.

GERMAN BUNDT AND SUGAR CAKE

Kathy Glassburn
Padroni E.H.

1/2 c. butter or oleo	3 c. sifted flour
1/4 c. Crisco	5 eggs
2 1/2 c. sugar	1 tsp. vanilla
1 c. milk	1 tsp. almond or lemon flavoring

Cream together butter, Crisco and sugar. Add rest of ingredients. Beat eggs one at a time then add.

Bake in greased and floured tube pan or bread pan. Bake
1 hour and 15 minutes at 325°. Makes 3 bread pans full. Dust top
with powdered sugar when done.

OATMEAL CHOCOLATE CHIP CAKE

Betty Robinett
Highland Lassies

1 3/4 c. boiling water	1 3/4 c. unsifted flour
1 c. uncooked oatmeal	1 tsp. soda
(quick or old fashioned kind)	1/2 tsp. salt
1 c. lightly packed brown sugar	1 Tbsp. cocoa
1 c. granulated sugar	1-12 oz. pkg. semi-sweet
1 stick (1/2 c.) margarine	chocolate bits
2 extra large eggs	3/4 c. chopped walnuts

Pour boiling water over oatmeal. Let stand at room temperature 10 minutes. Add brown and white sugar and margarine.
Stir until margarine melts. Add eggs; mix well. Sift together flour,
soda, salt and cocoa. Add flour to sugar mixture; mix well. Add
about half of the package of chocolate bits or chips. Pour batter
into greased and floured 9x13 inch pan. Sprinkle walnuts and remaining chocolate chips on top.

Bake in oven preheated to 350°, about 40 minutes or until
wooden pick inserted in center comes out clean.

RED VELVET CAKE AND FROSTING

Juanita Pyle
Proctor E.H. Club

3-1/2 oz. bottle red food coloring	
1/2 c. butter	1 tsp. vinegar
2 eggs	3 Tbsp. cocoa
1 tsp. salt	1 1/2 c. sugar
1 c. buttermilk	2 1/4 c. sifted cake flour

1 tsp. baking soda   1 tsp. vanilla

Mix food coloring, cocoa and let stand. Cream butter and sugar; add eggs, then coloring and cocoa mixture and beat well. Sift together cake flour, salt and soda. Add creamed mixture alternately with buttermilk. Stir in vanilla and vinegar but do not beat. Pour batter into two greased and paper lined 9 inch cake pans. Bake at 350° for 35 minutes.

Top with the following Creamy Whipped Frosting:

1/2 c. flour	dash of salt
1 c. milk	1 c. butter
1 c. sugar	1 tsp. vanilla

Mix the flour with the milk and cook until thick. Cool. Cream the sugar and the butter and add the salt and vanilla. Add cooled flour mixture and beat at high speed until frosting is light and fluffy. You may use peppermint extract in place of the vanilla.

DUTCH BABIES

Lillie Manuello
Southsiders

Pan size 2 to 3 qt.:

1/4 c. butter	3/4 c. milk
3 eggs	3/4 c. flour

Pan size 3 to 4 qt.:

1/3 c. butter	1 c. milk
4 eggs	1 c. flour

Pan size 4 to 4 1/2 qt.:

1/2 c. butter	1 1/4 c. milk
5 eggs	1 1/4 c. flour

Pan size 4 1/2 to 5 qt.:

1/2 c. butter	1 1/2 c. milk
6 eggs	1 1/2 c. flour

Put butter into pan. Set into 400° oven while mixing batter. Put eggs in blender at high speed for 1 minute.. Gradually pour in milk; slowly add flour and salt. Continue whirling 30 seconds. Pour batter slowly into pan with melted butter. Bake until puffy and brown, 20 to 25 minutes. Serve with syrup, powdered sugar and frozen strawberries.

CHOCOLATE SHEET CAKE

Hilda Bredehoft
Pep and Progress

2 c. sugar
2 c. sifted flour
1 c. cold water
1/2 c. margarine
1/2 c. salad oil

1 tsp. soda
2 eggs
1/2 c. buttermilk
4 Tbsp. cocoa

Sift together sugar, flour and cocoa in bowl. In saucepan, bring to boil the water, margarine and oil. Pour over dry ingredients and beat until creamy. Add buttermilk, soda and eggs; beat well.

Bake in jelly roll pan, 11x14 inches. Bake at 400° for 15 to 20 minutes. Frost while warm. Bring to boil 1/2 cup margarine, 1/4 cup cocoa and 1/3 cup buttermilk. Add 1 pound box powdered sugar and 1 1/2 teaspoons vanilla. Mix well. Add finely chopped nuts (1/2 cup).

BUTTERMILK CHOCOLATE CAKE AND FROSTING

Bonnie Janda
X-tra X-amples X-tension Club

2 sticks oleo
1 c. water

3 Tbsp. cocoa

Boil and pour over the following:

2 c. flour
2 c. sugar

1/2 tsp. salt

Add the following ingredients:

2 eggs, beaten
1 tsp. soda

1/2 c. buttermilk
1 tsp. vanilla

Grease and flour sheet cake pan. Bake for 20 minutes at 350°.

Frosting:

3/4 stick oleo
3 Tbsp. cocoa
5 Tbsp. milk

powdered sugar
1 tsp. vanilla
1/2 c. nuts (opt.)

Heat first 3 ingredients until hot. Then add sugar, vanilla and nuts.

NO FROST CHOCOLATE CHIP CAKE

Helen Fehringer
Hearth and Home
Marilyn Crane, Creative Homemakers

1 c. dates, cut up
1/2 c. nuts
1 tsp. soda
1 c. shortening
1 c. sugar
1 Tbsp. vanilla

1/2 tsp. salt
2 c. flour
2 eggs
1 Tbsp. cocoa
1 c. plus 3 Tbsp. hot water
1 c. chocolate chips

Add soda to dates, then pour hot water over them. Cream shortening and sugar; add eggs, flour and salt, cocoa, vanilla and beat well. Add date mixture and 1/2 cup of chips. Pour into greased and floured 9x13 inch pan. Sprinkle chips and nuts over top. Bake at 350° for 40 minutes.

ROCKY ROAD SHEET CAKE AND FROSTING

Norma Nab
Pep and Progress

2 c. sifted flour
1/2 tsp. salt
1 3/4 c. sugar
4 Tbsp. cocoa

1 c. water
1/2 c. salad oil
1/4 c. margarine
2 eggs

Sift together ingredients in left column. Cook ingredients in right column together. Pour cooked mixture over flour mixture. Beat till creamy.

1/2 c. buttermilk
1/2 tsp. soda

2 eggs

Mix together and beat into first mixture. Place in greased 17x11 inch cookie sheet. Bake at 375° for 18 minutes.

Frosting:

1/2 c. margarine
1/3 c. buttermilk
1/4 c. cocoa

3 c. powdered sugar
1/2 c. nuts
1/2 tsp. vanilla

Place margarine, buttermilk and cocoa in saucepan. Bring to easy boil. Remove from heat and add 3 cups powdered sugar and 1/2 cup nuts with 1/2 teaspoon vanilla. Mix till smooth. Stir in 2 cups miniature marshmallows. Spread on warm cake immediately.

CHOCOLATE SHEET CAKE
Mrs. R. Burkholder
Kelly Woman's Improvement E.H.C.

2 c. flour
1/2 tsp. salt
1 3/4 c. sugar
3 Tbsp. cocoa
1 c. water

1/2 c. salad oil
1/4 c. oleo
1/2 c. buttermilk
1/2 tsp. soda
2 eggs

Sift together flour, salt, sugar and cocoa. Bring to easy boil . Add to flour mixture the water, oil and oleo; beat until creamy. Then add buttermilk, soda and eggs to the batter and beat it till smooth. Pour into greased 9x13 inch pan and bake 35 minutes at 375°.
Note: Submitted by Mrs. Lorin Lindstrom.

CHOCOLATE SHEET CAKE AND FROSTING
Florence Annan
Home Hustlers

2 c. sugar
2 c. flour
1 cube oleo
4 Tbsp. cocoa
1 c. water

1/4 c. Crisco
1/2 c. buttermilk or
    sour milk
1 tsp. cinnamon
2 eggs
1 tsp. soda
1 tsp. vanilla

Mix and boil 1 cube oleo, 4 tablespoons cocoa, 1 cup water, 1/4 cup Crisco. While hot, pour in flour and sugar mixture. Then add 1/2 cup buttermilk or sour milk, 1 teaspoon cinnamon. Mix all together; then add 2 eggs, 1 teaspoon soda and 1 teaspoon vanilla Bake 20 to 25 minutes at 325°.

Frosting:

1 cube oleo
4 Tbsp. cocoa

5 Tbsp. milk
1 lb. powdered sugar
1/4 c. nuts
1 tsp. vanilla

Mix and boil the oleo, cocoa and milk. Then add powdered sugar, nuts and vanilla. Pour on cake while hot.

MUD CAKE

Kenda Stoltenberg
Padroni E.H.

3 c. flour
2 tsp. soda
1 tsp. salt
1/2 c. cocoa
2 c. sugar

1 tsp. vanilla
2 Tbsp. vinegar
3/4 c. salad oil
2 c. water

Measure flour, soda, salt, cocoa and sugar into 9x13 inch cake pan. Make 3 holes in dry ingredients; pour vanilla, vinegar and oil, one in each hole. Pour water over batter and blend with fork until smooth. Bake 30 to 40 minutes at 350°.

SOUR CREAM CHOCOLATE CAKE

Rachel Schuppe
Proctor

2 c. cake flour
1 tsp. soda
1 tsp. salt
1 c. sugar
1 c. sour cream

1 egg, well beaten
3 sqs. chocolate, melted
3/4 c. sweet milk
1 tsp. vanilla

Sift, then measure flour. Sift three times with soda and salt. Beat the sour cream until it thickens. Slowly add sugar, beating after each addition. Blend in well beaten egg. Add chocolate. Combine vanilla and milk. Add dry and liquid ingredients alternately, beating until smooth. If natural sour cream is not available, use 1 1/3 tablespoons vinegar to 1 cup sweet cream.

Pour into 9x13 inch cake pan or two layer pans. Bake at 350° for about 25 minutes. (Commercial sour cream not recommended.)

CAN'T LAST CAKE

Norma Ruf
Home Hustlers

3 c. flour
2 c. sugar
3 eggs
1 1/2 c. oil
1 tsp. each, salt, soda,
  cinnamon and vanilla

2 c. mashed bananas (real ripe)
1-8 oz. can crushed pineapple,
  drained
1 c. nuts

Mix dry ingredients in large bowl. Make a well in the center. Add eggs, pineapple, nuts, oil, vanilla and bananas. Stir (do not beat), it takes only a few stirs to mix. Pour into a greased, floured tube pan. Bake at 350° for 60 minutes. Can use a Bundt pan.

SHEATH CAKE AND ICING

**Dorothy Miller
Highland Lassies**

2 c. sifted flour
2 c. sugar
3 to 4 Tbsp. cocoa
1 c. water
1 stick margarine
1/2 c. Crisco shortening

1 tsp. soda
1/2 c. buttermilk or
   sour milk
2 eggs, slightly beaten
1 tsp. cinnamon (opt.)
1 tsp. vanilla

Combine flour and sugar. Combine cocoa, water, margarine, and shortening. Bring to rapid boil. Add to flour mixture. Dissolve soda in buttermilk. Add with eggs, cinnamon and vanilla to batter; mix well. Pour into greased, floured, 11x19x1 inch pan.
Bake at 350° to 400° for 20 minutes.

Icing for Sheath Cake:

3 to 4 Tbsp. cocoa
6 Tbsp. milk
1 stick margarine

1 lb. box powdered sugar
1 tsp. vanilla
1/2 to 1 c. chopped nuts

Bring cocoa, milk and margarine to a boil. Add sugar and vanilla; mix well. Add nuts. Spread on cake when removed from oven while still hot.

BASIC CAKE MIX

**Iris Lambert
Rainbows of Happiness**

3 1/2 c. flour
1/3 c. cornstarch
2 tsp. salt
3 c. sugar

2/3 c. dry milk
1 Tbsp. baking powder
1 1/3 c. shortening

Blend until mixture is in fine crumbs.

Yellow Cake:

2 c. mix
1/2 c. water

1 egg
1/2 tsp. vanilla

Lemon-Poppy Seed Cake:

2 c. mix
1/2 c. water
1 egg

2 Tbsp. poppy seed
1 1/2 tsp. grated lemon peel

Chocolate Cake:

2 c. mix
1/2 oz. unsweetened
  chocolate, melted

1/4 tsp. soda
1/3 c. water
1/4 c. sour cream
1 egg
1/2 tsp. vanilla

Pour into greased 8 inch round glass pan. Microwave at 50% power for 5 minutes and 100% power for 4 minutes.

CHOCOLATE ANGEL FOOD CAKE

Annabelle Miller
Padroni E.H.

7/8 c. cake flour
1/3 tsp. salt
1 1/2 tsp. cream of tartar
1/4 c. cocoa

1 1/2 c. egg whites
1 1/4 tsp. vanilla
1 1/2 c. sugar

Beat egg whites until frothy. Add cream of tartar and salt. Continue beating until egg whites are glossy, and fine grained and will stand up in stiff point as the beater is pulled out. With wire whip, gradually fold in 2/3 cup sugar. Whip until a frothy meringue form. Sift flour, remaining sugar and cocoa and fold into meringue. Fold in vanilla. Pour into ungreased 10 inch tube pan. Cut through batter with knife to release large air bubbles and even up batter.

Bake in a moderate oven about 35 minutes. Invert pan and allow to cool 1 hour.

ANGEL FOOD CAKE AND TOPPING

Ardis Bazata
Highland Lassies

1 c. flour
1 1/2 c. powdered sugar
1 1/2 c. egg whites
1 1/2 tsp. cream of tartar

1/3 tsp. salt
1 1/2 tsp. vanilla
1/2 tsp. almond flavoring
1 c. granulated sugar

Sift together 3 times the flour and powdered sugar. Combine the egg whites, cream of tartar, salt and flavorings. Beat egg whites until foamy; add the granulated sugar, a little at a time and keep beating until stiff. Fold in flour and sugar mixture in small amounts. Turn into a large ungreased tube pan and bake 35 minutes at 375°. This cake is much moister than most angel foods.

(Cont.)

Topping for Angel Food Cake:

1 c. whipping cream
3 plain Hershey bars

Melt Hershey bars. Whip cream and fold in chocolate. Spread on cake and set in refrigerator.

YELLOW ANGEL FOOD

Mrs. John Felzien (Deceased)
Kelly Woman's Improvement Club

1 1/4 c. sugar
1/2 c. water
1 c. Swans Down cake flour

7 eggs
1 tsp. cream of tartar
flavor as desired

Boil sugar and water until it spins a thread. Beat egg yolks while syrup boils. Beat syrup into yolks pouring slowly. Cool thoroughly and add flour. Beat egg whites until frothy and add cream of tartar then beat stiff. Add flavoring and fold into yolk mixture. Bake in angel food cake pan at degree and time as for angel food.

CRANBERRY CAKE AND FROSTING

Eva M. Guenzi
Home Hustlers

2 1/4 c. flour
1 c. sugar
1/4 tsp. salt
1 tsp. soda
1 tsp. baking powder
1 c. walnuts, chopped

1 c. dates, chopped
1 c. cranberries (whole)
grated rind of 2 oranges
2 eggs, beaten
1 c. buttermilk
3/4 c. salad oil

Frosting:

1 c. orange juice
3/4 c. granulated sugar

Sift dry ingredients. Stir in chopped dates, cranberries and nuts into dry mixture. Add together eggs, oil and buttermilk; add to first mixture. Bake in well greased and floured angel food cake pan. Bake at 350° for 1 hour. Cool to lukewarm. Take out of pan and frost (takes several applications before it soaks into the cake.)

BUTTERLESS, EGGLESS, AND MILKLESS CAKE   Sammy Shaw

1 c. brown sugar
1 c. water
1 tsp. cloves
1 tsp. cinnamon
1 c. chopped raisins
1/2 tsp. nutmeg

1/3 c. lard
pinch of salt
1 tsp. soda
2 c. flour
1/2 tsp. vanilla
1/2 c. black walnuts

Mix together the brown sugar, water, spices, raisins, lard and salt in a saucepan and boil for 3 minutes. Let cool; add the soda. Stir in the flour and baking powder. Add the nuts.

Bake in a 9 inch pan in a slow 350° oven for 30 to 40 minutes or until done.

APPLESAUCE CAKE

Libby Lindstrom (Deceased)
Kelly Woman's Improvement Club

1 1/2 c. unsweetened
  applesauce
2 level tsp. soda
1 c. sugar
1/2 c. shortening
1/2 tsp. salt

2 3/4 c. flour
1 tsp. cinnamon
1 tsp. cloves
1 c. raisins

Cream together the sugar and shortening. Add soda to apple-sauce and add alternately with flour, spices and salt to the creamed mixture. Add raisins and bake in a 9x13 inch pan at 350° until toothpick inserted in middle comes out clean.
Note: To make a Christmas cake, add nuts and citron.

RAW APPLE CAKE

Bonnie Bollig
Pep and Progress

1/2 c. shortening
1 c. sugar
1/2 c. strong coffee
2 eggs
1 tsp. cinnamon
1 1/2 c. flour
1 tsp. soda

1/2 tsp. cloves
1 c. raw apples, grated
  or chopped
1/4 c. nuts
1/2 c. coconut
1 c. dates, currants or
  raisins

Cream together shortening and sugar. Add 1/2 cup strong coffee, eggs, cinnamon, flour, soda and cloves.

In a separate dish, mix the raw apples, nuts, coconut, dates, currants or raisins. Mix all together. Bake in large pan. Bake at 350° for 1 hour.

AUTUMN APPLE CAKE

Irene Golgart
Kelly Woman's Improvement Club

1 c. sugar
2 c. chopped apples
1 1/2 c. sifted flour
1 tsp. baking soda
1 tsp. vanilla

1/2 tsp. salt
1/2 c. vegetable oil
1/2 c. chopped nuts
1/2 c. flaked coconut

Put sugar over finely chopped (unpeeled) apples and let stand for 10 minutes. To this, add the flour, soda and salt after sifting together. Stir in the oil, nuts, coconut and vanilla.

Bake in a 9x13 inch pan at 350° for about 30 minutes. Serve it with whipped cream or ice cream on top if desired.

APPLE CAKE
Jackie Waitley
Proctor

4 Tbsp. shortening or butter
1 c. sugar
2 eggs
3/4 c. sweet milk
cinnamon

2 c. flour
2 tsp. baking powder
1 tsp. salt
1/4 c. sugar

Cream sugar and shortening. Add eggs, dry ingredients and milk alternately. Peel two apples and core and cut into fourths. Slice each fourth into wedges 1/4 inch thick. Insert wedges into batter in greased and floured cake pan. Sprinkle 1/4 cup sugar mixed with cinnamon over top of batter and apples.

Bake 25 to 30 minutes at 350°.

RHUBARB CAKE AND TOPPING
Bette McBride
Proctor

1 1/2 c. rhubarb, cut fine
1/2 c. sugar
2 c. flour
1 1/2 c. sugar
1/2 c. vegetable oil
1 tsp. salt

1 egg
1 c. sour milk or buttermilk
1 tsp. soda
1 tsp. cinnamon
1 tsp. vanilla

Combine rhubarb and 1/2 cup sugar. Mix together rest of ingredients. Add rhubarb, mixing until well blended. Pour into greased and floured 9x13 inch pan. Bake at 350° for 1 hour.

Topping:

6 Tbsp. butter or margarine
2/3 c. brown sugar
1 c. coconut

1/4 c. milk
1 c. nuts

Cook together for 3 minutes. Pour over warm cake.

RHUBARB CAKE AND TOPPING
Betty Robinett
Highland Lassies

1 c. brown sugar
1/2 c. shortening

2 eggs
2 c. flour

1 tsp. soda
1/4 tsp. salt

1 c. sour milk or buttermilk
1 1/2 to 2 c. diced rhubarb

Cream sugar and shortening. Add eggs and beat well. Sift flour, soda and salt. Add eggs and beat well.

Add alternately with buttermilk. Add diced rhubarb with last bit of flour.

Place in 8x10 or 9x9 inch greased pan. Sprinkle with topping. Bake in 350° oven for 45 minutes.

Topping:

1 c. brown sugar
1 tsp. cinnamon

1 Tbsp. butter

DATE CAKE

Betty Ballinger
Hearth and Home

2 c. chopped dates
2 c. sugar
2 Tbsp. butter

2 c. flour
2 tsp. vanilla
2 c. hot water
2 tsp. soda
1 c. nuts

Cream butter and sugar together. Add flour. Pour 1 cup of hot water over dates. Add 2 teaspoons soda to other cup hot water and pour over dates. Stir in flour mixture gradually. Add vanilla and nuts. Bake at 350° for 30 minutes.

PLUM CAKE

Juanita Pyle
Proctor E.H. Club

2 c. self rising flour
1 tsp. cloves
1 c. cooking oil
1/2 tsp. red food coloring
nuts (opt.)

2 c. white sugar
1 tsp. cinnamon
3 whole eggs
2 small jars red plum baby food

Mix sugar and oil. Then add eggs, sifted flour, and spices. Add the food coloring and plum baby food. Last add the nuts, if desired. Bake in a Bundt pan for 1 hour at 300°. Top with a glaze made up of 1 cup powdered sugar thinned with a little lemon juice.

CHOCOLATE ZUCCHINI CAKE AND ICING   Connie Lechman
Yvonne Davidson, Nite Owls

2 1/2 c. flour
1/2 c. cocoa
2 1/2 tsp. baking powder
1 1/2 tsp. baking soda
1 tsp. salt
1 tsp. cinnamon
3/4 c. oleo

2 c. sugar
3 eggs
2 tsp. vanilla
2 tsp. grated orange peel
2 c. shredded zucchini
1/2 c. milk
1 c. chopped nuts

Mix flour, cocoa, baking powder, soda, salt and cinnamon. Set aside. Mix sugar and oleo till smooth. Add eggs, one at a time, beating well after each addition. Using a spoon, stir in vanilla, orange peel and zucchini. Alternately stir in dry ingredients and milk. Add nuts. Pour into greased and floured tube or Bundt pan. Bake at 350° for 1 hour.

Glaze:

2 c. powdered sugar
3 Tbsp. milk

1 tsp. vanilla

Glaze with powdered sugar icing.

CHOCOLATE ZUCCHINI CAKE   Connie Lechman
Proctor E.H. Club

2 1/2 c. flour
1/2 c. cocoa
2 1/2 tsp. baking powder
1/2 tsp. soda
1 tsp. salt
1 tsp. cinnamon
3/4 c. soft oleo

2 c. sugar
3 eggs
2 tsp. vanilla
2 tsp. grated orange rind
2 c. grated zucchini
1/2 c. milk
1 c. nuts, chopped

Cream sugar and shortening; add eggs one at a time. Add the vanilla, orange rind, zucchini, dry ingredients, milk and the nuts; mix well. Pour into a floured Bundt pan.
Bake for 1 hour at 350°. Cool 15 minutes before adding the following Glaze to the cake.

3 Tbsp. milk
2 c. powdered sugar

1 tsp. vanilla

PRUNE CAKE

Sammy Shaw
Sterling Homemakers

3 eggs
1 c. cooking oil
1 c. buttermilk
1 1/2 c. sugar
2 c. unbleached flour
1 tsp. salt

1 tsp. soda
1 tsp. cinnamon
1 tsp. nutmeg
1 tsp. allspice
1 tsp. vanilla
1 c. mashed stewed prunes
(about 24)

Beat eggs with oil in a bowl. Add buttermilk and sugar and set aside.

Mix flour, salt, soda, cinnamon, nutmeg and allspice in another bowl and stir together with a fork. Beat into the liquid ingredients. Add vanilla and prunes and stir until thoroughly mixed. Pour into a greased and floured Bundt pan or a 9x12 inch rectangular pan.

Bake in a preheated oven at 350° for 45 minutes for a Bundt pan or 30 minutes for a rectangular pan. Remove from oven. Cool on rack thoroughly before unmolding.

CAKE

Joyce Jones
Sterling Homemakers

1 chocolate cake mix
1-1 lb. 5 oz. can cherry pie
    filling

2 Tbsp. water
2 eggs

Mix all ingredients. Cook in microwave 13 minutes in Bundt pan; turn once. Other variations can be used.

CARROT CAKE AND FROSTING

Connie Lechman
Proctor E.H. Club

4 eggs
1 c. salad oil
2 tsp. soda
1/2 tsp. salt

2 c. sugar
2 c. flour
1 tsp. cinnamon
3 small jars strained baby
    carrots

Combine the eggs, sugar and oil and beat for 1 minute. Add the remaining ingredients and mix well. Bake at 350° for 30 to 40 minutes.

Frosting:

1 stick oleo
1-6 oz. pkg. softened
  cream cheese

1/2 tsp. vanilla
3 1/2 to 4 c. powdered sugar

163

(Cont.

Mix frosting ingredients together and beat with beater until creamy.

CHOCOLATE YOGURT CAKE AND ICING
Opal Vance
Sterling Homemakers

2 c. flour
2 c. sugar
1/2 c. margarine
1/4 c. oil or shortening
1/4 c. cocoa
1 c. water

1/2 c. yogurt
2 eggs
1 tsp. vanilla
1 tsp. baking soda

Yogurt Icing:

1/4 c. margarine
2 Tbsp. cocoa

3 Tbsp. yogurt
powdered sugar

Mix flour and sugar in large bowl. Combine in saucepan the margarine, oil, cocoa and water. Bring to rapid boil. Pour over sugar and flour; beat well. Add yogurt, eggs, vanilla and baking soda; mix well. Pour into greased 9x13x2 inch pan.

Bake at 350 to 400° for 25 to 30 minutes. Cool in pan. When cool, ice with Yogurt Icing.

Icing: Bring to boil margarine, cocoa and yogurt. Remove from heat and add powdered sugar for desired consistency.

WACKY CAKE
Kathy Glassburn
Padroni E.H.

3 c. flour
2 c. sugar
2 tsp. soda
1/2 c. cocoa
1 tsp. salt

1 c. cooking oil
2 c. boiling water
2 tsp. vanilla
2 tsp. vinegar

Mix cake in same pan you use to bake it. Do not grease pan.

Sift together flour, sugar, soda, cocoa and salt. Add cooking oil, boiling water, vanilla and vinegar.

Bake at 350° for 30 minutes in 13x9 inch pan.

WACKY CAKE
Carrie Terrell
Creative Homemakers

1 1/2 c. flour
1 tsp. soda
1 c. sugar

3 Tbsp. cocoa
1/4 tsp. salt

Sift first 5 ingredients into pan cake is to be baked in. Make 3 holes in dry ingredients. In 1st hole, put 1 tablespoon vinegar, 2nd hole, 1 teaspoon vanilla, 3rd hole put 5 tablespoons melted butter. Pour 1 cup cold water over all ingredients and mix well. Bake at 350° for about 30 minutes.

CRAZY CAKE

Mrs. Lorin Lindstrom
Kelly Woman's Improvement E.H.C.
(from Mrs. Elgin Boegler, former member)

1 1/2 c. flour	6 Tbsp. oil
1 c. sugar	1 Tbsp. vinegar
3 Tbsp. cocoa	1 tsp. vanilla
1 tsp. soda	1 c. water
1/2 tsp. salt	

Sift dry ingredients in 9x9 inch baking dish. Make 3 holes in the mixture. Put oil in one, vinegar in one and vanilla in last one. Pour water over entire mixture. Stir with a fork. Do not beat. Bake 30 minutes at 350°. Chocolate chips may be sprinkled over the top of the batter for a topping.

PUMPKIN CAKE ROLL

Marilyn Hutt
Busy Bees

3 eggs	1 tsp. ginger
1 c. sugar	1/2 tsp. nutmeg
2/3 c. pumpkin	1/2 tsp. salt
1 tsp. lemon juice	3/4 c. finely chopped walnuts
3/4 c. flour	1 c. powdered sugar
1 tsp. baking powder	1-8 oz. pkg. cream cheese
2 tsp. cinnamon	4 Tbsp. butter or margarine
	1/2 tsp. vanilla

Beat eggs on high speed 5 minutes. Gradually beat in sugar. Stir in pumpkin and lemon juice. Stir together flour, baking powder, cinnamon, ginger, nutmeg, and salt. Fold into pumpkin mixture.

Spread in greased and floured 15x10 1/2 x 1 inch pan. Top with nuts. Bake at 375° for 15 minutes.

Turn out on towel sprinkled with powdered sugar. Starting with narrow end, roll towel and cake together. Cool in refrigerator for 1 hour. Unroll.

Filling: Combine and beat smooth the powdered sugar, cream cheese, margarine and vanilla. Spread over cake, then roll. Chill and serve.

BREAD SPONGE CAKE

Iva Helst
Kelly Home Improvement Club

1 1/2 c. sugar
1 c. shortening
3 eggs
2 c. bread sponge
flour to make a rather
  stiff batter (1 1/2 c. to
    begin with)

1 tsp. soda in a little
  hot water
1 tsp. cinnamon
3/4 tsp. cloves
1 tsp. nutmeg
1 c. raisins

Cream shortening and sugar; add eggs and beat well. Stir in the bread sponge. Add the soda and water. Sift the flour and spices together. Mix in the raisins. Add to first ingredients.

Grease a 9x13 inch pan and flour it. Put batter in the pan and let rise 2 hours. Bake in a 300 to 350° oven for 1 hour. Test with a toothpick for doneness. Ice with any favorite icing.

TOMATO SOUP CAKE

Rosie Nicholas
Creative Homemakers

1 1/2 c. sugar
2 Tbsp. shortening
1 egg
1 can tomato soup
1 1/2 c. flour

1 tsp. cinnamon
1/2 tsp. nutmeg
1 tsp. ground cloves
1 tsp. soda

Cream sugar and shortening. Add egg and soup. Combine rest of ingredients and add gradually to creamed mixture. Bake at 375° for 30 to 35 minutes.

GUM DROP FRUIT CAKE

Ann Ruf
Pep and Progress

1 lb. white raisins
2 lbs. large gum drops,
  cut up (no black ones)
1 c. pecans
2 c. sugar
1 c. butter
2 eggs, well beaten
1 tsp. vanilla

1/4 tsp. each, salt, cloves,
  nutmeg
1 tsp. cinnamon
4 c. flour (use 1 c. to dredge
  raisins)
1 1/2 c. applesauce,
  unsweetened
1 tsp. soda, dissolved in
 1 Tbsp. hot water

Cream butter and sugar; add well beaten eggs, then alternate dry ingredients (that have been sifted together) with applesauce.

Add soda and vanilla and fruits. Bake in a tube angel food pan in a slow 300 to 325° oven for 2 hours. Do Not Cut or take out of pan until cold (24 hours). If desired, use 3/4 pound candied cherries and 1/4 pound candied pineapple.

FRUIT CAKE

Margaret Lueck
Hearth and Home

3/4 c. sugar
3/4 c. flour
1/2 tsp. salt
1 Tbsp. baking powder

2-8 oz. pkgs. whole dates
8 oz. jar maraschino cherries
1 pkg. dried apricots
2 1/2 to 3 c. pecans or dried nuts

Mix dry ingredients with fruit and nuts. Add 3 eggs and mix well. Pour into greased loaf pan. Bake at 350° for 45 to 60 minutes.

SCOTCH SHORTBREAD COOKIES

Barb Korrey
X-tra X-amples X-tension Club

1/2 c. granulated sugar
1/2 lb. (1 c.) butter

2 c. flour

Cream sugar and butter. Add flour. Roll out and cut in tiny rounds. Bake at 350° for 10 minutes, till delicate brown. Roll while warm in powdered sugar

ORANGE SLICE COOKIES

Esther Pace

1 c. each brown and
  granulated sugar
1 c. shortening
2 eggs
2 c. quick oats
1 c. coconut
1 pkg. orange slices, diced

2 c. flour
1/2 tsp. salt
1 tsp. each soda and baking
  powder
1 tsp. vanilla
2 Tbsp. milk

Mix both sugars and shortening. Add eggs. Mix together flour, oats, coconut, salt, baking powder, soda and orange slices. Mix milk and vanilla into sugar mixture, then add dry ingredients. Drop by teaspoonfuls onto baking sheet. Bake 12 to 15 minutes at 350°.

DATE ROLL COOKIES

Helen Fehringer
Hearth and Home

1 lb. dates, cut fine
2/3 c. water
1/2 c. sugar
1/2 c. chopped nuts
1 c. white sugar

1 c. brown sugar
1 c. shortening
2 eggs
1 tsp. soda
4 c. flour
2 1/2 tsp. salt

Combine dates, water and sugar. Cook for 5 minutes. Remove from heat and add nuts.

In mixing bowl, cream together rest of ingredients. Toss dough lightly on floured board and roll 1/4 inch thick. Spread date filling on dough and roll like jelly roll. Wrap in waxed paper. Chill overnight. Cut into slices and bake on greased cookie sheet for 12 minutes in 400° oven.

MAH'MOOL (NUT FILLED COOKIES)

Minnie Korrey
Hearth and Home E.H.

2 c. rendered butter
1 box cake flour (5 c.)
1 1/2 c. powdered sugar
1 tsp. baking soda

1 egg
pinch of salt
Filling:
2 c. ground nuts
1 Tbsp. butter
1 tsp. almond

Combine all ingredients and mix very well. Mold into cookie shapes (circles). Mix filling well. Put 1 teaspoon filling into cookie circle. Pinch around edges to form ball or crescent shape.

Bake at 325° for 20 minutes. Then dip into powdered sugar.

BUTTER HORN COOKIES

Mary Ellen Breidenbach
Hearth and Home

Dough:

4 c. flour
1 pkg. dry yeast
1 1/4 c. butter
3 egg yolks

1/2 c. sour cream
1 tsp. vanilla

Filling:

3 egg whites
1 c. sugar
2 1/2 oz. dates, chopped

1 c. chopped nuts
1 tsp. vanilla

Dough: Combine flour and yeast. Cut in butter as for pie

crust. Add egg yolks, sour cream and vanilla; stir until dough forms. Divide dough into 6 or 8 equal portions. Chill at least 1 hour, or overnight, for easier handling.

Filling: Beat egg whites stiff. Add sugar gradually, beating until stiff and glossy. Fold in dates, nuts and vanilla . Roll portion of dough into circle as for a pie crust, on foil or pastry cloth dusted with powdered sugar. Cut into 12 wedges. Place rounded teaspoon of filling at wide end of wedge. Roll up into horn. Place on ungreased cookie sheet.

Bake at 350° for 15 to 20 minutes, until lightly browned. Sprinkle with confectioners sugar while horns are hot, or frost with confectioners icing. Store in tightly covered container.

HONEY AND SPICE CUT-OUTS
Debbie Breidenbach
Hearth and Home

2 1/4 c. sifted flour	1/2 c. sugar
1/2 tsp. baking soda	1 egg
1 tsp. ground ginger	1/4 c. light corn syrup
1/2 tsp. ground cinnamon	1/4 c. honey
1/2 c. butter, softened	1 Tbsp. vinegar

Sift flour, soda, ginger, cinnamon, cloves onto waxed paper. Beat butter, sugar and egg in large bowl until fluffy. Beat in corn syrup, honey, vinegar, and stir into flour mixture until soft dough forms. Refrigerate several hours. Roll out dough (small portions) onto lightly floured cookie cutters. Place on greased cookie sheet 1/2 inch apart. Bake at 375° for 5 minutes. Makes 5 dozen.

CHERRY PUFFS
Bonnie Bollig
Pep and Progress

2 c. sifted flour	2/3 c. milk
1/3 c. sugar	1 egg
1/2 tsp. salt	1/2 tsp. vanilla
1/4 c. salad oil	1 c. frozen or canned
3 tsp. baking powder	cherries, well drained

Sift flour, sugar, salt and baking powder together. Add salad oil, egg and milk. Mix with fork. Add vanilla and cherries. Drop by teaspoonfuls into deep hot fat, 375°. Fry until golden brown, about 3 minutes. Drain on absorbent paper. Roll warm puff in sugar or glaze by dipping into thin confectioners sugar icing.

MACAROONS

Bonnie Bollig
Pep and Progress

2 egg whites
1/4 tsp. cream of tartar
pinch of salt
1 tsp. vanilla
3/4 c. sugar

1 c. coconut
2 1/2 c. corn flakes
1/2 c. chopped nuts

Beat egg whites until foamy. Add salt and cream of tartar; beat until stiff. Add vanilla. Beat and add gradually the sugar. Fold in corn flakes, coconut and nuts. Drop on well buttered baking sheet. Bake in slow oven about 350° until firm.

KAYLE COOKIES

Doris Seghi
Night Owls

1 c. shortening
2 c. sugar
2 c. raisins (cooked)
5 Tbsp. raisin juice

4 c. flour
2 tsp. soda
2 tsp. cinnamon
2 eggs

Add soda to hot raisin juice. Combine and mix ingredients. Drop on greased cookie sheet. Bake at 350° for 10 to 12 minutes.

CHOCOLATE COVERED CHERRY COOKIES

Marilyn Hutt
Busy Bees

1 1/2 c. flour
1/2 c. cocoa
1/4 tsp. salt
1/4 tsp. baking powder
1/4 tsp. baking soda
1/2 c. oleo

1 c. sugar
1 egg
1 1/2 tsp. vanilla
1-10 oz. jar maraschino cherries
1-6 oz. pkg. chocolate chips
1/2 c. Eagle Brand sweetened
    milk

In a large bowl, stir together flour, cocoa, salt, baking powder and baking soda. Beat together oleo and sugar till fluffy. Add egg and vanilla; beat well. Gradually add dry ingredients to creamed mixture; beat till well blended. Shape dough into 1 inch balls and place on ungreased cookie sheet. Press down center of dough with thumb (I pressed with the cherry). Drain cherries, reserving juice. Place a cherry in center of each cookie.

In small saucepan, combine sweetened condensed milk and chocolate chips. Heat till chocolate is melted. Stir in 4 teaspoons cherry juice. Spoon about 1 teaspoon frosting over each cherry, covering cherry after baked. Thin with more juice if necessary.

Bake at 350° for 10 minutes. Makes 48 cookies.

UNBELIEVABLE COOKIES

Alice E. Lindstrom
Kelly Woman's Improvement Club

1 c. crunchy peanut butter
1 c. white granulated sugar
1 egg, beaten

Mix the above 3 ingredients. Roll out into 26 balls about the size of a walnut. Flatten slightly on cookie sheet. Bake 12 to 15 minutes at 325°.

CHOICE COOKIES

Luella Sonnenberg
Night Owls

1 c. shortening
3/4 c. sugar
3/4 c. brown sugar
2 eggs
1 Tbsp. hot water
1 tsp. vanilla
1 1/2 c. flour
1 tsp. soda
1 tsp. salt
1 c. chopped nuts
2 c. quick oatmeal
1 c. chocolate chips
1 c. bran flakes
1 c. coconut

Cream sugars and shortening until light and fluffy. Add eggs, one at a time, beating after each. Add hot water and vanilla, then add flour, soda and salt. Stir in nuts, oatmeal, chips, bran flakes and coconut; mix well. Drop by teaspoonfuls on greased cookie sheets. Bake at 375° for 8 to 10 minutes.

REFRIGERATOR COOKIES

Deana Rasmussen
Rainbows of Happiness

1 c. margarine or butter
1 c. brown sugar
1 c. white sugar
2 eggs, beaten
1 tsp. vanilla
3/4 c. chopped nuts
1 c. chopped dates
1 tsp. soda
1 tsp. baking powder
3 c. flour, sifted

Cream margarine and sugars; stir in beaten eggs, vanilla, nuts and dates. Sift together soda, baking powder and flour. Stir into mixture. Mix well. Form into rolls and chill for several hours or overnight. Slice and bake about 10 minutes at 375°.

This dough may be wrapped in foil and frozen. Will keep 3 months. Makes 5 1/2 dozen cookies.

NO-BAKE COOKIES

Rosie Nicholas
Creative Homemakers

2 c. sugar
1/2 c. milk
1/2 c. margarine
3 Tbsp. cocoa

3 c. quick oats
1/2 c. peanut butter
1 tsp. vanilla

Bring first 4 ingredients to full boil. Cook 1 full minute. Take off heat and add remaining ingredients. Spoon immediately by teaspoonfuls onto waxed paper.

NO BAKE COOKIES

Phyllis Moore
Pep and Progress

1 1/2 c. sugar
1/2 c. oleo
1/2 c. milk
1 tsp. vanilla

1 Tbsp. cocoa
1-6 oz. pkg. chocolate chips
1 c. marshmallows
3 c. quick oats

Combine 1 1/2 cups sugar, 1/2 cup oleo, 1/2 cup milk, 1 teaspoon vanilla. Bring to a boil and boil 1 minute, then add the cocoa, chocolate chips, marshmallows and oats. Mix well. Drop on foil. Cool until set.

BUSY DAY CHOCOLATE COOKIES

Glennis Lechman
Sterling Homemakers

2 c. sugar
1 stick margarine
1/4 tsp. salt
1/2 c. milk

1/4 c. cocoa
1/2 c. peanut butter
1 tsp. vanilla
3 1/2 c. rolled oats

Mix sugar, margarine, salt, milk and cocoa in a large saucepan. Stir until sugar is dissolved. Bring to a boil, stirring occasionally. Remove from heat. Stir in peanut butter and oats and vanilla; mix well. Drop by teaspoonfuls onto waxed paper. Cool. Makes 3 dozen.

DATE REFRIGERATOR PINWHEELS

Phyllis Jones
Night Owls

2 1/4 c. pitted dates, cut
1 c. water
1 c. shortening
3 eggs
1/2 tsp. salt

1 c. white sugar
1/2 c. chopped nut meats (opt.)
2 c. brown sugar
3 1/2 to 4 c. flour
1/2 tsp. soda

Cook dates, white sugar and water until thick, about 10 minutes. Add nuts. Set aside to cool. Mix and chill dough (remaining ingredients). After it is chilled, roll thin and spread filling. Roll as a jelly roll and chill in refrigerator. Cut into thin slices. Bake 10 minutes at 400°.

FRUITED PINWHEELS
Mrs. William Lester
Former member of Kelly Woman's Improvement E.H.C.

2 1/2 c. chopped dates or raisins
1 c. hot water
1/2 c. sugar
1 c. white sugar
1 c. brown sugar
1 c. shortening

3 eggs
1 tsp. soda
1 tsp. cinnamon
1 tsp. allspice
4 c. flour
1 c. nuts
1/2 tsp. salt

Cook fruit and sugar in one cup water until thick. Cool. Cream sugars and shortening. Add eggs. Add sifted dry ingredients and mix well. Roll dough into an oblong shape about 1/2 inch thickness. Spread fruited mixture over the dough. Roll the dough into a long roll. Chill and slice in 1/4 inch slices for baking at 350° for about 15 to 20 minutes. They burn easily.

MOLASSES COOKIES
Alice Folladori
Proctor

1 c. sugar
1 c. shortening
1 c. dark molasses
1 Tbsp. vinegar
6 c. sifted flour
1/2 tsp. salt

1 tsp. baking soda
1/2 tsp. baking powder
1 tsp. ginger
1 tsp. cinnamon
2 beaten eggs

Combine sugar, shortening, molasses and vinegar in a saucepan. Bring to a boil and cook 2 minutes. Cool. Sift together flour, salt, baking powder and spices. Add eggs and cooled molasses mixture. Add dry ingredients and mix well. Chill. Roll out on lightly floured board about 1/8 to 1/4 inch thick. Cut with cookie cutters and put on greased baking sheet.
Bake at 375° for 10 minutes or till done. Makes 12 dozen 2 1/2 inch cookies.

OATMEAL COOKIES

Connie Lechman
Proctor E.H. Club

3 eggs
1 1/2 c. brown sugar
3 c. oatmeal
2 1/4 c. flour
1 1/2 tsp. soda

1 1/2 c. white sugar
1 1/2 c. shortening
1 1/2 tsp. vanilla
1 1/2 tsp. salt

Preheat oven to 375°. Cream the sugars and the shortening. Add the eggs and the remaining ingredients; mix well. Bake for 10 minutes at 375°.

BOB'S OATMEAL COOKIES

Jackie Waitley
Proctor

1 c. shortening (all oleo
   or 1/2 Crisco)
1 c. white sugar
1 c. brown sugar (don't pack)
1 tsp. vanilla
3 eggs
2 c. sifted flour

1 tsp. soda
1 tsp. salt
1 tsp. cinnamon
1/2 tsp. ground cloves
2 c. quick cooking oatmeal
2 c. raisins

Cream shortening, sugars and vanilla. Beat in eggs. Sift flour, soda, salt, cinnamon, cloves together and add. Stir in oatmeal and raisins. Drop by teaspoonfuls on ungreased cookie sheet.
   Bake at 375° for 10 to 12 minutes.

RANGER COOKIES

Charlotte Lambrecht
Rainbows of Happiness

1 c. shortening
1 c. white sugar
1 c. brown sugar
2 eggs
2 tsp. vanilla
2 c. flour
2 tsp. baking powder

1 tsp. baking soda
1/2 tsp. salt
2 c. oatmeal
2 c. corn flakes or Rice Krispies
1 c. coconut

Melt shortening. Pour over sugars; mix well. Add eggs and vanilla. Stir dry ingredients together. Add to sugar mixture. Add oatmeal, corn flakes and coconut; mix well. Drop by teaspoonfuls on a greased cookie sheet.
   Bake at 350° for 10 to 12 minutes. Makes 4 to 5 dozen cookies.

OATMEAL COOKIES

Dorothy Miller
Highland Lassies

1 c. shortening or oleo
1 c. sugar
2 eggs
1 c. raisins, cooked
   and cooled
6 Tbsp. raisin juice
1 tsp. soda

2 c. flour
2 c. oatmeal
vanilla
salt

Cream sugar and shortening; add 2 eggs and beat well. Add cooled, cooked raisins and 6 tablespoons raisin juice. Add soda, flour, oatmeal, vanilla and salt. Mix well. Drop by spoonfuls on greased cookie sheet. Bake at 350° for 10 to 12 minutes.

GUMDROP OATMEAL COOKIES

Bette McBride
Proctor

1 c. brown sugar
1 c. white sugar
1 c. butter or margarine
2 eggs
1 tsp. vanilla
2 c. flour
1 tsp. soda

1 tsp. baking powder
1/4 tsp. salt
2 c. quick oatmeal
1 c. flaked coconut
1 c. chopped nuts
1 c. colored gum drops, cut up
(don't use black ones)

Mix ingredients in order listed. Bake at 375° for 10 minutes. Makes 6 dozen.

OATMEAL CHOCOLATE CHIP COOKIES

Olive Myers
Sterling Homemakers

1/2 c. shortening
1/2 c. white sugar
1/2 c. brown sugar
3/4 c. sifted flour
1 egg, beaten
1 1/2 c. quick oatmeal

1 1/4 c. chocolate chips
1 Tbsp. water
1/2 tsp. vanilla
1/2 tsp. salt
1/2 tsp. soda

Cream shortening and sugars. Add egg, water and vanilla. Sift dry ingredients and add. Then add oatmeal and chips last. Bake 10 to 12 minutes at 375°. Do not overbake.

CHOCOLATE CHIP COOKIES

Earline Schuppe
Proctor

3 c. flour
1 tsp. baking powder
1 tsp. baking soda
1 tsp. salt
1/2 c. shortening
1/2 c. margarine

3/4 c. sugar
3/4 c. brown sugar
3 eggs
1 1/4 tsp. vanilla
1 tsp. water
1 c. chocolate chips

Sift together flour, baking powder, baking soda and salt. Cream together shortening, margarine, sugar and brown sugar. Beat in eggs. Add and beat water and vanilla. Add flour mixture and mix well. Stir in 1 cup of chocolate chips or more, to taste.

Bake at 350° for 8 to 10 minutes on ungreased cookie sheet. Makes about 5 dozen.

RUSSIAN TEA CAKES

Marilyn Brehe
Padroni E.H.

1 c. soft butter
1 tsp. vanilla
2 1/4 c. sifted flour

1/2 c. powdered sugar
1/4 tsp. salt
3/4 c. finely chopped nuts

Mix butter and vanilla well. Sift and stir in the flour. Mix in powdered sugar and salt. Add nuts mixing well. Chill dough and roll into 1 inch balls. Place on ungreased baking sheets.

Bake at 400° for 10 to 15 minutes, till set but not brown. Roll in powdered sugar. Cool and roll in powdered sugar again.

CORN MEAL COOKIES

Cecilia Pyle
Padroni E.H.

1 c. shortening
1 1/2 c. sugar
3 eggs
1/2 tsp. vanilla
3 c. flour

1 c. yellow corn meal
1 1/2 tsp. baking powder
1 tsp. nutmeg
1/2 tsp. salt
1 tsp. lemon extract

Cream together shortening and sugar; add eggs, one at a time, beating until light and fluffy. Add lemon and vanilla. Stir in flour, corn meal, baking powder, nutmeg and salt. Roll dough on floured surface 1/8 inch thick. Cut cookies with a cutter of your choice. Place on lightly greased baking sheet. Sprinkle with sugar if you are not going to decorate them.

Bake at 350° for about 10 minutes. Makes about 80.

HEALTH COOKIES

Rosabelle Smith
Kelly Woman's Improvement Club

1 1/2 c. whole wheat flour
3/4 c. wheat germ
1 1/2 tsp. baking powder
3/4 tsp. salt
1/2 c. coconut
3/4 c. margarine
  (at room temp.)

1 c. brown sugar
1 egg
2 Tbsp. orange juice
1 tsp. vanilla
1 c. raisins
1/2 c. sunflower seeds (raw)

Combine flour, wheat germ, baking powder, salt, coconut and set aside. Beat margarine, sugar, egg, juice and vanilla. Stir in dry ingredients; add raisins and seeds. Mix until well blended. Bake on greased cookie sheet after dropping by spoonfuls. Bake at 350° for 10 to 12 minutes.

AMISH SUGAR COOKIES

Enid Lindstrom
Kelly Woman's Improvement Club

1 c. granulated sugar
1 c. powdered sugar
1 c. margarine
1 c. cooking oil
2 eggs

4 1/2 c. flour
1 tsp. baking soda
1 tsp. cream of tartar
1 tsp. vanilla

Combine the first 4 ingredients and beat well. Add eggs and beat again. Add remaining ingredients and mix well. Drop small balls of dough on cookie sheet and flatten slightly with a fork. Bake at 375° for 10 to 12 minutes.

SUGAR COOKIES

Jennifer Felzien
X-tra X-amples X-tension Club

3/4 c. softened shortening
2 eggs
2 1/2 c. flour
1 tsp. salt

1 c. sugar
1/2 tsp. vanilla
1 tsp. baking powder

Mix shortening, sugar, eggs and vanilla together. Blend in flour, baking powder and salt; mix all ingredients together until well blended. Chill at least 1 hour. Roll dough 1/8 inch thick on floured board. Cut with cookie cutter. Place on an ungreased cookie sheet. Bake 6 to 8 minutes at 375°. Makes about 4 dozen.

CHEWY PEANUT BUTTER STRIPS

Marilyn Hutt
Busy Bees

1 c. butter
1 1/2 c. peanut butter
1 c. honey
2 c. sugar
2 eggs
1 tsp. vanilla

1 1/4 tsp. baking powder
3 c. flour
3/4 tsp. salt
1 1/2 c. coconut
nuts, if desired
powdered sugar

Blend butter, peanut butter, sugar, honey, eggs and vanilla. Mix dry ingredients and add to peanut mixture. Stir in coconut and nuts. Spread in greased 9x13 inch pan.

Bake at 350° for 45 to 50 minutes. Dust with powdered sugar and cut into strips.

CHERRY CHEWY BARS

Katherine Kalinowski
Sterling Homemakers

1 box quick nut bread (plain)
1 egg
1/2 c. oleo

1-21 oz. can cherry pie filling
1 c. canned milk
1 1/2 c. coconut

Mix nut bread, egg and oleo. Press in bottom of 9x13 inch pan. Bake 10 minutes at 350°. Then put on crust the cherry pie filling, canned milk and coconut. Bake 30 minutes at 350°.

CHERRY FUDGE CAKE (BARS)

Catherine Nab
Pep and Progress

1 fudge cake mix
1 tsp. almond extract

2 eggs
21 oz. can cherry fruit pie
    filling

Combine ingredients and mix well. Grease and flour 15x10 inch jelly roll pan or 13x9 inch pan. Bake at 350° for 25 to 30 minutes.

Frosting:

1 c. sugar
1/2 c. milk

5 Tbsp. butter or margarine

Combine and boil, stirring constantly for one minute. Remove from heat. Stir in 16 ounce package semi-sweet chocolate pieces. Pour over cake.

BLUEBERRY SQUARES

Katherine Kalinowski
Sterling Homemakers

1 3/4 c. sugar
1 c. butter or oleo
4 eggs
1 tsp. vanilla
3 c. flour
1/2 tsp. salt
1 1/2 tsp. baking powder

1-21 oz. can blueberry filling
sprinkle of nutmeg
1 recipe of Lemon Icing
1 1/4 c. powdered sugar
1 Tbsp. butter
1 Tbsp. lemon juice

Spread 1/2 of mixture in 15x10x1 inch pan. Put filling on top of mixture and spread remaining mixture on top of filling.
Bake in ungreased pan at 350° for 40 to 45 minutes.
For topping, mix powdered sugar, butter and lemon juice. Spread on squares while still warm.

SIX LAYER BARS (MICROWAVE)

Pam Fey
X-tra X-amples X-tension Club

1/2 c. butter or margarine, melted
1 1/2 c. graham cracker crumbs
1-14 oz. can sweetened condensed milk

1 c. (6 oz.) semi-sweet chocolate chips
1 c. flaked coconut
1 c. finely chopped nuts

Power Select: Medium; Approximate Cooking Time: 12 minutes. Makes 32 bars.
Set Power Select at medium. In each of two (8 inch) square baking dishes, pour 1/2 of butter. Sprinkle with 3/4 cup crumbs; pour 1/2 of condensed milk evenly over crumbs. Top with 1/2 of chocolate chips, coconut, and nuts; press down slightly. Heat, one dish at a time, 5 to 6 minutes. Let stand, covered, 5 minutes. Then chill. Cut into squares to serve.

DANISH APPLE BARS

Ardis Bazata
Highland Lassies

10 to 12 apples
3 c. flour
1 1/4 c. lard
1 tsp. salt
1 egg
1/2 c. milk

crushed corn flakes
1/2 c. sugar
1 1/2 tsp. cinnamon
butter

Pare and slice apples thin; set aside.

179   (Cont.)

In a mixing bowl, put 3 cups flour, 1 1/4 cup lard and 1 teaspoon salt; blend these well. Add 1 egg yolk, beaten with 1/2 cup milk. Add this and mix with the dry ingredients. Now divide dough into 2 parts. Roll out to fit cookie sheet. Line the pan with dough, then sprinkle crushed corn flakes on the dough. Add sliced apples on the corn flakes. Sprinkle sugar and cinnamon mixture on apples. Dot with butter. Roll out other half of dough and cover the apples with it. Pierce the top of dough. Beat egg white till fluffy. Take a pastry brush and spread on top dough.

Bake at 350° for 40 to 45 minutes. When cool, drizzle with powdered sugar frosting.

DATE SQUARES

Mrs. Gilbert Lindstrom
Kelly Woman's Improvement E.H.C.

4 c. Rice Krispies
4 oz. chopped dates

4 oz. butter or margarine
1/2 c. sugar

Melt butter; add sugar and dates and cook till dates are mushy. Pour over Rice Krispies and stir until they are covered with mixture. Press into greased 9x13 inch pan. When cooled, they may be cut. Note: Recipe submitted by Mrs. Lorin Lindstrom.

OATSIES

Pam Clark
X-tra X-amples X-tension Club

2 c. oatmeal
1/2 c. brown sugar, packed
1/2 c. margarine, melted
1/4 c. corn syrup
1/2 tsp. salt

1 tsp. vanilla
6 oz. semi-sweet
  chocolate pieces, melted
1/4 c. chopped nuts

Heat oven to 400°. Grease baking pan 9x9 inches. In medium bowl, mix oats and brown sugar. Stir together butter, syrup, salt and vanilla. Mix thoroughly into oat mixture. Press dough evenly in bottom of pan.

Bake 8 to 10 minutes or until top bubbles. Cool. Spread chocola on top. Sprinkle nuts on chocolate. Chill one hour. Cut into bars. Makes 32 bars.

GUM DROP BARS

Marilyn Brehe
Padroni E.H.

4 eggs
2 c. brown sugar
1/4 tsp. salt
1 c. pecans

1 Tbsp. cold water
2 c. flour
1 tsp. cinnamon
1 c. sliced gum drops
  (no black ones)

Beat eggs till light; add water. Beat in sugar. Keep 1 tablespoon to dredge gum drops in and also nuts. Sift dry ingredients; add to egg mixture. Fold in nuts and gum drops. Put in 10x14 inch pan lined with well oiled waxed paper.

Bake at 325° for 30 minutes. Cool. Remove from pan. Cut into bars, 1x3 inches. Sprinkle with powdered sugar. Makes 4 dozen bars.

CHOCOLATE CHIP CHEESECAKE BARS

Rosalie Wolfe
Home Hustlers

1-12 oz. pkg. chocolate chips
1/3 c. margarine or butter
2 c. graham cracker crumbs
1 c. chopped nuts

1-8 oz. pkg. cream cheese, softened
1-14 oz. can Eagle Brand sweetened condensed milk
1 tsp. vanilla extract
1 egg

Preheat oven to 350° (325° for glass dish). In medium saucepan, melt chips and margarine; stir in crumbs and nuts. Press half the mixture firmly onto bottom of greased 13x9 inch baking pan.

In large mixer bowl, beat cheese until fluffy; beat in Eagle Brand, vanilla and egg; mix well. Pour into prepared pan. Top with remaining crumb mixture.

Bake 25 to 30 minutes or until toothpick inserted near center comes out clean. Cool to room temperature. Chill before cutting into bars. Refrigerate left overs.

NO BAKE PEANUT BARS

Phyllis Jones
Night Owls

1 c. chopped salted peanuts
4 c. graham cracker crumbs
1 c. evap. milk
1/2 c. peanut butter

2 c. miniature marshmallows
1 c. powdered sugar
1-12 oz. pkg. butterscotch chips
1/3 c. finely chopped salted peanuts

Mix 1 cup peanuts, marshmallows, cracker crumbs and powdered sugar in large mixing bowl. Mix butterscotch chips and milk in small saucepan. Cook over low heat, stirring constantly until smoothly blended. Remove from heat. Add peanut butter and stir. Pour in bowl with other ingredients and stir until all cracker crumbs are blended in. Turn into a well buttered pan, 13x9x2 inches and sprinkle 1/3 cup chopped peanuts over top. Chill until firm, about 1 1/2 hours. Cut into 1 inch squares to serve.
Note: One 13 3/4 ounce package graham crackers or 52 two inch squares may be used.

PEANUT BUTTER CUPS

Rena Morrison
Padroni E.H.

2 sticks margarine
1 lb. powdered sugar
 (4 c. sifted)
1 c. peanut butter

1/3 lb. (1 pkg.) graham
 crackers, crushed
1-8 oz. Hershey bar or
 2 c. chocolate chips

Melt margarine; add powdered sugar, peanut butter, crushed graham crackers and mix well. Put into jelly roll pan. Melt Hershey bar or chocolate chips and spread over first mixture.

PEANUT BUTTER BON BONS

Dorothy A. Harms
Home Hustlers

1 cube margarine
1 lb. powdered sugar
3 c. Rice Krispies,
 crush after measuring
2 c. chunky peanut butter

8 oz. Hershey chocolate bar
6 oz. chocolate chips
1/3 stick paraffin

Mix first 4 ingredients and form about 1 teaspoonfuls into a ball. Set on waxed paper on cookie sheet and place into refrigerator to chill thoroughly.

Melt chocolate bar, chips and paraffin very slowly on low in microwave, stirring every 30 seconds. Dip peanut butter balls in chocolate and return to waxed paper to set.

CRISPY DELIGHTS (MICROWAVE)

Jill Distel
Creative Homemakers

1/3 c. butter
3 c. miniature marshmallows

4 c. crisp rice cereal
1 c. peanuts

Place butter and marshmallows in a 2 quart casserole. Microwa on high (100%) for 2 to 3 minutes or until melted. Stir until smooth. Stir in cereal and nuts. Mix until cereal is covered. Pour into a greased 11 3/4 x 7 1/2 x 1 3/4 inch baking dish. Cool and cut into squares.

CHEWIES

Marilyn Crane
Creative Homemakers

5 c. corn flakes
2 c. krispies
2 c. salted peanuts

1 c. corn syrup
1 c. cream
1 c. brown sugar

Cook last 3 ingredients to soft ball stage. Pour over dry ingredients and press into 9x13 inch greased pan.

CEREAL BALLS

Margaret Lueck
Hearth and Home

1 c. dates, cut up
1/2 c. sugar

1/3 c. butter

Cook slowly stirring all the time, until thick. Add 2 cups Rice Krispies. Butter hands and roll into balls the size of walnuts. Roll in coconut or ground nuts.

DELICIOUS MARSHMALLOW TREATS

Eva Korrey
Rainbows of Happiness

1/4 c. margarine or butter
1-10 oz. pkg. (about 40)
  regular marshmallows
or 4 c. miniature marshmallows

5 c. Kellogg's Rice Krispies
  cereal

Melt margarine in large saucepan over low heat. Add marshmallows and stir until complteely melted. Cook over low heat 3 minutes longer, stirring constantly. Remove from heat. Add cereal. Stir until well coated. Using buttered spatula or waxed paper, press mixture evenly into buttered 9x13 inch pan. Cut into squares when cool. Makes 24 squares.

CANDY BAR COOKIES

Ginny Anderson
X-tra X-amples X-tension Club

Cookies:

3/4 c. butter
3/4 c. sifted powdered sugar
1 tsp. vanilla

2 Tbsp. evap. milk
1/4 tsp. salt
2 c. flour

Caramel Filling:

1/2 lb. light candy caramels
1/4 c. evap. milk

1/4 c. butter
1 c. sifted powdered sugar
1 c. pecans, chopped

Chocolate Icing:

1 big Hershey chocolate
  bar
1/4 c. evap. milk

2 Tbsp. butter
1 tsp. vanilla
1/2 c. powdered sugar

(Cont.)

For cookies: Cream butter and sugar; add vanilla, milk and salt; mix well. Add flour. Pat in cookie sheet (ungreased) and bake at 325° for 12 to 15 minutes or until light brown. Cool. Spread on Caramel Filling, then top with Chocolate Icing.

For Filling: Combine caramels and milk in double boiler; heat till caramels melt, stirring occasionally. Remove and add butter and sugar; mix well. Stir in pecans. Keep over hot water. Spread over cookies.

For Icing: Melt chocolate over low heat; add butter, vanilla and powdered sugar. Spread over caramel filling. Make in 15 1/2 x 10 1/2 inch pan.

HERSHEY BARS

Diane Freeman
Southsiders of Iliff

1 c. butter   1/2 c. white sugar
1/2 c. brown sugar

Cream the above together, then add:

2 egg yolks   1 c. oatmeal
1 c. flour

Spread into greased 9x13 inch pan. Bake at 325° for 20 minutes. Frost with 4 Hershey bars (just lay bars on hot mixture till they are melted enough to spread.)

SALTED PEANUT CHEWS

Connie Lechman
Proctor E.H. Club

1 yellow cake mix   1/3 c. oleo
1 egg   3 c. marshmallows, small
2/3 c. corn syrup   1/4 c. oleo
2 tsp. vanilla   12 oz. pkg. peanut butter chips
2 c. Rice Krispies   2 c. salted peanuts

Combine the cake mix, egg and oleo. Press in bottom of 9x13 inch pan. Bake 12 to 18 minutes. Remove from oven and add marshmallows. Put back in oven 1 to 2 minutes. Cool.

In saucepan, heat corn syrup, 1/4 cup oleo, vanilla and chips until chips are melted and mixture is smooth, stirring constantly. Remove from heat. Add cereal and nuts. Immediately spoon warm topping over marshmallows. Spread to cover. Chill. Cut into bars. Store covered.

CARAMEL BARS

Dorothy J. Robinson
Home Hustlers

1 German chocolate cake mix
60 light caramels
1/2 c. evap. milk
3/4 c. melted butter

1/3 c. evap. milk
1 c. chopped nuts
1 c. semi-sweet chocolate
chips

Combine 1/2 cup evaporated milk with caramels; melt. Grease and flour 9x13 inch pan. Combine cake mix, butter, 1/3 cup evaporated milk and nuts. Press 1/2 of dough into pan. Bake at 350° for 8 minutes. Remove and sprinkle with chocolate chips. Spread caramel mix over chips. Cover with remaining dough. Bake 20 minutes. Cut and wrap bars and store for 24 hours.

CARAMEL CHEWIES

Louise Ebbers
Padroni E.H.

1 c. Rice Krispies
1 c. coconut

1 c. corn flakes
1 c. nuts

Blend together. Melt 36 caramels and 3 tablespoons cream. Shape with spoon. Wrap each in plastic wrap.

YUMMY CARAMEL BARS

Mabel Karg
Southsiders

32 caramels
1 c. sifted all purpose flour
3/4 c. firmly packed dark
brown sugar
3/4 c. butter or margarine
1/2 c. coarsely chopped pecans

1/3 c. light cream or
evap. milk
1/2 tsp. baking soda
1 c. uncooked old fashioned
oats
1-6 oz. pkg. semi-sweet chocolate
pieces

Combine caramels and cream in the top of a double boiler. Heat over simmering water until caramels are melted, stirring occasionally to blend smooth. Remove from heat and set aside. Heat oven to 350°. Lightly butter an 11x7x1 1/2 inch baking pan. Sift flour, baking soda and salt together into a large mixing bowl. Stir in brown sugar and oats. Using a pastry blender or two knives, cut in butter until mixture looks like coarse crumbs. Turn half of the oat mixture into prepared pan and press evenly over the bottom.
Bake 10 to 15 minutes or until lightly browned. Remove from oven; sprinkle evenly with chocolate pieces and pecans and

then spread with reserved caramel mixture. Sprinkle remaining oat mixture evenly over the caramel. Return to oven and bake about 20 minutes or until lightly browned. Set pan on wire rack to cool slightly, about 30 to 40 minutes. Chill in refrigerator 1 1/2 to 2 hours or until caramel layer is set. Cut into bars. Store in an air tight container. Makes 24.

TOFFEE STICKS

Alice Folladori
Proctor

3/4 c. softened butter
1/2 c. brown sugar
1 egg yolk
1 tsp. vanilla
1/4 tsp. salt
1 1/2 c. sifted flour
2 tsp. vegetable shortening

1-6 oz. pkg. butterscotch chips
1/4 c. light corn syrup
1 Tbsp. water
1/4 tsp. salt
toasted slivered almonds

Blend together softened butter, brown sugar, egg yolk, vanilla and salt. Stir in flour. Spread mixture in 9x13 inch pan. Bake at 350° for 20 minutes or until browned. Cool slightly.

Combine shortening, butterscotch chips, corn syrup, water and salt in saucepan. Heat and stir until sauce is smooth. Spread over top of baked dough. Sprinkle with almonds. Allow topping to set. Cut into 48 (1x2 inch) sticks.

CAROB FRUIT-NUT BARS

Sammy Shaw
Sterling Homemakers

1 c. unsifted flour
1/2 tsp. baking powder
1/8 tsp. soda
1/2 tsp. salt
1/3 c. melted butter
 or cooking oil
3/4 c. firmly packed brown
 sugar

1 Tbsp. hot water
1 egg
1 tsp. vanilla
1/2 c. finely cut dates or figs
1/2 c. chopped nuts
6 oz. carob baking chips

Sift together flour, baking powder, soda and salt. Combine butter, brown sugar, water, egg and vanilla; beat well. Gradually add flour mixture. Add dates and nuts. Spread mixture in greased 8 or 9 inch square pan. Sprinkle carob chips over the top. Lightly press chips into dough. Bake in oven, preheated to 350°, for 30 to 35 minutes or until lightly browned and wooden pick inserted in center comes out clean. Cool in pan. Cut into bars. Makes about 2 dozen bars, 1x2 inches in size.
Note: You may substitute any flavor chips for the carob chips,

or any dried fruits for dates and figs.

MILK DUD BARS (TOFFE NUT BARS)
Sharon Roberts
Creative Homemakers

1/4 c. butter, softened
1/2 c. brown sugar, packed
1 c. sifted flour
2 eggs, beaten
1 c. brown sugar, packed
1 tsp. vanilla

2 Tbsp. flour
1 tsp. baking powder
1/2 tsp. salt
1/2 c. chopped nuts
1/2 c. moist flaked coconut
2/3 c. Milk Duds
(3-1.6 oz. pkgs.)

Mix until well blended the butter, 1/2 cup packed brown sugar, and flour. Press into buttered 9x13 inch pan. Bake in 350° oven for 5 minutes; cool.

Beat together remaining ingredients and spread over baked crust. Bake 25 minutes until golden brown. Cool. Sift confectioners sugar over top and if desired, place a Milk Dud into top of each bar. Makes 30 bars.

LEMON SQUARES
Sharon Roberts
Creative Homemakers

1 c. flour
1/2 c. butter, softened
1/4 c. powdered sugar
1 c. sugar
2 eggs

2 tsp. grated lemon peel
2 Tbsp. lemon juice
1/2 tsp. baking powder
1/4 tsp. salt

Mix flour, butter, powdered sugar. Press into ungreased 8x8 inch pan. Build up 1/2 inch edge. Bake 20 minutes. Beat remaining ingredients until light and fluffy, about 3 minutes. Bake just until no indentation remains when touched in center, about 25 minutes. Cool. Sprinkle with powdered sugar.

LEMON SOUR BARS
Lorraine Johnston
Home Hustlers

1 c. flour
1/3 c. butter or margarine
2 Tbsp. powdered sugar
2 eggs, beaten
3/4 c. brown sugar
3/4 c. flaked coconut
1/2 c. chopped nuts

1/4 c. flour
1/4 tsp. baking powder
1/2 tsp. vanilla
1/2 tsp. grated lemon rind
1 Tbsp. lemon juice
1 c. powdered sugar
1 Tbsp. milk

187   (Cont.)

Mix flour, butter and 2 tablespoons powdered sugar and spread in 11x7 inch pan. Bake in moderate oven, 350°, for 10 minutes.

Mix together eggs, brown sugar, coconut, nuts, 1/4 cup flour, baking powder and vanilla. Pour over baked layer. Bake at 350° for 15 minutes. Remove and frost while warm.

Frosting: Combine lemon peel, lemon juice, and powdered sugar. Add enough milk to make mixture a glaze of spreading consistency. Let cool, then cut into squares.

MOIST BROWNIES

Marilyn Hutt
Busy Bees

4 eggs
2 c. sugar
1 c. melted oleo

1 1/2 c. flour
1/2 c. cocoa
1/2 c. nuts

Beat eggs; add melted oleo. Sift flour, sugar and cocoa together and add to egg mixture. Add nuts. Pour into greased 9x13 inch pan. Bake 35 minutes at 325°.

CHOCOLATE BROWNIES

Julie Schaefer
X-tra X-amples X-tension Club

4 eggs
2 c. sugar
1 tsp. vanilla
1 c. margarine, melted
1 c. flour

2/3 c. cocoa
1/2 tsp. baking powder
1/2 tsp. salt
1 c. nuts (opt.)

Grease 9x13 inch pan. Beat eggs and add sugar and vanilla. Add dry ingredients and mix well. Add nuts last.

Bake at 350° for 35 to 40 minutes or until brownies pull away from sides of pan.

BLONDE BROWNIES

Anne Stieb
Hearth and Home

2 c. brown sugar
2/3 c. margarine or butter
2 eggs, slightly beaten
1 tsp.. salt

1/4 tsp. salt
1 tsp. baking powder
2 c. flour
1 c. chopped nuts
1 c. chocolate chips

Mix together. Bake at 350° for 25 to 30 minutes in a 13x9 inch pan.

PEANUT BUTTER BROWNIES

Phyllis Moore
Pep and Progress

3 eggs
3/4 c. brown sugar
1/4 c. oleo
2 c.flour
1/2 tsp. salt
2 tsp. baking powder

1 c. sugar
1/2 c. peanut butter
2 tsp. vanilla
walnuts or peanuts

Mix the eggs, brown sugar, oleo, sugar, peanut butter and vanilla. Add the flour, salt, baking powder and mix well. Add nuts. Spread in greased 9x13 inch pan. Bake at 350° for 25 minutes. Cut while still warm.

BROWNIES

Kenda Stoltenberg
Padroni E.H.

2 c. sugar
4 eggs
1 c. flour
4 Tbsp. oil

1 c. shortening
1 tsp. vanilla
8 Tbsp. cocoa

Preheat oven to 325°. Cream sugar and shortening. Stir in eggs and vanilla. Add flour, cocoa and oil. Stir well. Bake in 9x13 inch pan for 35 to 40 minutes. Do not over bake.

MOIST 'N CHEWY BROWNIES

Norma Penner
Rainbows of Happiness

1 c. chocolate chips
1/4 c. margarine
2 c. biscuit mix
1 can Eagle Brand milk

1 egg, beaten
1 c. chopped walnuts
vegetable cooking spray

Preheat oven to 350°. Melt chocolate chips and margarine. Remove from heat. Add biscuit mix, milk and egg. Stir well. Stir in nuts. Spray 9x13 inch baking dish with vegetable spray. Pour mixture into dish and bake 20 to 25 minutes. Makes 40 brownies.

BIRTHDAY PARTY BROWNIES

Janet Weingardt
Rainbows of Happiness

2 c. sugar
1/2 c. cocoa
1 stick margarine
4 large eggs

1 Tbsp. vanilla
1 1/4 c. flour
chocolate icing
M&M's

189   (Cont.)

Mix sugar and cocoa; add melted butter. Beat eggs in one at a time. Add vanilla and flour. Mix well. Turn onto greased 15 1/2 x 10 1/2 x 1 inch cookie pan. Bake 20 minutes at 350°. Cut while warm with 3 inch round donut cutter (with center removed). Ice sides and top with chocolate powdered sugar icing and make Happy Faces with M&M's.

CHOCOLATE ZUCCHINI BROWNIES

Carrie Ferrell
Creative Homemakers

2 c. flour
1 1/4 c. sugar
1 1/2 tsp. soda
1/2 c. cocoa
1/2 tsp. salt

1/2 c. chopped nuts
2 tsp. vanilla
1/2 c. salad oil
2 c. grated zucchini
1 egg

Mix all of the above. Pour into greased 9x13 inch pan. Bake at 350° for 35 to 40 minutes. Frost with chocolate icing.

APPLESAUCE BROWNIES

Mrs. Lorin Lindstrom
Kelly Woman's Improvement Club

1 c. shortening
1 1/2 c. sugar
2 eggs
1 c. applesauce
1 tsp. vanilla

2 c. flour
3 Tbsp. cocoa
1 tsp. baking powder
1/2 tsp. soda
1/4 tsp. salt
1/2 c. chopped nuts

Topping:

1 Tbsp. margarine
1 Tbsp. applesauce

1 Tbsp. cocoa
1 c. powdered sugar

Cream shortening and sugar. Add eggs, applesauce and vanilla creaming after each addition. Sift dry ingredients and add to creame mixture. Spread into greased and floured 9x13 inch pan.

Bake 35 minutes in 350° oven. While warm, cut into squares or bars. When cool, frost with topping. Nuts may be sprinkled over the topping.

BROWNIES

Nell Berdine Druyff
Sterling Homemakers

1/4 lb. butter or margarine
1 c. sugar
4 eggs (2 at a time)

1 tsp. vanilla
1-1 lb. can chocolate
  syrup

1 c. plus 1 Tbsp. flour
1/2 tsp. baking powder

1/2 c. nuts

Frosting:

1/3 c. margarine
1/3 c. milk

1 1/2 c. sugar
1/2 c. chocolate chips

Beat together butter or margarine, sugar and eggs, two at a time. Add vanilla, chocolate syrup, flour, baking powder and nuts. Bake at 350° for 30 minutes in 15 1/2 x 10 1/2 inch pan. While hot, frost with frosting.

Frosting: Mix together margarine, milk and sugar. Bring to boil 30 seconds. Add chocolate chips. Beat smooth. Spread on brownies.

DOUBLE CHOCOLATE BROWNIES

Annie Neff
Southsiders E.H. Club

1/2 c. Crisco
1 c. sugar
4 eggs
1 can chocolate flavored
   syrup (16 oz.)

1 1/4 c. sifted flour
1/2 tsp. salt
1 c. chopped walnuts
Quick Frosting

Preheat oven to 350°. In mixing bowl, blend Crisco and sugar. Beat in eggs and vanilla. Blend in chocolate syrup, flour and salt; stir in nuts. Pour into greased 13x9x2 inch baking pan. Bake at 350° for 30 to 35 minutes. Cool slightly, about 5 minutes. Top with Quick Frosting. Cool and cut into bars. Makes 32 brownies.

Quick Frosting:

2/3 c. sugar
3 Tbsp. milk
2 Tbsp. Crisco

1/4 tsp. salt
1/2 c. semi-sweet chocolate
   pieces
1/2 tsp. vanilla

Combine sugar, milk, Crisco and salt. Bring to boiling and boil 30 seconds. Remove from heat. Stir in semi-sweet chocolate pieces and vanilla till melted. Cool 10 minutes. Spread over brownies.

BROWNIES

Jennifer Felzien
X-tra X-amples X-tension Club

1 cube margarine
2 eggs
1/2 c. flour

2-1 oz. sqs. chocolate
1 tsp. vanilla

(Cont.)

Melt margarine and chocolate together. Beat in the eggs and vanilla. Then add the flour. Mix well. Bake at 350° for 15 to 20 minutes in 8x8 inch pan.

BROWNIES
Mary Beam Proctor

2 c. sugar
1 cube oleo or butter
8 Tbsp. cocoa
4 beaten eggs

dash of salt
1 c. flour
1 c. nuts
2 tsp. vanilla

Cream sugar, oleo and cocoa. Add eggs, salt, flour, nuts and vanilla. Pour in 9x13 inch pan and bake at 350° for 30 minutes.

GINGER SNAPS
Mary Heist
Kelly Home Improvement Club

2 c. sugar
2 c. lard
2 c. syrup
1 c. hot water
1 tsp. soda
flour (to make a stiff dough)

2 tsp. ginger
2 tsp. cinnamon
1/2 tsp. cloves
1 tsp. nutmeg
1/2 tsp. salt

Cream the first 3 ingredients. Sift the spices with 2 cups flour. Add the soda to the water and put into the first mixture. Add the flour mixture and add more flour to make a stiff dough. Divide into lumps. Roll out onto bread board and cut with a cookie cutter. Bake at 375° for 10 to 12 minutes.

GINGERSNAPS
Helen Davis
Highland Lassies

1 1/2 c. shortening
2 c. sugar
2 eggs, beaten
1/2 c. molasses
4 c. flour

2 tsp. soda
2 tsp. cinnamon
2 tsp. cloves
2 tsp. ginger

Cream shortening and sugar and beat in the eggs. Add molasses Sift together flour, soda and spices and add to the other mixture. Roll into 1 inch balls. Dip in sugar and place on greased cookie sheet. Flatten the balls slightly with the bottom of a glass dipped in sugar. Bake at 375° for 8 to 10 minutes.

OLD FASHIONED GINGER SNAPS

Opal Vance
Sterling Homemakers

1 c. sugar
1 c. molasses
1 c. oleo
6 c. flour (approx.)

1 Tbsp. ginger
1 Tbsp. soda
1 egg

Mix in order given. Add enough flour, about 6 cups, to make a very stiff dough. Roll into very small balls. Bake in 350° oven until brown. Allow to cool before removing from pan.

GINGERSNAPS

Sammy Shaw
Sterling Homemakers

1 stick margarine
1/4 c. Crisco
1 c. light brown sugar
1 egg
1/4 c. light molasses

2 1/4 c. flour
2 tsp. soda
1/4 tsp. salt
1 tsp. ginger
1 tsp. cinnamon
1/2 tsp. cloves

Mix together the margarine, Crisco, brown sugar, molasses and egg until light in color. Add the flour, soda, salt and spices. Chill dough for about 1 hour. Roll into walnut sized ball. Dip into granulated sugar and sprinkle with a few drops of water. Bake in 375° oven for 10 to 12 minutes.

WHIPPED CREAM ICING

Annabelle Miller
Padroni E.H.

1/2 c. milk
dash of salt
1 c. powdered sugar

2 Tbsp. flour
1 stick margarine
1 tsp. vanilla

Shake milk, flour and salt in small jar. When smooth, heat in pan, stirring until thick. Cool. Beat margarine in another bowl for 3 minutes. Add milk mixture and beat 3 more minutes. Add powdered sugar and beat 3 more minutes. Add vanilla and beat again.

QUICK FUDGE ICING

Barb Korrey
X-tra X-amples X-tension Club

c. sugar
/4 c. cocoa
/4 c. butter

2 Tbsp. light corn syrup
1 1/2 c. sifted confectioners
sugar

193   (Cont.)

1/2 c. milk   1 tsp. vanilla

Boil granulated sugar, cocoa, butter, milk and corn syrup 3 minutes, stirring occasionally. Remove from heat. When you can hold your hand on the bottom of the pan, stir in the confectioners sugar and vanilla. If too thin, add more confectioners sugar.

SEA SPRAY FROSTING

Jackie Waitley
Proctor

1/2 c. sugar   1/4 tsp. cream of tartar
1/4 c. light corn syrup   2 egg whites
1/4 c. water   1/2 tsp. vanilla

Combine sugar, corn syrup, water and cream of tartar. Place over low heat and stir until sugar is dissolved. Cook until syrup spins a thread. Beat egg whites until stiff but not dry. Pour syrup over egg whites while beating. Add vanilla.

Write your extra recipes here:

DESSERTS

To days Special:
CONE ..... 5¢
DOUBLE DIP. 7¢

HAND CRANKED DAILY
FRESH CREAM USED

© ardi ORIGINALS

A leaf of lettuce dropped into the pot absorbs the grease from the top of the soup. Remove the lettuce and throw it away as soon as it has served its purpose.

To prevent splashing when frying meat, sprinkle a little salt into the pan before putting the fat in.

Small amounts of leftover corn may be added to pancake batter for variety.

To make bread crumbs, use fine cutter of the food grinder and tie a large paper bag over the spout to prevent flying crumbs.

When bread is baking, a small dish of water in the oven will help to keep the crust from getting hard.

Rinse a pan in cold water before scalding milk to prevent sticking.

When you are creaming butter and sugar together, it's a good idea to rinse the bowl with boiling water first. They'll cream faster.

To melt chocolate, grease pan in which it is to be melted.

Dip the spoon in hot water to measure shortening, butter, etc., the fat will slip out more easily.

When you buy cellophane-wrapped cupcakes and notice that the cellophane is somewhat stuck to the frosting, hold the package under the cold-water tap for a moment before you unwrap it. The cellophane will then come off clean.

When you are doing any sort of baking, you get better results if you remember to preheat your cooky sheet, muffin tins, or cake pans.

Chill cheese to grate it more easily.

The odor from baking or boiling salmon may be eliminated by squeezing lemon juice on both sides of each salmon steak or on the cut surface of the salmon and letting it stand in the refrigerator for one hour or longer before cooking.

Use the type can opener that leaves a smooth edge and remove both ends from a flat can (the size can that tuna is usually packed in) and you have a perfect mold for poaching eggs.

Use the divider from an ice tray to cut biscuits in a hurry. Shape dough to conform with size of divider and cut. After baking biscuits will separate at dividing lines.

A clean clothespin provides a cool handle to steady the cake tin when removing a hot cake.

Try using a thread instead of a knife when a cake is to be cut while it is hot.

DESSERTS

DUMP CAKE

Nell Berdine Druyff
Sterling Homemakers

2-1 lb. 6 oz. cans prepared
cherry pie filling
1-1 lb. 4 oz. cans pineapple
chunks, drained
1-1 lb. 2 1/2 oz. pkgs. yellow
cake mix

1 c. melted butter or margarine
1 c. flaked coconut
1 c. chopped nuts

Preheat oven to 350°. Spread pie fillings evenly in bottom of a greased 13x9x2 inch baking pan. Arrange pineapple chunks over cherries. Sprinkle cake mix over evenly. Cover with melted butter or margarine. Top with coconut and walnuts. Bake 1 hour or until done.

GOOD CAKE

Mrs. Helen Koester
Padroni E.H.
Betty Ballinger, Hearth and Home

4 eggs
2 c. Bisquick or
similar product

1 box brown sugar
(2 1/3 c.)
1 c. nuts or raisins

Beat eggs until foamy; add brown sugar and beat, then add Bisquick and beat a little. Add nuts and spread in greased 9x12 inch pan. Bake at 350° for 30 minutes. Cut while warm.

GOOD CAKE

Betty Ballinger
Hearth and Home

4 eggs
2 1/2 c. brown sugar

2 c. Bisquick
1 c. nuts

Beat eggs; add brown sugar and blend. Add Bisquick. Stir in nuts. Pour into 9x13 inch greased pan. Bake at 350° for 45 minutes.

FRUIT COCKTAIL PUDDING

Dorothy Bartholomew
Pep and Progress

1 can fruit cocktail
(juice and all)
1 egg
3/4 c. sugar

1 c. flour
1 tsp. soda
1/2 c. brown sugar
1/2 c. chopped nuts or coconut

Mix; pour into 10 inch square pan. Top with 1/2 cup brown sugar, 1/2 cup nuts or coconut. Bake at 350° until done. Serve with whipped cream.

MYSTERY PUDDING

Mrs. Lorin Lindstrom
Kelly Woman's Improvement E.H.C.

1 c. flour
1 c. sugar
1 tsp. soda
1/4 tsp. salt
3/4 c. brown sugar
1/2 c. chopped nuts
1 egg

1 #2 can fruit cocktail
  or 2 c. diced fruit (such as
  pears, peaches or apples,
  combination of fruits and syrup
  of fruits)
whipped cream
1/2 c. maraschino cherries

Sift dry ingredients 3 times. Combine fruit and syrup with the slightly beaten egg; mix thoroughly. Spoon batter into 9x9 inch greased baking dish. Sprinkle brown sugar combined with the nuts over the batter. Bake 45 minutes in 350° oven. Garnish with whipped cream and maraschino cherries.
Note: Recipe submitted by Mrs. Lorin Lindstrom.

MYSTERY DESSERT

Olive Myers
Sterling Homemakers

1 1/2 c. flour
1 c. sugar
1 tsp. soda
1 tsp. vanilla
1 egg

1-17 oz. can fruit cocktail
  Topping:
3/4 c. brown sugar
1 c. chopped nuts

Place all ingredients in a bowl and mix together. Pour into a 9x12 inch pan. Top with brown sugar and nuts. Bake at 325° for 45 to 60 minutes.

ANGEL FOOD CAKE DESSERT

Ellen Luft
Night Owls

Make custard of:

1 c. sugar
4 egg yolks
1 env. gelatin in 1/2 c.
  cold water

1 Tbsp. cornstarch
1 1/2 c. milk
4 egg whites
1 pt. whipped cream

Tear up cake and put in bottom of 8 1/2 x 12 inch pan. Sprinkle with crushed drained pineapple, fruit cocktail or other

196

fruit. Add custard mixture with gelatin and egg whites (stiffly beaten). Add whipped cream. Pour mixture over cake and set in ice box. Sprinkle nuts and coconut on top. Serves 14 to 16 persons.

SPRING FLING CAKE

Annabelle Miller
Padroni E.H.

1 yellow cake mix
4 eggs
1/2 c. cooking oil
11 1/2 oz. can mandarin oranges

1-3 oz. pkg. instant vanilla pudding
1 flat can crushed pineapple
1-8 oz. tub Cool Whip
nuts

Combine cake mix, eggs, oil and oranges, with juice. Mix until smooth. Bake at 350° for about 25 minutes or until done in 9x13 inch pan. After cake has cooled, mix the instant pudding with the pineapple plus juice. Mix well, then fold into the Cool Whip. Spread over cake and sprinkle with nuts.

EASY CAKE DESSERT

Sadie Slice
Shamrock

1 large can sliced peaches
1 Betty Crocker butter
pecan cake mix

1 cube margarine
1 c. coconut
3/4 c. chopped walnuts

Spread peaches in oblong cake pan evenly. Pour dry cake mix over peaches evenly. Melt margarine and drizzle over cake. Try to get this spread evenly. Mix coconut and nuts and sprinkle on cake. Bake at 325° for 30 to 35 minutes. Serve cold and top if desired.

CHERRY DELIGHT CAKE

Florence Lindstrom
Kelly Woman's Improvement Club

1 or 2 cans cherry pie filling
1 large box yellow cake mix

1 cube margarine

Spread pie filling in bottom of a 9x13 inch pan. Add cake mix spreading evenly over the pie mix. Slice margarine and place evenly over the cake mix. Bake in 350° oven for 45 to 50 minutes.

ICEBOX CAKE

Marlene Allen
Padroni E.H.

20 marshmallows
1 c. graham cracker crumbs

1 env. unflavored gelatin
1 c. crushed pineapple

(Cont.)

1 c. milk   1 c. chopped walnuts
1/2 pt. whipping cream

Heat marshmallows in milk until melted. Cool. Beat cream. Dissolve gelatin. Mix all together and put into baking dish lined with crumbs. Sprinkle crumbs over top and refrigerate several hours.

COCONUT MOUSSE

Ardis Bazata
Highland Lassies

1 1/2 Tbsp. plain gelatin   1/2 tsp. almond flavoring
1/4 c. cold water   1 c. flaked coconut
1 1/2 c. hot pineapple juice   1 c. well drained crushed
1/2 c. sugar   pineapple
pinch of salt   juice of one lemon
                                   1 c. whipping cream

Dissolve gelatin in cold water. Add gelatin to hot pineapple juice. Add sugar, salt, flavoring, coconut, pineapple and lemon juice. Cool until it begins to thicken but not set. Whip cream and fold into gelatin mixture. Pour into ring mold. When unmolded, sprinkle with coconut and decorate as desired. This is pretty if you set a small bowl of gelatin cubes in the center (1 or 2 colors). This can be used as a salad or a dessert.

FRUIT DESSERT

Werdna Montgomery
Shamrock

1-3 oz. pkg. lemon jello   1 large can milk
1 c. boiling water   1 can crushed pineapple
juice of one lemon   1 c. nuts
1 c. any fruit juice   vanilla wafers

Mix jello, boiling water, lemon juice and fruit juice. Let set until it begins to get thick. Whip very foamy. Whip 1 can very cold milk until thick. Combine the 2 mixtures; add pineapple and nuts. Roll vanilla wafers and spread on bottom of pan. Pour the mixtures and cover with crumbs. Set in refrigerator. Can be made the day before.

RHUBARB TORTE

Jo Ann Rizzolo
Home Hustlers

1 c. sugar   4 c. sliced rhubarb
3 Tbsp. cornstarch   1/2 c. water

few drops red food coloring
1 recipe graham cracker
   crust
1/2 c. whipping cream

1 1/2 c. tiny marshmallows
1-3 3/4 or 3 5/8 oz. pkg.
   instant vanilla pudding mix

Combine sugar and cornstarch; stir in rhubarb and water. Cook and stir till thickened. Reduce heat; cook 2 to 3 minutes. Add food coloring. Spread on cooled graham cracker crust. Cool. Whip cream; fold in marshmallows. Spoon on rhubarb mixture. Prepare pudding according to package directions. Spread over all. Sprinkle with reserved crumbs; chill. Makes 9 servings.

To make Graham Cracker Crust: Combine 1 cup graham cracker crumbs, 2 tablespoons sugar and 4 tablespoons melted butter or margarine. Reserve 2 tablespoons. Pat remainder in 9x9x2 inch pan. Bake at 350° for 10 minutes. Cool.

FRUIT SOUFFLE

Mabel Karg
Southsiders

1 env. Knox unflavored gelatin
3/4 c. hot pineapple juice
1/4 tsp. salt
1/2 c. chopped nuts
1 c. cream, whipped

1/4 c. cold water
1/2 c. sugar
1 flat can crushed pineapple,
   drained
1/2 c. halved maraschino
   cherries, well drained
1 egg white

Soften gelatin in cold water. Add sugar and hot pineapple juice and stir until dissolved. Cool. When it begins to thicken, fold in the whipped cream, maraschino cherries and pineapple. Fold in stiffly beaten egg whites. Sprinkle with chopped nuts. Put into pan and refrigerate.

HOT FUDGE PUDDING

Carrie Terrell
Creative Homemakers

1 c. flour
1/4 tsp. salt
1/2 c. milk

2 tsp. baking powder
2 Tbsp. cocoa
2 Tbsp. oil

Mix above and put in 9x9 inch pan. On top, add 1 cup brown sugar with 1/4 cup cocoa. Pour 1 3/4 cups hot water on top. DO NOT STIR. Bake at 350° for 45 minutes.

CHOCOLATE PUDDING DESSERT

Norma Ruf
Home Hustlers

1 cube oleo
1 c. flour
1 c. chopped nuts
2 Tbsp. sugar
8 oz. pkg. cream cheese,
    soft
1 c. powdered sugar

1 c. Cool Whip
1 small pkg. instant vanilla
    pudding
1 small pkg. instant chocolate
    pudding
3 1/2 c. milk

Mix oleo, flour, nuts and sugar and put into a 9x12 inch greased pan. Bake at 350° for 15 minutes; cool. Cream together cream cheese, powdered sugar and Cool Whip. Spread onto cooled crust. Mix instant pudding with milk and pour over creamed mixture. Cover with Cool Whip. Any kind of instant pudding can be used.

FOUR LAYER DESSERT

Mrs. Helen Koester
Padroni E.H.

1 c. flour
3/4 c. nuts

1 stick margarine
1/2 c. sugar

Melt margarine and add flour, nuts and sugar. Press into 9x13 inch pan. Bake at 350° for 15 minutes. cool crust.

8 oz. pkg. cream cheese
1 c. powdered sugar

1 c. Cool Whip

Soften cream cheese; beat with Cool Whip and powdered sugar and spread over crust.

1-3 oz. pkg. instant
    pudding

1-3 oz. pkg. instant chocolate
    pudding (or nay other flavor)

Mix puddings with 2 1/2 cups milk and spread over cream cheese mixture. Top with Cool Whip and sprinkle nuts over Cool Whip.

TUTTI FRUTTI DESSERT

Florence Mette
Southsiders

1 c. flour
1 tsp. soda
1 c. sugar
1/8 tsp. salt

1 #2 can fruit cocktail
1 egg
1/3 c. nuts
1/2 c. brown sugar

Drain can of fruit cocktail. Beat 1 egg and add to cocktail.

Stir in dry ingredients. Put in a buttered loaf pan and sprinkle with mixture of 1/3 cup nuts and 1/2 cup brown sugar. Bake at 350° for 30 minutes. Cut in squares and serve with whipped cream.

COCONUT PUDDING DESSERT
Werdna Montgomery
Shamrock

Crust:

1 c. flour
2 tsp. sugar

1/2 c. butter or margarine
1/2 c. pecans, chopped fine

2nd Layer:

8 oz. cream cheese
1 c. powdered sugar

1 c. Cool Whip

3rd Layer:

2 pkgs. coconut cream
     pudding

3 c. milk

Mix crust ingredients and press into 9x13 inch pan. Bake 15 minutes at 350°. Cool.

Second layer: Blend cheese and sugar; add Cool Whip and spread on cooled crust.

Third layer: Mix pudding according to package directions with 3 cups of milk. Spread on cheese layer. Cover with Cool Whip. Sprinkle with chopped pecans.

PINEAPPLE SQUARES
Thelma Davis
Sterling Homemakers

1 c. fine vanilla wafer crumbs
1 1/4 c. flaked coconut
1/2 c. oleo or butter
1 1/2 c. sifted powdered sugar
2 eggs

1 c. crushed pineapple, drained
1/2 c. broken walnuts
1 c. whipping cream, whipped
1/4 c. maraschino cherries

Place half of the crumbs in a 9x9x2 inch pan. Sprinkle with half the coconut. Cream butter gradually; add sugar and cream till light. Add one egg at a time, beating well after each. Spread mixture over coconut. Fold pineapple, walnuts and cherries into whipped cream. Spread over mixture in pan. Sprinkle with remaining coconut and crumbs. Chill about 4 hours. Serves 12.

FOOD FOR THE GODS

Helen Fehringer
Hearth and Home

2 c. sugar
1 pkg. chopped dates
6 eggs, well beaten

9 tsp. cracker crumbs
  (not fine)
2 tsp. baking powder
1 lb. walnuts, chopped up

Mix all ingredients except eggs. Mix them very well. Add the 6 well beaten eggs and pour into 9x12 inch baking pan, ungreased. Bake at 350° for 30 minutes.

COCOA MARBLE CHEESECAKE

Kathy Martinez

2-8 oz. pkgs. cream cheese,
  softened
1 c. sugar, divided
2 Tbsp. cornstarch
2 eggs, slightly beaten

1 tsp. vanilla
1/3 c. cocoa
1-9" baked graham
  cracker crust

Beat cream cheese, 3/4 cup sugar and cornstarch in large mixer bowl till smooth. Beat in eggs and vanilla. Measure 1 cup batter; set aside.

Combine cocoa and remaining 1/4 cup sugar. Beat cocoa mixture into remaining 2 cups batter in bowl till well blended. Pour dark and reserved light batter alternately into crust. Swirl with spatula. Bake at 350° for 30 to 35 minutes or till center is firm. Cool completely on wire rack. Refrigerate 4 hours or overnight. Makes 12 servings.

CHEESE CAKE

Doris Seghi
Night Owls

1-3 oz. pkg. lemon jello
1 c. boiling water
3 Tbsp. lemon juice
1-8 oz. pkg. cream cheese

1 c. sugar
1 tsp. vanilla
1 can chilled Milnot or
  Carnation

Dissolve jello in boiling water and addd lemon juice; cool. Cream together cheese, sugar and vanilla. Add jello mixture and mix well. Fold in whipped Milnot or Carnation with jello mixture.

Crust: Mix 1 package graham crackers with 1/4 cup sugar and 1/3 cup margarine. Put in 9x13 inch pan and bake 10 minutes. Cool before adding cheese mixture. This will freeze well.

GRAHAM CRACKER JELLO DESSERT

Luverta Wilson
Sterling Homemakers

1/2 cube butter or margarine
1/2 c. sugar
1 small can crushed pineapple
    (8 oz.)
1 egg

1 c. cottage cheese
1-3 oz. box jello
1/2 c. nuts
16 to 18 graham crackers

Cream butter and sugar; beat in egg. Add pineapple, nuts and cheese. Line pan with crackers. Pour in mixture. Cover with more crackers. Pour nearly set jello over and refrigerate. Serve with whipped cream.

PECAN PIE SURPRISE

Philomena Sewald
Pep and Progress

1 pkg. yellow cake mix
(less 2/3 c.)
1/2 c. melted butter
    or margarine
1 egg

Filling:
2/3 c. cake mix
1/2 c. brown sugar, packed
1 1/2 c. dark syrup
3 eggs
1 tsp. vanilla
1 c. pecans

Mix ingredients in left column together. Press into 9x13 inch cake pan. Bake 15 to 20 minutes in 350° oven.
Mix filling ingredients together except nuts. Pour over baked cake. Add nuts on top of cake mixture. Bake again in 350° oven for 30 to 35 minutes. Cool. Top with Cool Whip.

COCONUT CRUNCH TORTE

Eva M. Guenzi
Home Hustlers

1/2 c. graham cracker crumbs
1/2 c. chopped moist shredded
    coconut
1/2 c. chopped California
    walnuts
4 egg whites

1/4 tsp. salt
1 tsp. vanilla
1 c. sugar
1 pt. butter brickle ice cream

Combine graham cracker crumbs, coconut and nuts. Beat egg whites with salt and vanilla until foamy; gradually add sugar and continue beating until egg whites form stiff peaks. Fold graham cracker mixture into egg white mixture. Spread in well greased inch pie plate or 10x6x1 1/2 inch baking pan. Bake in moderate

350° oven for 30 minutes. Cool. Cut in wedges and top with scoops of ice cream. Makes 6 to 8 servings.

BLUEBERRY JELLO

Reva Roland
Rainbows of Happiness

1-3 oz. pkg. raspberry jello
1 can blueberries

1 small can crushed pineapple
1 c. Cool Whip

Mix jello with 1 cup boiling water. Drain fruit but save 1/3 cup of juice from each can of fruit. Add to jello. Set slightly. Stir in Cool Whip.

LEMON FRUIT FREEZE

Philomena Sewald
Pep and Progress

2/3 c. butter or margarine
1/3 c. sugar
7 c. Rice or Corn Chex cereal, crushed to make 3 c.
1-14 oz. can Eagle Brand condensed milk

1/2 c. real lemon juice
1-21 oz. can lemon pie filling
1-17 oz. can fruit cocktail, well drained
2 c. whipped topping

In medium saucepan, melt butter. Stir in sugar and cereal crumbs. Reserve 1/3 cup of this mixture for garnish. Pat rest of mixture firmly in bottom of 13x9 inch cake pan. Bake at 300° for 12 minutes; let cool.

In large bowl, mix condensed milk and fruit cocktail. Pour over crust. Top with whipped topping. Garnish with remaining crumbs. Freeze for 4 hours. Remove from freezer 20 minutes before serving.

PEACHES AND CREAM CRESCENT DESSERT

Hazel Pyle
Proctor E.H. Club

8 oz. can crescent rolls
8 oz. pkg. cream cheese, softened
1/2 c. sugar
2 tsp. almond extract
21 oz. can fruit pie filling
 (peach, cherry, apple, etc.)

1/2 c. flour
1/4 c. brown sugar
3 Tbsp. margarine
1/2 c. chopped nuts

Use a 13x9 inch pan. Separate dough into two rectangles and press into an ungreased pan. Blend cream cheese, sugar, almond extract until smooth. Spread over dough. Spread fruit filling over cheese. Combine flour, brown sugar, margarine, and mix until crumbly. Stir in nuts. Sprinkle crumb mixture over fruit. Bake 25 to 30 minutes at 375°.

BAKED COBBLER DESSERT

Debbie Garcia
Creative Homemakers

1/2 stick oleo, melted
   in pan
1 c. flour
1 c. sugar
1 c. milk

2 tsp. baking powder
1 can fruit (cherry pie mix,
   peaches, etc.)

Melt butter in pan. Mix flour, sugar, milk, baking powder and pour batter onto butter. Spoon the fruit on top of batter. Bake at 350° for 30 minutes or until golden brown. Use square cake pan.

LAZY DAY COBBLER

Doris Seghi
Night Owls

1 c. sugar
1 c. flour
3/4 c. milk
1 tsp. vanilla plus 1/4
   tsp. lemon extract

1/2 tsp. salt
2 tsp. baking powder

Melt 1/2 cup butter in baking dish or 9x13 inch pan. Pour ingredients into pan with hot butter. Add 1 can of fruit plus juice over top. Do Not Stir. Bake 1 hour or less, at 350°.
Note: No eggs are in this recipe. Blue plums and apricots are delicious. I also use sliced fresh or frozen apples and cinnamon.

QUICK PEACH COBBLER

Mary Beam
Proctor

1 cube butter
1 c. flour
1 c. sugar

1 c. milk
1 tsp. baking powder
1 can peaches

Put butter in pan. Put in oven and melt; add flour. Mix together sugar, milk, and baking powder. Pour over meldted butter. Pour peaches over that and bake at 350° for 30 minutes.

RHUBARB DESSERT

Rena Morrison
Padroni E.H.

1 c. flour	1 tsp. baking powder
1/4 tsp. salt	2 Tbsp. margarine
1 egg, beaten	2 Tbsp. milk
3 c. rhubarb	1 pkg. red gelatin

Topping:

1 c. sugar	1/2 c. flour
1/3 c. margarine	

Blend flour, baking powder, salt and margarine as in making pie crust. Add milk and egg. Pat mixture into 9 inch pan. Place rhubarb over layer and sprinkle dry jello over it. Mix topping mix together until crumbly; sprinkle over filling. Bake at 350° for 45 minutes. Serve with ice cream or cream topping.

BAKED APPLE SQUARES

Jama Marvel
X-tra X-amples X-tension Club

1 3/4 c. sugar	1/2 tsp. salt
3 eggs	1 tsp. vanilla
2 c. sifted flour	1 c. cooking oil
1 tsp. baking powder	1 c. chopped nuts
1 tsp. cinnamon	2 c. thinly sliced apples

Beat eggs; add sugar gradually. Beat until mixture is light and fluffy. Add sifted dry ingredients. Add oil and vanilla. Fold in chopped nuts. Fold in apples. Turn into greased 9x13 inch pan. Bake at 350° for 40 to 45 minutes. Place pan on rack to cool. Cut into squares. These freeze well.

APPLE CRISP

Olive Myers
Sterling Homemakers

2 c. apples	1/4 tsp. salt
1/2 tsp. cinnamon	1/2 c. water
6 Tbsp. shortening	1/2 c. brown sugar
1/4 c. flour	

Peel, core and slice apples in a greased baking dish. Add 1/4 cup brown sugar, cinnamon and water. Mix 1/4 cup brown sugar and shortening and flour till crumbly. Spread over apples. Bake at 350° for 45 minutes.

BAKED FUDGE PUDDING

Pearly Breidenbach
Hearth and Home

1 c. flour
2 tsp. baking powder
1/4 tsp. salt
3/4 c. sugar
1/2 c. milk

2 tsp. melted shortening
1 c. nuts
1 c. brown sugar
4 tsp. cocoa
1 3/4 c. hot water
1/4 c. cocoa

Sift flour, baking powder, salt, sugar and cocoa; add milk, shortening and nuts; mix well. Spread in greased pan. Mix 4 tablespoons cocoa and brown sugar; sprinkle on top and pour 1 3/4 cups hot water over it. Bake at 350° for about 45 minutes.

HASTY PUDDING

Mrs. Gilbert Lindstrom
Kelly Woman's Improvement Extension H.C.

2 c. water
1 c. brown sugar
2 Tbsp. butter
1 c. raisins
1/2 c. milk

1 c. flour
2/3 c. sugar
1 1/2 tsp. baking powder
1/4 tsp. salt

Make sauce of water, brown sugar and butter. Heat it until sugar is dissolved. Sift dry ingredients together. Add raisins and milk and pour batter into greased 9x9 inch baking dish. Pour the sauce over batter. Bake 35 minutes at 375°. Serve warm with topping or cream.
Note: Recipe submitted by Mrs. Lorin Lindstrom.

COTTAGE PUDDING

Amelia Vendegna
Pep and Progress

c. flour
tsp. baking powder
Tbsp. shortening
c. milk

1/2 c. sugar
1/8 tsp. salt
1 egg

Sift together flour, sugar, salt and baking powder. Add milk, beaten egg and shortening. Beat well. Bake in greased pan at 375° or about 20 minutes. Serve with sauce.

Sauce:

/2 c. sugar
Tbsp. butter
anilla

2 Tbsp. flour
hot water

(Cont.)

Mix sugar and flour. Pour on a little boiling water and cook, stirring constantly until mixture begins to thicken. Add the butter and more boiling water until it thickens like a sauce. Flavor with vanilla.

OLD FASHIONED STEAMED PUDDING

Luverta Wilson
Sterling Homemakers

1 c. bread crumbs
1/2 c. sour milk
1/4 c. shortening
1/2 c. sugar
1/2 tsp. vanilla
1 egg
1/2 c. flour

1/2 tsp. salt
1/2 tsp. cinnamon
1/16 tsp. nutmeg
1/2 tsp. soda
1/2 c. raisins or other fruit
1/2 c. nuts

Soften crumbs in milk. Cream shortening and sugar well. Add vanilla. Add beaten egg. Blend all together. Sift together flour, salt, cinnamon, nutmeg, and soda. Combine with first mixture. Add raisins or other fruit and nuts. Blend well and steam in greased mold for 1 hour. Serves 6. Serve with Lemon Sauce.

DATE PUDDING

Luella Sonnenberg
Night Owls

1 c. dates
1/2 c. hot water
1 tsp. soda
1 egg
1 c. sugar
1 1/2 c. flour
1 c. dates

1/2 c. sugar
3/4 c. water
1 tsp. vanilla
1/2 c. sour cream
1 tsp. baking powder
1/2 c. nut meats

Put the first 3 ingredients together and let stand 15 minutes. Make a batter by creaming the sugar and eggs and sour cream. Sift the flour and baking powder 4 times. Mix this and the soaked dates and nuts all together. Bake in a greased 9x13 inch pan for 30 minutes at 375°. While the cake bakes, make a sauce by cooking the 1 cup dates, sugar and water into a paste. Cool. Add the vanilla. Spread on the cake after it has cooled. Serve with whipped cream.

SUET PUDDING WITH TOPPING

Helen Davis
Highland Lassies

1 c. ground suet
1 c. dark syrup
1/2 c. sugar

1 tsp. soda
1/2 c. raisins
1 tsp. cinnamon

1 c. sweet milk	3 c. sifted flour
1 tsp. soda	pinch of salt

Topping:

1 c. brown sugar	3 c. boiling water
1/2 c. dark syrup	nutmeg to taste
1/2 c. flour or cornstarch	1 tsp. vinegar (or to taste)
1 tsp. butter	1/4 c. pecans or walnuts, chopped

Pudding: Mix suet, syrup and sugar. Sift dry ingredients together and add alternately with milk. Add raisins. Grease cheese cloth well (large enough to place pudding in center and tie securely, leaving enough room inside for pudding to rise). Steam 3 hours in a colander in a kettle, or in a blanching kettle. Slice and serve hot with hot topping.

Topping: Mix all ingredients together except the nuts. Cook until slightly thickened and smooth, stirring often. Just before serving, add the nuts. Can be served over the pudding, spice cake or ginger bread.

UNCOOKED PLUM PUDDING

Eleanor Carlson
Home Hustlers

1 pkg. orange jello	2 c. dates
1 c. Grape Nuts	1/2 tsp. cloves
3/4 c. sugar	1/2 tsp. cinnamon
1 c. nut meats	1/2 tsp. nutmeg
1 pt. boiling water	

Mix jello, Grape Nuts and sugar in mixing bowl. Pour over this 1 pint boiling water. Stir to dissolve jello. Add remaining ingredients and mix well. Spoon into serving dishes and chill. Top with whipped cream.

MAPLE NUT ICE CREAM

Esther Pace
Night Owl

8 eggs	4 tsp. Rawleigh Maple Flavoring
4 c. sugar	1 c. chopped pecans
2 pts. whipping cream	
3 1/2 pts. milk	

Beat eggs; add sugar and beat well. Add cream and beat until well mixed. Add milk and maple; mix well. Add pecans. Pour into freezer can and freeze according to freezer directions. Makes 1 gallon. A little more milk may be needed.

PARTY DESSERT

Opal Vance
Sterling Homemakers

3 oz. pkg. lemon gelatin
1 c. hot water
1 c. cold water
1 pt. heavy cream, whipped
1/2 lb. tiny marshmallows
1 c. drained, crushed
  pineapple

1 c. chopped nuts
1 small bottle maraschino
  cherries, drained and chopped
red food coloring for desired
  pink shade (opt.)
8" Baker's angel food cake

Dissolve gelatin in hot water. Stir in cold water. Chill almost firm. Beat fluffy. Blend in whipped cream, marshmallows, pineapple, nuts, cherries and food coloring. Break angel food cake into bite size pieces. Arrange cake pieces in 9x13 inch pan. Cover with half of gelatin mix. Cover with remaining cake pieces. Cover with remaining half of gelatin mix. Refrigerate overnight. Cut in squares to serve and garnish with additional whipped cream if desired. Serves 12 to 15.

RASPBERRY DESSERT

Thelma Davis
Sterling Homemakers

1-3 oz. pkg. raspberry Jell-O
1 c. vanilla ice cream
  (not homemade)
1-9 oz. can crushed pineapple

1 med. sliced banana
1 c. hot water
3 Tbsp. orange juice
1/2 c. chopped pecans

Combine jello and hot water. Add ice cream and stir until thoroughly dissolved. Add orange juice. Set aside until partially thickened. Add fruits and nuts. Pour into a 1 quart mold. Chill until firm. Serves 8 to 10.

RASPBERRY SWIRL

Alba DeSoto
Southsiders

3/4 c. graham cracker crumbs
2 Tbsp. sugar
1-8 oz. pkg. cream cheese
1/8 tsp. salt
1-10 oz. pkg frozen
  raspberries, partially thawed

3 Tbsp. butter, melted
3 eggs, separated
1 c. sugar
1 c. heavy cream

Combine thoroughly the crumbs, melted butter and 2 table-spoons sugar. Lightly press mixture into well greased 7x11x1 1 1/2 inch pan. Bake in a 375° oven about 8 minutes. Cool thoroughly.

Beat egg yolks untl thick. Add cream cheese, sugar and salt; beat until smooth and light. Beat egg whites until stiff peaks form. Whip cream till stiff and thoroughly fold with egg whites into cheese mixture.

In a mixer or blender, crush raspberries to a pulp. Gently swirl half of fruit pulp through cheese filling and spread mixture into crust. Spoon remaining puree over top. Swirl with a knife. Freeze, then cover and return to freezer. Makes 6 to 8 servings.

STRAWBERRY CREAM BAVARIAN

Sandy Schneider
Hearth and Home

1-3 oz. pkg. strawberry Jell-0
1 c. boiling water
1-8 oz. strawberry yogurt
4 c. sliced strawberries

6 Tbsp. sugar
1 pt. whipping cream, whipped
1 angel food cake

Dissolve jello in boiling water. Chill until consistency of unbeaten egg white. Whip jello until frothy. Fold in yogurt. Add strawberries that have been sweetened with 6 tablespoons sugar. Fold in whipped cream. Break cake into 1 inch pieces and fold into mixture. Pour into 9x13 inch pan. Refrigerate several hours or overnight. May be frozen if desired. To serve, top with additional strawberries and whipped cream.

CREAMY FRUIT DESSERT

Gail Wagner
Pep and Progress

2 c. coarsely crushed
   pretzels
3/4 c. melted margarine
2 Tbsp. sugar
1-8 oz. pkg. cream cheese
1-8 oz. tub Cool Whip

1 large box strawberry jello
2 c. boiling water
2 pkgs. (10 oz.) frozen
   strawberries

Mix pretzels, margarine and sugar. Press into 9x13 inch pan. Bake at 400° for 8 minutes. Combine cream cheese and Cool Whip. Spread cream cheese and Cool Whip. Spread over crumb mixture. Add jello to boiling water; cool slightly. Add frozen strawberries. Pour over cheese mixture and chill.

FROZEN STRAWBERRY DESSERT

Marilyn Gerk
X-tra X-amples X-tension Club

. c. flour
/4 c. brown sugar

1/2 c. chopped nuts
1/2 c. margarine

(Cont.)

Crust: Cut ingredients together with a fork to make crumbs. Spread on cookie sheet and bake at 350° till brown. Cover bottom of 13x9 inch pan with 2/3 of the crumbs.

2 egg whites
2/3 c. sugar
2 Tbsp. lemon juice

10 oz. pkg. strawberries,
　partially thawed
1 c. whipped cream
　or 2 pkgs. Dream Whip, prepared

Filling: Beat egg whites, sugar, lemon juice and strawberries together until thick. Fold in prepared Dream Whip. Pour over crumbs. Sprinkle with remaining crumbs. Freeze until ready to serve.

YIPPEE YOGURT POPS

Patty Craven
Creative Homemakers

16 oz. carton (2 c.) plain
　or vanilla yogurt
1-6 oz. can frozen apple,
　pink lemonade, pineapple
　or grape juice concentrate

10-3 oz. cold drink cups
10 wooden sticks

In small bowl, combine yogurt and juice concentrate; stir to blend. Fill cups 1/2 to 2/3 full. Place in freezer until partially frozen, about 1 hour. Insert sticks and freeze completely. To serve, peel off paper cups.

CREME DE MENTHE DESSERT

Kathy Martinez

1-10 oz. pkg. large marshmallows
1 c. milk
1/2 cube margarine
1-15 oz. pkg. chocolate
　Oreo cookies

1-8 oz. carton Cool Whip
6 Tbsp. creme de menthe
　or 1 tsp. flavoring
green food coloring

Combine marshmallows and milk in heavy saucepan. Set on moderate heat until marshmallows are melted, stirring frequently. Cool. Crush cookies into fairly fine crumbs. Melt margarine and mix with 3/4 of cookie crumbs. Spread in 9x13 inch pan. Combine whipped cream, marshmallow mixture, flavoring and food coloring (to desired shade). Spoon evenly over crumbs. Sprinkle with remaining crumbs. Refrigerate overnight. Serves 12.

CHERRY TREAT

Janice Grauberger
Hearth and Home

1/2 c. melted butter
1 c. flour
1 c. sugar
1 1/2 tsp. baking powder
1/4 tsp. salt

2/3 c. milk
1 #1 can cherries,
  water packed, drained
1/2 c. sugar

Melt butter in 8x8 inch pan. Mix sifted dry ingredients with milk. Pour over butter. Mix 1/2 cup sugar with cherries. Pour over butter. Bake at 350° until brown, about 35 minutes. Serve warm or cold with whipped topping.

CHERRY DESSERT

Judy Larson
Hearth and Home

20 whole graham crackers
1/4 lb. butter, melted
36 marshmallows

1/2 c. milk
1 c. heavy cream, whipped
1 can cherry pie filling

Blend crackers and butter. Spread half in 9x9 inch pan. Melt marshmallows in milk and cool. Add whipped cream (to marshmallows.) Pour half of crackers. Pour cherry pie filling over marshmallow layer. Add remaining mixture and top with remaining crumbs. Refrigerate till set.

CHERRY DELIGHT

Glennie Lochman
Sterling Homemakers

3 egg whites, beaten fluffy
1/4 tsp. cream of tartar
1 c. sugar
1 c. soda crackers

1/2 tsp. vanilla
  Topping:
1 pkg. Dream Whip
1/2 c. cherry pie filling

Beat egg whites and cream of tartar. Beat at lower speed adding sugar. Fold in soda crackers and vanilla. Put in 7x9 inch pan. Bake 20 minutes at 350° and cool. For topping mix Dream Whip and cherry pie filling.

DESSERT SALAD

Mrs. Walter Browner
Sterling Homemakers

13 graham crackers
1/4 cube melted oleo
2 1/2 c. Cool Whip
3 oz. Phila. cream cheese

1 c. powdered sugar
1 tsp. almond flavoring
1-16 oz. can cherry or
  blackberry pie mix

213   (Cont.)

Crush crackers and mix with oleo. Add to Cool Whip, cream cheese. Fold in powdered sugar. Add almond flavoring. Line an 8x8 inch pan with crumb mixture. Save a few for the top. To the cream mixture add pie mix, and put on the crumbs. Sprinkle reserved crumbs over all and refrigerate.

CHERRY DESSERT

Mary Beam
Proctor

Crust:

1 c.flour   1 cube oleo

Filling:

8 oz. cream cheese   1 can cherry pie filling
1 c. powdered sugar
1 pkg. Dream Whip, prepared
   or 1 carton Cool Whip

Melt oleo; add flour and pat into pan. Bake at 350° until brown like a pie shell. Beat cream cheese, powdered sugar and Cool Whip together. Pour over cooled shell and top with pie filling.

CHERRY DESSERT

Doris Harms
Night Owls

Sift into bowl:

1 c. flour   2 tsp. baking powder
1 c. sugar   1/2 tsp. salt

Add 2/3 cup milk and mix. Pour into baking dish.

Sauce:

1 can red sour cherries   1 c. sugar

Heat sauce and pour over batter. Bake 45 minutes at 350°. Serve warm. Great with ice cream.

CHERRY DESSERT

Carol Lambrecht
Rainbows of Happiness

1 c. shortening   1/2 tsp. salt
1 c. brown sugar   1 tsp. baking powder
1 3/4 c. flour   2 cans cherry pie filling
1 3/4 c. oatmeal

Mix all ingredients except cherry pie filling and place half

214

of the mixture in a 9x13 inch baking dish. Pour the pie filling on dry mixture. Pour the other half of the dry mixture over the pie filling. Bake 40 minutes at 350°.

BANANA SPLIT DESSERT

Barb Schaefer
Home Hustlers

1/2 c. butter
2 c. graham cracker crumbs
2 eggs
2 c. powdered sugar
1/2 c. softened oleo

1 tsp. vanilla
1-20 oz. can crushed pineapple, drained
4 med. bananas, sliced
1-9 oz. Cool Whip
1/2 c. chopped pecans
1-4 oz. jar maraschino cherries

Combine oleo and cracker crumbs. Put in 9x13x2 inch pan. Beat eggs on high till light. Add powdered sugar, softened oleo and vanilla. Beat 5 minutes. Spread pineapple over creamed mixture. Arrange bananas over pineapple. Cover with Cool Whip. Sprinkle with nuts. Garnish with cherries.

BANANA SPLIT DESSERT

Alice Folladori
Proctor

1/2 c. butter , melted
2 c. graham cracker crumbs
2 eggs
2 c. sifted powdered sugar
3/4 c. softened butter
1 tsp. vanilla

1-20 oz. can crushed pineapple, drained
4 med. bananas (3 c. sliced)
1-9 oz. carton whipped topping
1/2 c. chopped nuts
1-4 oz. jar maraschino cherries, drained

Combine melted butter and cracker crumbs. Pat in bottom of 9x13 inch pan. Beat eggs till light; add powdered sugar, softened butter and vanilla. Beat 5 minutes. Spread over crumbs then chill 30 minutes. Spread pineapple over creamed mixture. Arrange bananas over pineapple; cover with whipped cream and sprinkle with nuts. Cover and refrigerate 6 hours or overnight. Garnish with cherries.

BANANA SPLIT CAKE

Darlene Denton
X-tra X-amples X-tension Club

2 c. vanilla wafer crumbs
1 stick (1/2 c.) melted butter
2 sticks (1 c.) softened butter

1 box powdered sugar
1-20 oz. can well drained, crushed pineapple
5 bananas

2 unbeaten egg whites
1-12 oz. tub whipped cream

pecans and cherries,
enough to decorate top

Combine crumbs and 1 stick melted butter in a 9x13x2 inch pan. Flatten it on the bottom to form a crust. Then beat the egg whites, softened butter and powdered sugar for about 5 minutes. Spread this mixture smoothly over the crust. Then spread the pineapple over the filling. Slice the bananas lengthwise and dip in lemon juice (or the saved pineapple juice) to keep them fresh longer. Cover the pineapple and filling by placing the bananas close together, and on top. Cover with whipped cream, enough to cover the bananas. Garnish with cherries and pecans. Keep refrigerated until serving. Makes 16 servings. This is very rich, but tastes almost exactly like a banana split.

FROZEN BANANA SPLIT

Mrs. Joe Gerk
Hearth and Home

Crust:

2 c. crushed creme-filled
chocolate cookies

3 Tbsp. butter, melted

Combine and press into 9x13 inch pan.

Filling:

3 large bananas, peeled
and sliced
2 Tbsp. lemon juice

6 c. vanilla ice cream
6 c. strawberry ice
cream

Sprinkle bananas with lemon juice. Toss gently to coat and set aside. Stir vanilla ice cream to soften slightly. Spread over crust. Drizzle Fudge Sauce (recipe follows) over top and place bananas on top. Freeze until almost frozen. Top with softened strawberry ice cream. May be served with dollop of whipped cream.

Fudge Sauce:

6 oz. chocolate chips

1 c. whipping cream

Combine in top of double boiler. Heat over hot water until chocolate is melted and sauce well blended. Cool and use.

PINEAPPLE TORTE

Cheryl Monheiser
X-tra Xpamples X-tension Club

1 1/2 c. milk
1 lb. marshmallows

14 whole graham crackers,
crushed

1 1/2 c. drained, crushed
    pineapple

3/4 pt. whipping cream

Line 12x7 1/2 inch pan with graham cracker crumbs. (Reserve 1/3 cup crumbs for topping.) Heat milk. Add marshmallows and stir over medium heat until melted. Let cool. Add pineapple and whipping cream. Top with reserved graham cracker crumbs. Let set overnight.

PEPPERMINT BAVARIAN

Jan Nixon
Extension Home Economist

1 env. unflavored gelatin
1/2 c. cold water
1-8 oz. pkg. Neufchatel
    cheese
1/2 c. sugar

dash of salt
1 c. milk
1/2 c. crushed peppermint candy
1 c. heavy cream, whipped
    (may use thawed frozen substitute)

Soften gelatin in cold water; stir over low heat until dissolved. Combine softened Neufchatel, sugar and salt, mixing until well blended. Gradually add milk and gelatin; stir in candy. Chill until slightly thickened, stirring occasionally. Fold in whipped cream. Pour into 8 (6 ounce) custard cups. Chill until firm. Garnish with additional whipped cream and peppermint candy if desired.

MARSHMALLOW DESSERT

Deana Rasmussen
Rainbows of Happiness

1/2 lb. (or 24 large)
    marshmallows
1/2 c. milk
1 1/2 c. Cool Whip
1-8 1/4 oz. can pineapple

1/2 c. chopped nuts
1 tsp. vanilla
crushed graham crackers

Place marshmallows and milk in double boiler over hot water to dissolve marshmallows. Stir until all are dissolved. Cool! Fold 1 1/2 cups Cool Whip into marshmallow mixture. Add pineapple, nuts and vanilla; mix well. Put crushed graham crackers in bottom of a 7x11 inch baking pan. Pour the marshmallow mixture over the graham cracker crumbs and top with more crumbs. Cool for 3 hours or more. Cut into squares and serve.

DESSERT

Pearly Breidenbach
Hearth and Home

2 c. pretzels, rolled
    (not too fine)

3/4 c. melted margarine
3 tsp. sugar

217   (Cont.)

Mix ingredients and bake 15 minutes at 350°.

1-8 oz. pkg. cream cheese
1/2 c. powdered sugar

1-12 oz. tub Cool Whip
2 c. miniature marshmallows

Carefully spread on pretzel base. Prepare 6 ounce package of strawberry jello with 2 1/2 cups of boiling water. Add at once 1 package of frozen strawberries. When started to stiffen, pour over cream cheese, marshmallow mixture. Let stand all night.

PISTACHIO DESSERT

Eleanor Carlson
Home Hustlers

60 Ritz crackers
2 cubes oleo
2 pkgs. pistachio instant
   pudding
1 1/2 c. milk

4 c. vanilla ice cream
Cool Whip
chocolate candy bars

Crush crackers and add 2 cubes melted oleo. Line a 9x13 inch pan and bake 10 to 15 minutes. Cool thoroughly. Blend 2 packages instant pudding with 1 1/2 cups milk until thickened. Add the ice cream. Spread on baked crust. Chill 1 hour. Spread Cool Whip over mixture and sprinkle shredded chocolate for garnish. Freeze. Remove from freezer 1 hour before serving.

FRUIT COCKTAIL PARFAIT PIE

Mabel Karg
Southsiders

1-1 lb. can (2 c.) fruit cocktail
1/2 c. cold water
vanilla wafer crust

1-3 oz. pkg. lemon flavored
   jello
1 pt. vanilla ice cream

Drain fruit cocktail; reserve syrup. Add water to syrup to make 1 cup. Heat to boiling; add jello and stir till dissolved. Add cold water. Cut ice cream in 6 pieces and add to hot mixture; stir till melted. Chill till mixture mounds slightly when spooned, about 15 to 20 minutes. Fold in fruit. Turn into vanilla wafer crust. Chill till firm (45 minutes for creamy filling, to a few hours for a firmer gelatin kind).

FRUIT SALAD PIE

Diane Freeman
Southsiders of Iliff

1 lb. can tart pie cherries
   and juice
1 lb. can crushed pineapple
   and juice

3/4 to 1 c. sugar, mixed
   with 1/4 c. flour
1 box cherry* jello powder

Mix tart pie cherries and juice, crushed pineapple and juice with sugar-flour mixture. Cook in large pan until thickened, about 5 minutes, stirring constantly. Add jello powder. Stir until jello is dissolved. Set aside to cool on counter. (This can set all day or overnight.)
*Any red jello is okay.

3 large bananas, diced   1/2 c. chopped pecans

When mixture has cooled, add the bananas and pecans. Mix well. Put into two butter crumb crusts. Chill till set. Top with Cool Whip to serve. Cover. Will keep several days. Makes 2 pies, or to make 3, just add more fruit.

FRUIT PIZZA
Bonnie Amen
Proctor

1 pkg. slice and bake sugar   1/3 c. sugar
  cookie dough   1/4 c. apricot preserves
1 pkg. cream cheese   fresh or thoroughly drained,
1/2 tsp. vanilla   canned fruit of your choice

Cut cookie dough into 1/8 inch slices. Line bottom of a 12 inch pizza pan with slices. Press dough together as evenly as possible. Bake in preheated oven (375°) until golden brown. Cool crust at room temperature then refrigerate until chilled. Beat together cheese, sugar and vanilla. Spread mixture over crust. Arrange fruit in circles on top. Mix together apricot preserves and enough water to make them of spreading consistency. Carefully drizzle preserves over top of fruit to glaze it. Refrigerate until chilled.

Write your extra recipes here:

Write your extra recipes here:

WEIGHTS AND MEASURES

AVOIRDUPOIS

1 pound = 16 ounces
1 hundredweight = 100 pounds
1 ton = 20 hundredweight = 2000 pounds
1 long ton = 2240 pounds

EQUIVALENT VALUES

1 square mile = 640 acres = 102,400
        square rods = 3,097,600 square yards
1 square mile = 27,878,400 square
       feet = 4,014,489,600 square inches

Inches	Feet	Yards	Rods	Furlongs	Miles
36 =	3	= 1			
198 =	16.5	= 5.5	= 1		
7,920 =	660	= 220	= 40	= 1	
63,360 =	5280	= 1760	= 320	= 8	= 1

APOTHECARIES

1 scrupple = 20 grains
1 dram = 3 scruples
1 ounce = 8 drams
1 pound = 12 ounces

METRIC

1 centigram = 10 milligrams
1 decigram = 10 centigrams
1 gram = 10 decigrams
1 dekagram = 10 grams
1 hektogram = 10 dekagrams
1 kilogram = 10 hektograms
1 metric ton = 1000 kilograms
1 kilogram = 2.20 pounds
1 pound avoirdupois = 0.45 kilogram

(English Units)
LINEAR MEASURE

1 foot = 12 inches
1 yard = 3 feet
1 rod = 5 ½ yards = 16 ½ feet
1 mile = 320 rods = 1760 yards = 5280 feet
1 nautical mile = 6080 feet
1 knot = 1 nautical mile per hour
1 furlong = ⅛ mile = 660 feet = 220 yards
1 league = 3 miles = 24 furlongs
1 fathom = 2 yards = 6 feet
1 chain = 100 links = 22 yards
1 link = 7.92 inches
1 hand = 4 inches
1 span = 9 inches

SQUARE MEASURE

1 square foot = 144 square inches
1 sq. yard = 9 sq. feet
1 sq. rod = 30 ¼ sq. yards = 272 ¼ sq. inches
1 acre = 160 sq. rods = 43560 sq. feet
1 sq. mile = 640 acres = 102400 sq. rods
1 sq. rod = 625 square links
1 sq. chain = 16 square rods
1 acre = 10 square chains

CUBIC MEASURE

1 cubic foot = 1728 cubic inches
1 cubic yard = 27 cubic feet
1 register ton (shipping measure) = 100 cu. feet
1 U.S. shipping ton = 40 cubic feet
1 cord = 128 cubic feet
1 perch = 24 ¾ cubic feet
1 cubic yard = 27 cu. feet = 46656 cu. inches
1 U.S. liquid gallon = 4 quarts = 231 cu. inches
1 imperial gallon = 1.20 U.S. gals. = 0.16 cu. ft.
1 board foot = 144 cubic inches

DRY MEASURE

2 pints = 1 quart
8 quarts = 1 peck
4 pecks = 1 bushel
1 bushel = 4 pecks
32 quarts = 64 pints
U.S. bushel = 2,150.42 cubic inches
British bushel = 2,218.19 cubic inches

(Metric Units)
LINEAR MEASURE

1 centimeter = 10 millimeters
1 decimeter = 10 centimeters
1 meter = 10 decimeters
1 dekameter = 10 meters
1 hektometer = 10 dekameters
1 kilometer = 10 hektometers
1 inch = 2.54 centimeters
1 meter = 39.37 inches
1 yard = 0.914 meter
1 mile = 1609 meters = 1.61 kilometers

SQUARE MEASURE

1 square centimeter = 100 square millimeters
1 square decimeter – 100 square centimeters
1 sq. meter = 100 sq. decimeters = 1 centar
1 ar = 100 centars
1 hektar = 100 ars
1 square kilometer = 100 hektars
1 square centimeter = 0.15 square inch
1 square meter = 1.20 square yards
1 square kilometer = 0.39 square mile
1 hektar = 2.47 acres
1 square inch = 6.45 square centimeters
1 square yard = 0.84 square millimeter
1 square mile = 2.59 square kilometers
1 acre = 0.40 hektar

CUBIC MEASURE

1 cubic centimeter = 1000 cubic millimeters
1 cubic decimeter = 1000 cubic centimeters
1 cubic meter = 100 cubic decimeters
1 cubic yard = 0.76 cubic meter
1 cubic meter = 1.31 cubic yards
1 liter = 1.06 U.S. liquid quarts
1 hektoliter = 100 liters =
               26.42 U.S. liquid gallons
1 U.S. liquid quart = 0.94 liter
1 U.S. liquid gallon = 3.76 liters

CANDY, JELLY, JAM, PRESERVES

CREAM CANDY

Alice E. Lindstrom
Kelly Woman's Improvement Club

4 c. sugar
2/3 c. light corn syrup
1/4 tsp. salt
2 c. whipping cream (heavy)

1 1/2 Tbsp. butter or oleo
1 1/2 tsp. vanilla
1/4 c. chopped nuts (opt.)

Boil all ingredients except butter and vanilla in a heavy saucepan at medium boil, until a hard ball forms (almost brittle in cold water). It may take 1 1/2 hours but it is well worth the time. Add butter and vanilla; beat until stiff. Pour immediately into greased pan. If nuts are desired, add before beginning to beat.

Microwave: Use large bowl. Cook on High. Turn every 3 to 4 minutes. Takes about 20 to 25 minutes.

CHINESE FRIED NUTS

Annabelle Miller
Padroni E.H.

6 c. water
4 c. walnuts
salt

1/2 c. sugar
salad oil

In a 4 quart saucepan, heat water to boiling. Add walnuts and boil one minute. Rinse nuts under hot water; drain.

In large bowl, with rubber spatula, gently stir warm nuts with the sugar until it is dissolved.

In a saucepan, over medium heat, heat about one inch of salad oil to 350°. Add 1/2 of the nuts to the oil and fry 5 minutes or until golden brown. With a slotted spoon, place the nuts in a sieve over a bowl to drain. Salt lightly. Toss nuts to keep from sticking together. Cool on paper towels. Repeat with rest of nuts.

CARAMEL FUDGE
(Very Old Recipe)

Dorothy Miller
Highland Lassies

6 c. white sugar
1 pt. white Karo syrup

1 qt. sweet cream

Mix all together and bring to a slow boil. Boil slowly to a hard ball stage. It should be a caramel color at this time. Remove from heat and beat constantly until it thickens like fudge. It takes a lot of beating. Pour into large buttered pan. It makes around 5 pounds. I make this at Christmas time each year.

221

OLD FASHION FUDGE

Deana Rasmussen
Rainbows of Happiness

3 Tbsp. margarine
3 c. sugar
2 Tbsp. corn syrup
  (at room temp)

3/4 c. milk
1 tsp. vanilla
3 Tbsp. cocoa
1 c. chopped nuts

Place butter, sugar, syrup and cocoa and milk in heavy 3 quart saucepan. Cook over medium heat, stirring constantly until mixture boils. Continue cooking, stirring occasionally, to soft ball stage (238°) or until a small amount of mixture makes soft ball in cold water. Remove from heat. Add vanilla. Cool to 110° or lukewarm. Beat until fudge begins to thicken and loses gloss. Fold in nuts. Quickly pour in greased pan, 8x8x2 inches. For best results, do not spread fudge or scrape the sides of pan. Cut in squares. Makes 2 pounds.

PEANUT BUTTER KISSES

Katherine Kalinowski
Sterling Homemakers

1 c. honey
1 tsp. vanilla
1 tsp. maple flavoring

1 c. peanut butter
2 c. powdered milk

Combine honey, vanilla and maple flavoring. Add to peanut butter and powdered milk. Knead until well mixed, then form the kisses.

TURTLE CANDY

Carol Lambrecht
Rainbows of Happiness

caramels
nuts

1-6 oz. bag chocolate chips
1/4 bar paraffin

Place one caramel on top of nuts on cookie sheet. Put in 250° oven until it just starts to melt. Remove from oven. Press caramel over nuts. Dip in melted chocolate chips and 1/4 bar of paraffin.

CARAMEL CORN

Fran Hofmann
Hearth and Home

2 c. brown sugar
2 sticks oleo

1/2 c. white corn syrup
1 tsp. salt

Boil 5 minutes. Take off stove and add 1/2 teaspoon soda.

Pop 1 1/2 cups of popcorn. Pour syrup mixture over popped corn. Bake in 200° oven for 1 hour. Stir every 15 minutes.

CARAMEL POPCORN

Mrs. Walter Browner
Sterling Homemakers

2 sticks butter or margarine
1/2 c. white syrup
2 c. brown sugar
1/4 tsp. cream of tartar

1 tsp. salt
1 tsp. soda
7 qts. popped corn

Mix butter, syrup and brown sugar. Bring to boil. Let boil for 6 minutes. Take off heat; add cream of tartar, salt, and soda. Stir until foamy and pour over corn. Spread on a cookie sheet after mixing well. Bake in 250° oven for 1 hour. This can be made in advance and stored in the freezer. Peanuts may be added if desired.

CARAMEL CORN

Reva Roland
Rainbows of Happiness

4 qts. popped corn
1 cube margarine
1 c. brown sugar

1/2 c. white corn syrup
1 tsp. soda

Cook margarine, brown sugar and syrup over low heat until blended. Turn up heat. Be sure it is boiling all over before timing for 5 minutes. Add 1 teaspoon soda to syrup mixture. Pour over popcorn. Place in warm oven at 200° for one hour. Stir every 15 minutes.

CRACKER JACKS

Ann Ruf
Pep and Progress

c. brown sugar
sticks margarine
/4 c. white syrup
/2 tsp. soda

1/2 tsp. salt
1/4 tsp. cream of tartar
popped corn

Combine brown sugar, margarine and white syrup. Bring to a boil and boil for 5 minutes. Add soda, salt, cream of tartar and stir. Pour over popped corn. Put in oven for 1 hour, stirring every 15 minutes at 250°.

CANDY MINTS

Ellen Luft
Night Owls

1/4 of an 8 oz. pkg.
  Phila. cream cheese
1/4 tsp. flavoring,
  or to taste

1 2/3 c. powdered sugar
2 drops coloring

Mash cheese; add flavoring and coloring. Mix in sugar finally kneading with hands until like pie dough. Roll into marble size or use molds to make desired shapes. Roll in granulated sugar and unmold on waxed paper to dry. More granulated sugar can be used if desired. Makes 25 roses and 25 leaves. For chocolate, use 3 teaspoons cocoa and 1 1/2 teaspoons vanilla.

MILLION DOLLAR FUDGE

Carole Quint
Pep and Progress

1 2/3 c. evap. milk
1 2/3 c. Marshmallow Creme
4 c. sugar
1 Tbsp. margarine

12 oz. chocolate chips
8 oz. Hershey bar (broken)
1 tsp. vanilla
1 2/3 c. chopped pecans

Combine milk, Marshmallow Creme, sugar and 1 tablespoon margarine in a 4 quart pan. Cook over medium heat, stirring constantly, until mixture comes to a full rolling boil. Boil and stir 7 minutes. Remove from heat and immediately add chocolate chips and Hershey bar, beating until completely melted. Blend in vanilla and pecans. Pour mixture into a buttered 9 inch pan and cool. Makes 4 1/2 pounds.

FUDGECICLES

Ginny Anderson
X-tra X-amples X-tension Club

1 qt. chocolate milk
1 c. sugar

2 egg yolks

Beat egg yolks well. Then add chocolate milk and sugar; stir well. Pour into cups or popcicle freezer containers and freeze. Makes 12. Great for kids and adults.

MICROWAVE POPCORN

Ginny Anderson
X-tra X-amples X-tension Club

4 qts. popped popcorn
1/2 c. oleo
1/4 tsp. soda

1/2 c. brown sugar
1/4 c. dark or white syrup
1/2 tsp. vanilla

Combine oleo, sugar and syrup in a casserole dish. Microwave 4 minutes on High, stopping and stirring every minute. Add soda and vanilla; mix well. Pour over popcorn in just a paper sack. Slash some holes in bag. Microwave 1 1/2 minutes on high; take out and shake well. Microwave 1 minute on high. Take out and shake well, micorwave 30 seconds on High. Shake well. Put in bowl and eat.

NEVER FAIL PEANUT BRITTLE

Betty Ballinger
Hearth and Home

1 c. sugar
1 c. peanuts

1 c. white Karo syrup

Boil until peanuts are suntanned, about 5 minutes. Stir in 1 teaspoon soda. Pour on cookie sheet.

15 MINUTE PEANUT BRITTLE

Patty Ament
Proctor E.H. Club

1 c. sugar
1/2 c. white corn syrup
1 c. raw peanuts
1/8 tsp. salt

1 tsp. butter
1 tsp. vanilla extract
1 tsp. baking soda

In 1 1/2 quart casserole, stir first 4 ingredients together. Microwave at High 4 minutes. Add butter and vanilla to syrup, blending well. Microwave on High 1 or 2 minutes longer. Peanuts will be light brown and syrup very hot. Add baking soda and gently stir until light and foamy. Pour mixture onto lightly greased cookie sheet, or unbuttered non-stick coated cookie sheet. Let cool 15 minutes to 1/2 hour. When cool, break into small pieces. Makes about 1 pound.

PEANUT BRITTLE

Fran Hofmann
Hearth and Home

2 c. white sugar
1 c. white corn syrup

2 c. raw peanuts

Cook until light brown. Remove from fire and add 2 teaspoons soda and 2 teaspoons oleo. Will bubble up. Pour into well greased cookie sheet. Spread out.

"FINGER" JELLO SQUARES

Cleta Carr
Pep and Progress

3 boxes (small) jello,
   any flavor

4 pkgs. Knox gelatin
   (1 box)
4 c. boiling water

Mix all together in large cake pan, 9x13 inches. Cool in refrigerator. Cut into squares. May be eaten with fingers.

PEANUT BRITTLE

Cleta Carr
Pep and Progress

2 c. sugar
1/2 tsp. soda

1 c. salted peanuts

Melt sugar over low heat in heavy skillet. Stir in quickly the soda and peanuts. Pour on buttered cookie sheet to cool. Break in pieces.

NEVER FAIL DIVINITY

Bonnie Bollig
Pep and Progress

2 1/2 c. white sugar
1/2 c. white corn syrup
1/2 c. cold water

1 tsp. vanilla
1 c. coarsely chopped nuts

Mix sugar, corn syrup and water together. Put on to cook until it spins a thread. While this is cooking, beat 2 egg whites until stiff. Pour 1/2 of cooked syrup over beaten egg whites and beat. Put other half syrup on to cook to hard ball stage and add to egg whites. Add 1 teaspoon vanilla and 1 cup coarsely chopped nuts.

FESTIVE FUDGE

Marge Rieke
Pep and Progress

2 c. sugar
2/3 c. Pet evap. skimmed
   milk
12 regular marshmallows
1/2 c. butter or margarine

few grains salt
1-6 oz. pkg. semi-sweet
   chocolate pieces
1 c. chopped nuts
1 tsp. vanilla

Mix in a heavy 2 quart saucepan the sugar, evaporated milk, marshmallows, butter and salt. Cook, stirring constantly over medium heat to a boil (mixture will be bubbling all over top).

Boil and stir 5 minutes longer. Take off heat. Stir in until completely melted, 6 ounces semi-sweet chocolate pieces. Stir in nuts and vanilla. Spread in a buttered 8x8 inch pan. Cool. Cut into 30 pieces.

OATMEAL CARAMELITAS

Marilyn Gerk
X-tra X-amples X-tension Club

1 c. flour
1 c. quick cooking rolled oats
3/4 c. firmly packed brown sugar
1/2 tsp. soda
1/4 tsp. salt

3/4 c. butter or margarine, melted
1 c. semi-sweet chocolate chips
1/2 c. chopped pecans or walnuts
3/4 c. caramel ice cream topping
3 Tbsp. flour

Set oven to 350°. In large mixer bowl, combine 1 cup flour, oats, brown sugar, soda, salt and melted butter. Blend well at low speed to form crumbs. Press half of crumbs into bottom of 11x7 inch pan. Bake at 350° for 10 minutes.

Remove from oven. Sprinkle with chocolate pieces and pecans. Blend caramel topping and 3 tablespoons flour. Pour back and forth over chocolate and pecans to cover. Sprinkle with remaining crumbs. Continue baking 15 to 20 minutes until golden brown. Chill 1 to 2 hours. Cut into 24 bars.

BACK PACK SNACK

Patty Craven
Creative Homemakers

3 c. granola cereal
1/2 c. peanuts
1/2 c. candy coated chocolate pieces or semi-sweet chocolate chips

1/2 c. seedless raisins
1/2 c. chopped dried apricots
1/2 c. chopped dates

In large bowl, combine all ingredients. Store covered in air tight container. Makes 5 1/2 cups.

CHERRY MASH

Marilyn Crane
Creative Homemakers

c. sugar
/3 c. evap. milk
2 large marshmallows

1/2 c. butter or oleo
dash of salt

Mix the above and boil 5 minutes. Add a 6 ounce package

227   (Cont.)

of cherry chips and 1 teaspoon vanilla. Stir until smooth, then pour into buttered 9x12 inch pan. Cool. Melt in a double boiler, a 12 ounce package milk chocolate chips, 3/4 cup peanut butter and add a package of chopped Spanish peanuts. Pour over the above mixture and cool.

PEANUT BUTTER FUDGE

Debbie Garcia
Creative Homemakers

1/2 c. honey
1/2 c. peanut butter

1 c. dry instant milk

Mix cold. Place in buttered pan. Chill. Cut.

JIM READ'S CORN COB JELLY

Jim Read
Logan County Extension Agent/Director
1963 – 1983

10 to 12 bright red field
  corn cobs (dry)
4 to 5 pts. water

1 pkg. pectin
3 c. sugar

Break cobs into 3 to 4 inch sections. Boil gently in the water about 30 minutes. Remove from heat and strain 3 cups of the red liquid into a pan through a cloth. Add pectin. Heat to a hard boil. Add sugar; stir until dissolved. Bring to rolling boil for 1 1/2 minutes. Remove from fire and skim. Pour into jars. Jelly will have an attractive reddish color and looks like wild apple jelly. Makes 3 pints.

TOMATO JUICE

Connie Lechman
Proctor E.H. Club

8 qts. tomatoes
2 Tbsp. salt
3/4 tsp. celery salt

1 med. onion
2 Tbsp. vinegar
2 Tbsp. sugar

Peel and slice the 8 quarts of tomatoes. Put in a large kettle and add one sliced medium onion. Cook until tender; strain. Add the remaining ingredients; mix well and boil. Pour hot into hot jars leaving 1/4 inch head space. Put on lids and process pints 10 minutes, quarts 15 minutes in boiling water bath.

BLUE PLUM CATCHUP
(Good Housekeeping)

Mrs. Lorin Lindstrom
Kelly Woman's Improvement Club

6 lbs. purple plums,
  halved and pitted
1 c. plus 2 Tbsp. cider
  vinegar
2 1/2 tsp. salt
1 small cinnamon stick

2 large cooking apples, diced
2 1/2 c. brown sugar
1/2 tsp. mace

Cook the plums and diced apples in vinegar. Mixture may be blended or sieved or left chunky to be used as a relish. Add sugar, salt and spices. Boil to desired consistency and can. Makes 3 pints.

GARDENERIA

Dorothy A. Harms
Home Hustlers

mixture of your choice of
  vegetables, such as: carrots,
  celery, peppers, cauliflower,
  onions

1 c. canning salt
1 gal. water
2 qts. white vinegar
1 qt. water

Cut vegetables into strips or slices. Place into brine made with canning salt and water; soak overnight.

Drain and pack into jars. Pour vinegar-water mixture over vegetables in jars. Release air bubbles in jar with knife. Seal tightly. Place into canner and cover with water. Process 10 minutes after water has come to a boil.

Write your extra recipes here:

Write your extra recipes here:

BEVERAGES
MISCELLANEOUS

EVERYDAY USE WITH THE METRIC SYSTEM

FOOD

Milk	1 liter	1.06 quarts
Butter	1 kilogram	2.2 pounds
Lemon juice	1 gram	0.035 ounces
Flour	1 liter	4.23 cups
Sugar	1 milliliter	0.067 tablespoons
Salt	1 milliliter	0.203 teaspoons
Water	1 liter	2.1 pints

DISTANCE

1 centimeter	0.4 inches
1 meter	3.3 feet
1 meter	1.1 yards
1 kilometer	0.6 mile

AREA

1 sq. centimeter	0.16 sq. inch
1 sq. meter	1.2 sq. yards
1 sq. kilometer	0.4 sq. mile
1 hectare	2.5 acres

TEMPERATURE

0 degree Celsius	32 degrees Fahrenheit
37 degrees Celsius	98.6 degrees Fahrenheit
100 degrees Celsius	212 degrees Fahrenheit

CLOTHING

		METRIC Size	U.S. Size
Women			
	Dresses	38	10
		40	12
		42	14
		44	16
	Stockings	2	9
		4	10
		6	11
	Shoes	35	5
		36	6
		38	7
Men			
	Shirts	35	14
		37	15
		40	16
	Socks	25.5	10
		28	11
		29.25	11 ½
	Shoes	41	8
		44	10
		46	12

Measuring cups will most likely show both ounces and grams or cups (and their fractions) and milliliters:

1 cup	=	250 milliliters (ml)
1/4 cup	=	62-1/2 ml
1 teaspoon	=	5 ml
1 tablespoon	=	15 ml
1 pint	=	0.47 liter (l)
1 quart	=	0.95 l
1 gallon	=	3.8 l
1 liter	=	2.1 pint
1 liter	=	1.06 quart
1 liter	=	0.26 gallon

BEVERAGES, MISCELLANEOUS

WATERMELON PUNCH
Eva Korrey
Rainbows of Happiness

1 can orange juice, frozen	ginger ale
1 can Hawaiian Punch	7-Up
1 can pink lemonade	vodka
1 can pineapple juice	water

Mix all juices together. Add ginger ale, 7-Up, vodka and water to taste. Use hollowed out melon for punch bowl.

SPICED TEA
Jackie Waitley
Proctor

2 c. Tang	2-6 oz. pkgs. lemonade mix
3/4 c. instant tea	1 tsp. ground cloves (opt.)
1 tsp. cinnamon	

Combine ingredients and mix well. Store in tight container and use 2 teaspoons in 1 cup hot water to serve.

HOT SPICED TEA
Hazel Pyle
Proctor E.H. Club

2 c. Tang	2 c. instant tea
2 c. sugar	1 pkg. (6 oz.) instant lemonade
1 tsp. cinnamon	1 tsp. cloves

Mix well and store in a tight plastic container.
To serve, mix 2 teaspoons with a cup of boiling water. May be steeped in a teapot for a few minutes using the same measurements.

HOT SPICED TEA
Phyllis Jones
Night Owls

1 lb. 2 oz. Tang or Start	1/2 c. dry instant tea
1 1/2 oz. dry lemonade	1 1/2 c. sugar
2 tsp. cinnamon	1 tsp. ground cloves

Mix all ingredients together. Store in a covered container. Place 2 or 3 teaspoons mix in a cup and add hot water.

ORANGE JULIUS

Carol Lambrecht
Rainbows of Happiness

1/2 c. milk
1/4 c. sugar
1/4 tsp. vanilla

1/3 of a 6 oz. can frozen orange
  juice
6 ice cubes

Blend the above ingredients in a blender until smooth.

ORANGE JULIUS

Debby Fehringer
Hearth and Home

1/2 can of 12 oz. frozen
  orange juice
1/2 c. milk
1/2 c. water

1/2 c. sugar
1/2 tsp. vanilla
8 ice cubes

Combine everything together except the cubes; mix well.
Then add ice cubes one at a time.

PUNCH

Doris Harms
Night Owls

6 pkgs. Kool Aid
  (strawberry)
1-6 oz. can frozen orange
  juice
1-46 oz. can pineapple juice
1 qt. 7-Up

4 1/2 c. sugar
1-6 oz. can frozen lemonade
7 qts. cold water

Pour 1 quart boiling water over the Kool Aid and sugar (be
sure they are dissolved). Add orange juice, lemonade, pineapple
juice and 7 quarts cold water. Just before serving, add 1 quart
7-Up and ice. Makes a clear, bright red punch, a large batch.

ORANGE JULIUS

Carol Atkin
Home Hustlers

1 small can frozen orange
  juice
1/3 c. sugar

1 tsp. vanilla
1 egg
1 c. milk

Combine all ingredients in blender with crushed ice. Blend
and serve.

HOT CRANBERRY DRINK

Ginny Anderson
X-tra X-amples X-tension Club

3 c. pineapple juice
1 1/2 c. water
1 tsp. whole cloves
dash of salt

3 c. cranberry juice
1/4 c. brown sugar
1 stick cinnamon (broken up)

Put the juices and water in a coffee pot. Put the sugar and spices in the coffee strainer. Let your coffee pot perk before serving.

ORANGE MILK PUNCH

Sandy Schneider
Hearth and Home

1/2 pt. vanilla ice cream
1-6 oz. orange juice concentrate

2 c. milk
1 c. ice

Blend in electric blender until smooth. Makes four 8 ounce servings.

COLORFUL, CHANGEABLE PUNCH
Serves 50

Marge Rieke
Pep and Progress

3-3 oz. pkgs. jello
  (any flavor)
6 c. boiling water
1-6 oz. can frozen lemonade
1-6 oz. can frozen orange
    juice

1 large can pineapple
  juice (46 oz.)
1 1/2 c. sugar
1 gal. water
2-28 oz. bottles ginger ale

Dissolve jello in hot water. Add other ingredients except ginger ale. Freeze. Take out of freezer and add ginger ale. Another freeze ahead recipe which requires no ice.

SLUSH

Mrs. Walter Browner
Sterling Homemakers

2 bananas, mashed
1 c. sugar
grated rind of 1 orange
    or lemon
1 Tbsp. lemon juice

1 pt. ginger ale or 7-Up
1-6 oz. can concentrated frozen
  orange juice
1-9 oz. can crushed pineapple
1 pt. crushed strawberries

Combine all ingredients and freeze. Chop finely when frozen. Refreeze. Serve in small cups and let it become slushy to serve. Good for breakfast in summer. Serves 12.

HOT PUNCH

Florence Lindstrom
Kelly Woman's Improvement Club

1 qt. apple cider
1 small can frozen orange
 juice plus water to
 reconstitute
1/3 c. red hots candy

1/2 c. lemon juice
1 can Hawaiian Punch, frozen
5 cans water

Combine ingredients. Heat, stirring until red hots are dissolved.

PLAY DOUGH

Jeri Breidenbach
Hearth and Home

2 c. flour
1 c. water

1 c. salt

May add food coloring. Mix all together well. Store in tight container.

Write your extra recipes here:

Basic Kitchen Information

Expression of Appreciation

For their help and cooperation in providing this indexed, up-to-date, authentic information of basic value to our book, our organization, the sponsors and compilers, wish to thank the home economists who worked on it, and the

National Live Stock and Meat Board.

U.S. Department of Agriculture.

Armour and Co.

Wheat Flour Institute.

Standard Kitchen Cover Scene If Used - Kitchens by Kleweno

THUMB INDEX

EQUIVALENTS, WEIGHTS and MEASURES, SUBSTITUTE INGREDIENTS

EVERYDAY HERB GUIDE

WHAT SHALL WE HAVE FOR DINNER?

TIME TABLE FOR MEAT COOKERY

SEA FOOD COOKERY, WAYS TO USE LEFTOVERS

QUANTITIES FOR 100 PEOPLE, SANDWICHES -- QUANTITY and FAMILY SIZE RECIPES

6 STEPS TO THE PERFECT PIE

DIET INFORMATION AND MENUS

FREEZING PREPARED FOODS and MAXIMUM HOME STORAGE FOR FROZEN FOOD

METRIC SYSTEM INFORMATION

STAIN CHART, FIRST AID and MISCELLANEOUS INFORMATION

EQUIVALENTS

3 tsps.	1 tbsp.
4 tbsps.	¼ cup
5⅓ tbsps.	⅓ cup
8 tbsps.	½ cup
10⅔ tbsps.	⅔ cup
12 tbsps.	¾ cup
16 tbsps.	1 cup
½ cup	1 gill
2 cups	1 pt.
4 cups	1 qt.
4 qts.	1 gal.
8 qts.	1 peck
4 pecks	1 bu.
16 ozs.	1 lb.
32 ozs.	1 qt.
8 ozs. liquid	1 cup
1 oz. liquid	2 tbsps.

(For liquid and dry measurements use standard measuring spoons and cups. All measurements are level.)

WEIGHTS AND MEASURES

Baking powder
1 cup = 5 ½ ozs.

Cheese, American
1 lb. = 2⅔ cups cubed

Cocoa
1 lb. = 4 cups ground

Coffee
1 lb. = 5 cups ground

Corn meal
1 lb. = 3 cups

Cornstarch
1 lb. = 3 cups

Cracker crumbs
23 soda crackers = 1 cup
15 graham crackers = 1 cup

Eggs
1 egg = 4 tbsps. liquid
4 to 5 whole = 1 cup
7 to 9 whites = 1 cup
12 to 14 yolks = 1 cup

Flour
1 lb. all-purpose = 4 cups
1 lb. cake = 4 ½ cups
1 lb. graham = 3 ½ cups

Lemons, juice
1 medium = 2 to 3 tbsps.
5 to 8 medium = 1 cup

Lemons, rind
1 lemon = 1 tbsp. grated

Oranges, juice
1 medium = 2 to 3 tbsps.
3 to 4 medium = 1 cup

Oranges, rind
1 = 2 tbsps. grated

Gelatin
3 ¼ oz. pkg. flavored = ½ cup
¼ oz. pkg. unflavored = 1 tbsp.

Shortening or Butter
1 lb. = 2 cups

Sugar
1 lb. brown = 2 ½ cups
1 lb. cube = 96 to 160 cubes
1 lb. granulated = 2 cups
1 lb. powdered = 3 ½ cups

One ingredient for another

For these	You may use these
1 whole egg, for thickening or baking	2 egg yolks. Or 2 tablespoons dried whole egg plus 2½ tablespoons water.
1 cup butter or margarine for shortening	⅞ cup lard, or rendered fat, with ½ teaspoon salt. Or 1 cup hydrogenated fat (cooking fat sold under brand name) with ½ teaspoon salt.
1 square (ounce) chocolate	3 or 4 tablespoons cocoa plus ½ tablespoon fat.
1 teaspoon double-acting baking powder	1½ teaspoons phosphate baking powder. Or 2 teaspoons tartrate baking powder.
Sweet milk and baking powder, for baking	Equal amount of sour milk plus ½ teaspoon soda per cup. (Each half teaspoon soda with 1 cup sour milk takes the place of 2 teaspoons baking powder and 1 cup sweet milk.)
1 cup sour milk, for baking	1 cup sweet milk mixed with one of the following: 1 tablespoon vinegar. Or 1 tablespoon lemon juice. Or 1¾ teaspoons cream of tartar.
1 cup whole milk	½ cup evaporated milk plus ½ cup water. Or 4 tablespoons dry whole milk plus 1 cup water. Or 4 tablespoons nonfat dry milk plus 2 teaspoons table fat and 1 cup water.
1 cup skim milk	4 tablespoons nonfat dry milk plus 1 cup water.
1 tablespoon flour, for thickening	½ tablespoon cornstarch, potato starch, rice starch, or arrowroot starch. Or 1 tablespoon granulated tapioca.
1 cup cake flour, for baking	⅞ cup all-purpose flour.
1 cup all-purpose flour, for baking breads	Up to ½ cup bran, whole-wheat flour, or corn meal plus enough all-purpose flour to fill cup.

EVERYDAY HERB GUIDE

FOUND IN Yugoslavia, Italy, Greece. Spain.

IT IS shrub of mint family, with pleasant aromatic odor and warm, slightly bitter taste.

TASTES GOOD WITH stuffings; pork roasts; sausages; poultry and hamburgers.

AVAILABLE as leaf; rubbed; powdered.

FOUND IN India, France, Argentina.

IT IS dried fruit of herb in parsley family; consists of tiny yellowish-brown seeds with licorice flavor.

TASTES GOOD WITH soups; fish dishes; sauces; sweet pickles; bread and rolls.

AVAILABLE whole; ground.

FOUND IN France, United States.

IT IS leaf and flower-top of plant; has pungent flavor resembling licorice.

TASTES GOOD WITH fish sauces; egg and cheese dishes; green salads; pickles; vinegar; chicken; tomatoes; sauces for meats and vegetables.

AVAILABLE whole; ground.

FOUND IN France, Spain.

IT IS member of mint family, with short brown leaves; has warm, aromatic odor, pungent flavor.

TASTES GOOD WITH soups; clam chowders; stuffings; beef, lamb, veal, and pork dishes; oysters; eggs; cheese; bean and vegetable soups; fish.

AVAILABLE whole; powdered.

FOUND IN United States, Europe,

IT IS tiny green leaf growing in clusters on low plant; mild, slightly tangy flavor.

TASTES GOOD WITH meat; vegetables; soups; eggs; cheese.

AVAILABLE whole; ground; as flakes.

FOUND IN France, Spain.

IT IS member of mint family; has aromatic odor, pungent flavor.

TASTES GOOD WITH eggs; meat; salads; chicken; soups; stuffings.

AVAILABLE whole; ground.

FOUND IN India, United States.

IT IS fruit of parsley family; has aromatic odor with delicate caraway flavor.

TASTES GOOD WITH fish dishes; cream and cottage cheese; potatoes; fish and vegetable salads; pickles; tomatoes.

AVAILABLE whole; ground.

EVERYDAY HERB GUIDE

FOUND IN India, Western Europe, United States.

IT IS member of mint family with leaves 1½" long; has mild aromatic odor; warm, sweet flavor with slight licorice taste.

TASTES GOOD WITH tomatoes; peas; squash; lamb; fish; eggs; tossed salad; cheese; duck; potatoes.
AVAILABLE whole; ground.

FOUND IN Turkey, Yugoslavia, Portugal, Greece.

IT IS green, aromatic leaf of laurel tree; has pungent flavor.

TASTES GOOD WITH vegetable and fish soups; tomato sauces and juice; poached fish; meat stews.
AVAILABLE as whole leaf.

FOUND IN France, United States.

IT IS member of parsley family with feathery leaves; has mild, delicate flavor.

TASTES GOOD WITH egg and cheese dishes; chicken; peas; spinach; green salads; cream soups.
AVAILABLE whole; ground.

FOUND IN Mexico, Italy, Chile, France.

IT IS member of mint family, light-green in color, with strong, aromatic odor and pleasantly bitter taste.

TASTES GOOD WITH tomato sauces; pork and veal dishes; pizza; vegetable and fish salads; chili.
AVAILABLE whole; ground.

FOUND IN all parts of the world.

IT IS dried leaf of peppermint or spearmint plant, with strong, sweet odor and tangy, cool taste.

TASTES GOOD WITH jellies; fruit juices; candies; frosting; cakes; pies; lamb; ice cream; potatoes; peas; and chocolate desserts.
AVAILABLE whole (dried); flaked; as fresh sprigs.

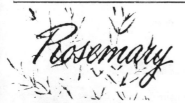

FOUND IN France, Spain, Portugal.
IT IS leaf of evergreen shrub, with appearance of curved pine needle; has aromatic odor with slightly piny taste.

TASTES GOOD WITH poultry stuffing; veal and lamb roasts; potatoes; cauliflower; fish; duck.
AVAILABLE whole; ground.

FOUND IN France, Germany, Chile.

IT IS member of mint family, with aromatic odor.

TASTES GOOD WITH fish chowders; vegetable soups; eggs; cheese dishes; stews; roast chicken; beef; lamb; pork; stuffings.
AVAILABLE whole; ground.

What Shall We Have For Dinner??
WHAT TO SERVE WITH *Meats*

ROAST PORK
Brown Potatoes, Applesauce or Fruit Salad
Sweet Potatoes, Sauerkraut
Mashed Potatoes, Celery or Apple Salad

PORK CHOPS
Scalloped Potatoes, Fried Apple Rings
Mashed Potatoes, Cabbage Salad

BAKED HAM
Sweet Potatoes, Spinach
Rice, Fried Pineapple Rings
Parsley Potatoes, Asparagus

COLD HAM
Baked Beans, Relish, Egg Rolls
Potato Salad, Dill Pickles

BACON
Corn Fritters, Maple Syrup

HAM STEAK
Buttered Rice, Glazed Pineapple
Fried Eggs, Hash Brown Potatoes
Hominy, Corn Muffins, Fried Bananas

SAUSAGE
Fried Apples, Corn Bread
Mashed Potatoes, Pickled Peaches

VEAL CUTLET
Baked Potato, Tossed Salad

LAMB CHOPS
Buttered Parsley Potatoes, Succotash
Browned Potatoes, Spinach, Peas

LAMB STEW
Dumplings, Green Salad

ROAST LAMB
Mashed Potatoes, Currant Jelly

LIVER
Bacon, Corn Bread

HAMBURGER
Toasted Buns, Sweet Onion Rings
Potato Salad, Carrots

CORN BEEF HASH
Poached Eggs, Green Salad

MEAT LOAF
Baked Potato, Canned Tomatoes
French Fried Potatoes, Asparagus

BOILED TONGUE
Buttered Noodles, Spinach

FRANKFURTER
Sauerkraut, Baked Beans

CHIPPED BEEF
Baked Potato, Green Salad

WHAT TO SERVE WITH *Chicken*

ROAST CHICKEN
Candied Sweet Potatoes, Cauliflower

FRIED CHICKEN
Lima Beans, Mashed Potatoes, Corn on the Cob and Biscuits

CHICKEN FRICASSEE
Dumplings, Corn on the Cob

CHICKEN PIE
Green Peas, Tossed Salad

CHICKEN SALAD
Potato Chips, Celery, Pickles, and Peas

What Shall We Have For Dinner??
WHAT TO SERVE WITH Fish

TROUT	Potatoes Diced in Cream, Asparagus, Pickle
BAKED SNAPPER	Broccoli with Hollandaise Sauce, Mashed Potatoes, Tossed Salad
LOBSTER	Steamed Clams, Baked Potato
LOBSTER NEWBURG	French Fried Onions, Watermelon Pickle
FRENCH FRIED SHRIMP	Mixed Vegetable, Tomato and Onion Salad
BROILED FILLETS	Baked Potatoes, Scalloped Tomatoes
CODFISH CAKES	Baked Beans, Bacon, Green Salad
CREAMED SALT COD	Boiled Potatoes, Cole Slaw, Toast and Green Salad
FILET OF SOLE	Cole Slaw or Dill Pickles, Tartar Sauce
BAKED SALMON	Baked Potato, Tossed Salad, Greens
BROILED SALMON	Hollandaise Sauce, Mashed Potatoes, Peas
BROILED HALIBUT	Broccoli, Corn Fried in Butter
FRIED FISH	French Fried Potatoes, Tossed Salad
SCALLOPED OYSTERS	Hashed Brown Potatoes, Broccoli

WHAT TO SERVE WITH Cheese or Eggs

CHEESE OMELET	Hash-brown Potatoes, Stewed Tomatoes
CHEESE SOUFFLE	Peas, Green Salad
SCRAMBLED EGGS	French Fried Potatoes, String Beans, Toast
SCRAMBLED EGGS WITH CUT—UP HAM	Rye or Pumpernickel Bread, Tossed Green Salad
WELSH RAREBIT	Dill Pickle or Stuffed Celery, Fruit Salad

WHAT TO SERVE WITH Miscellaneous

CONSOMME	French Omelet, Asparagus Tips
TOMATO SOUP	Chicken Salad or Tunafish Sandwich
CLUB SANDWICH	Celery, Potato Chips,
TOASTED HAM AND CHEESE SANDWICH	Tossed Salad, Potato Chips
WAFFLES	Canadian Bacon, Maple Syrup, Fruit Salad
CHOW MEIN	Pickled Peaches, Buttered Rice
BAKED MACARONI AND CHEESE	Pea Soup, Stewed Tomatoes, Lettuce Salad

Roasting

CUT	WEIGHT RANGE	COOKING TEMP.	INTERNAL MEAT TEMP.	APPROXIMATE TIME
BEEF				
Standing Ribs (3)	6-8 lbs.	325° F.		
Rare			140° F.	16-18 min. per lb.
Medium			160° F.	20-22 min. per lb.
Well Done			170° F.	25-30 min. per lb.
Rolled Rib	5-7 lbs.	325° F.		Add 10-12 min. per lb. to above time
Rump-boneless	5-7 lbs.	325° F.	170° F.	30 min. per lb.
VEAL				
Leg (center cut)	7-8 lbs.	325° F.	170° F.	25 min. per lb.
Loin	4½-5 lbs.	325° F.	170° F.	30-35 min. per lb.
Rack 4-6 ribs	2½-3 lbs.	325° F.	170° F.	30-35 min. per lb.
Shoulder-bone-in	6-7 lbs.	325° F.	170° F.	25 min. per lb.
Shoulder Boneless Roll	5-6 lbs.	325° F.	170° F.	35-40 min. per lb.
LAMB				
Leg	6-7 lbs.	325° F.	175-180° F.	30-35 min. per lb.
Shoulder Bone-in	5-7 lbs.	325° F.	175-180° F.	30-35 min. per lb.
Shoulder Boneless Roll	4-6 lbs.	325° F.	175-180° F.	40-45 min. per lb.
FRESH PORK				
Loin	4-5 lbs.	350° F.	185° F.	30-35 min. per lb.
Cushion Shoulder	4-6 lbs.	350° F.	185° F.	35-40 min. per lb.
Shoulder Boned & Rolled	4-6 lbs.	350° F.	185° F.	40-45 min. per lb.
Shoulder Butt	4-6 lbs.	350° F.	185° F.	45-50 min. per lb.
Fresh Ham	10-14 lbs.	350° F.	185° F.	30-35 min. per lb.
Spare Ribs (1 side)	1½-2½ lbs.	350° F.	185° F.	1-1½ hrs. total
SMOKED PORK				
Ham—whole	10-12 lbs.	325° F.	150-155° F.	18-20 min. per lb.
	14-16 lbs.	325° F.	150-155° F.	16-18 min. per lb.
Ham-half	6-8 lbs.	325° F.	150-155° F.	25-27 min. per lb.
Ham—2 inch slice	2½-3 lbs.	325° F.	170° F.	1½ hrs. total
Picnic	5-8 lbs.	325° F.	170° F.	33-35 min. per lb.
POULTRY				
Chickens stuffed weight	4-5 lbs.	325° F.	185° F.	35-40 min. per lb.
Chickens over 5 lbs.		325° F.	185° F.	20-25 min. per lb.
Turkeys stuffed weight	6-10 lbs.	325° F.	185° F.	20-25 min. per lb.
Turkey	10-16 lbs.	325° F.	185° F.	18-20 min. per lb.
Turkey	18-25 lb	325° F.	185° F.	15-18 min. per lb.

Geese—Same as turkey of similar weight.
Duck—Same as heavy chicken of similar weight.

Braising

CUT	WEIGHT RANGE	APPROXIMATE TIME
Beef Pot Roast, Chuck, Rump or Heel of Round	3-5 lbs.	Brown then simmer 3½-4 hours
Swiss Steak (round) 1 in. thick	2 lbs.	Brown then simmer 1½-2 hours
Flank Steak	1½-2 lbs.	Brown then simmer 1½ hours
Beef Short Ribs	2-2½ lbs.	Brown then simmer 2-2½ hours
Ox Tails	1-1½ lbs.	Brown then simmer 3-4 hours
Rolled Lamb Shoulder Pot Roast	3-5 lbs.	Brown then simmer 2-2½ hours
Lamb Shoulder Chops	4-5 oz. each	Brown then simmer 35-40 min.
Lamb Neck Slices	½ lb. each	Brown then simmer 1-1½ hours
Lamb Shanks	1 lb. each	Brown then simmer 1½ hours
Pork Rib or Loin Chops	4-5 oz. each (¾-1 inch)	Brown then simmer 35-40 min.
Pork Shoulder Steaks	5-6 oz. each	Brown then simmer 35-40 min.
Veal Rolled Shoulder Pot Roast	4-5½ lbs.	Brown then simmer 2-2½ hours
Cutlets or Round	2 lbs.	Brown then simmer 45-50 min.
Loin or Rib Chops	3-5 oz. each	Brown then simmer 45-50 min.

TIME TABLE FOR MEAT COOKERY

Broiling

CUT	THICKNESS	WEIGHT RANGE	APPROXIMATE TOTAL TIME (MINUTES)		
			RARE	MEDIUM	WELL DONE
BEEF					
Rib Steak	1 inch	1-1½ lb.	8-10	12-14	18-20
Club Steak	1 inch	1-1½ lb.	8-10	12-14	18-20
Porterhouse	1 inch	1½-2 lbs.	10-12	14-16	20-25
	1½ inch	2½-3 lbs.	14-16	18-20	25-30
	2 inch	3-3½ lbs.	20-25	30-35	40-45
Sirloin	1 inch	2½-3½ lbs.	10-12	14-16	20-25
	1½ inch	3½-4½ lbs.	14-16	18-20	25-30
	2 inch	5-5½ lbs.	20-25	30-35	40-45
Ground Beef Patties					
	¾ inch	4 oz. each	8	12	15
Tenderloin	1 inch		8-10	12-14	18-20
LAMB					
Rib or Loin					
Chops (1 rib)	¾ inch	2-3 oz. each	—	—	14-15
Double Rib	1½ inch	4-5 oz. each			22-25
Lamb Shoulder					
Chops	¾ inch	3-4 oz. each	—	—	14-15
	1½ inch	5-6 oz. each	—	—	22-25
Lamb Patties	¾ inch	4 oz. each	—	—	14-15
HAM, BACON & SAUSAGE					
Ham Slices	½ inch	9-12 oz. each	—	—	10-12
	¾ inch	1-1¼ lb.	—	—	13-14
	1 inch	1¼-1¾ lbs.	—	—	18-20
Bacon					4-5
Pork Sausage Links		12-16 to the lb.	—	—	12-15
Broiling Chickens (drawn) halves		1-1½ lbs.	—	—	30-35

Stewing

CUT	WEIGHT RANGE	APPROXIMATE TIME
Beef—1-1½ inch cubes from neck, chuck, plate or heel of round	2 lbs.	2½-3 hours
Veal or Lamb 1-1½ inch cubes from shoulder or breast	2 lbs.	1½-2 hours
Chicken	3½-4 lbs.	2-2½ hours

Simmering in Water

CUT	WEIGHT RANGE	APPROXIMATE TIME
Fresh Beef Brisket or Plate	8 lbs.	4-5 hours total
Corned Beef Brisket half or whole	4-8 lbs.	4-6 hours total
Cross Cut Shanks of Beef	4 lbs.	3-4 hours total
Fresh or Smoked Beef Tongue	3-4 lbs.	3-4 hours total
Pork Hocks	3/4 lbs.	3 hours total
Whole Ham	12-16 lbs.	18-20 min. per lb.
Ham Shanks	5-6 lbs.	25-30 min. per lb.
Smoked Pork Butt (boneless)	2-3 lbs.	40 min. per lb.
Picnic	7-8 lbs.	35-40 min. per lb.
Chicken	3½-4 lbs.	2-2½ hours total

Sea Food COOKERY

	BROILED	BAKED	BOILED STEAMED	FRIED SAUTED	MONTHS IN SEASON
BARRACUDA	2	1		3	VARIES
BLUEFISH	2	1		3	ALL YEAR
BONITO	2	1		3	ALL YEAR
BULLHEADS		2	1	3	APRIL – OCT.
BUTTERFISH	2	3		1	APRIL – DEC.
CARP	2	1		3	ALL YEAR
CATFISH			2	1	ALL YEAR
COD	1	2	3		ALL YEAR
CROAKER	2	3		1	FEB. – NOV.
EELS		2	3	1	ALL YEAR
FLOUNDER	2	3		1	ALL YEAR
GROUPER		1			NOV. – APRIL
HADDOCK	1	2	3		ALL YEAR
HALIBUT	1	2	3		ALL YEAR
HERRING	1	3		2	ALL YEAR
KINGFISH	1	2	3		JAN. – JUNE
LAKE TROUT	3	1		2	APRIL – NOV.
MACKEREL	1	2	3		ALL YEAR
MULLET	1	2		3	JUNE – OCT.
PERCH	2	3		1	ALL YEAR
PIKE	3	2		1	ALL YEAR
PICKEREL	3	2		1	ALL YEAR
POMPANO	1	2		3	ALL YEAR
PORGIES	2	3		1	ALL YEAR
RED SNAPPER		1	2		ALL YEAR
SALMON	2	1	3		ALL YEAR
SEA BASS	1	3		2	ALL YEAR
SEA TROUT	1	3		2	NOV. – MAY
SHAD	2	1		3	DEC. – JUNE
SHEEPSHEAD	3	2		1	ALL YEAR
SMELTS	2	3		1	SEPT. – MAY
SNAPPERS	2	1	3		ALL YEAR
SOLE	2	3		1	ALL YEAR
SPAN. MACKEREL	1	2		3	NOV. – APRIL
STRIPED BASS			1		ALL YEAR
STURGEON	2	1	3		APRIL – JAN.
SUNFISH	2			1	APRIL – OCT.
SWORDFISH	1	2	3		VARIES
TAUTOG	1	2		3	ALL YEAR
TROUT	2	3		1	APRIL – NOV.
TUNA	2	1	3		ALL YEAR
WEAKFISH	1	2		3	APRIL – NOV.
WHITING			1		MAY – DEC.
WHITEFISH	2	1		3	APRIL – DEC.

HOW TO COOK — 1 EXCELLENT   2 GOOD   3 FAIR

Ways to use left-overs

If it's good food, don't throw it away. Little left-overs, or big ones, fit into many dishes. A switch in recipes here or a novel dessert there—and your left-overs are put to work in interesting ways. Egg yolks can substitute for whole eggs, for example. If bread is a bit dry, then it's just right for french toast. Other left-overs have a way of adding food value or a fresh new touch—such as fruit in muffins or vegetables in omelet.

Listed below are some of the dishes in which left-overs may be used.

Cooked snap beans, lima beans, corn, peas, carrots, *in*

- Meat and vegetable pie
- Soup
- Stew
- Stuffed peppers
- Stuffed tomatoes
- Vegetables in cheese sauce

Cooked leafy vegetables, chopped, *in*

- Creamed vegetables
- Soup
- Meat loaf
- Meat patties
- Omelet
- Souffle

Cooked or canned fruits, *in*

- Fruit cup
- Fruit sauces
- Jellied fruit
- Quick breads
- Shortcake
- Upside-down cake
- Yeast breads

Cooked meats, poultry, fish, *in*

- Casserole dishes
- Hash
- Meat patties
- Meat pies
- Salads
- Sandwiches
- Stuffed vegetables

Cooked wheat, oat, or corn cereals, *in*

- Fried cereal
- Meat loaf or patties
- Sweet puddings

Cooked rice, noodles, macaroni, spaghetti, *in*

- Casseroles
- Meat or cheese loaf
- Timbales

Bread

- Slices, *for*
  - French toast
- Dry crumbs, *in*
  - Brown betty
  - Croquettes
  - Fried chops
- Soft crumbs, *in*
  - Meat loaf
  - Stuffings

Cake or cookies, *in*

- Brown betty
- Ice-box cake
- Toasted, with sweet topping, for dessert

Egg yolks, *in*

- Cakes
- Cornstarch pudding
- Custard or sauce
- Pie filling
- Salad dressing
- Scrambled eggs

Egg whites, *in*

- Custard
- Fruit whip
- Meringue
- Souffles

Hard-cooked egg or yolk, *in*

- Casserole dishes
- Garnish
- Salads
- Sandwiches

Sour cream, *in*

- Cakes, cookies
- Dessert sauce
- Meat stews
- Pie filling
- Salad dressing
- Sauce for vegetables

Sour milk, *in*

- Cakes, cookies
- Quick breads

Cooked potatoes, *in*

- Croquettes
- Fried or creamed potatoes
- Meat-pie crust
- Potatoes in cheese sauce
- Stew or chowder

Quantities to Serve 100 People

COFFEE	— 3 LBS.
LOAF SUGAR	— 3 LBS.
CREAM	— 3 QUARTS
WHIPPING CREAM	— 4 PTS.
MILK	— 6 GALLONS
FRUIT COCKTAIL	— 2 1/2 GALLONS
FRUIT JUICE	— 4 NO. 10 CANS (26 LBS.)
TOMATO JUICE	— 4 NO. 10 CANS (26 LBS.)
SOUP	— 5 GALLONS
OYSTERS	— 18 QUARTS
WEINERS	— 25 LBS.
MEAT LOAF	— 24 LBS.
HAM	— 40 LBS.
BEEF	— 40 LBS.
ROAST PORK	— 40 LBS.
HAMBURGER	— 30—36 LBS.
CHICKEN FOR CHICKEN PIE	— 40 LBS.
POTATOES	— 35 LBS.
SCALLOPED POTATOES	— 5 GALLON
VEGETABLES	— 4 NO.10 CANS (26 LBS.)
VEGETABLES	— 4 NO.10 CANS (26 LBS.)
BAKED BEANS	— 5 GALLON
BEETS	— 30 LBS.
CAULIFLOWER	— 18 LBS.
CABBAGE FOR SLAW	— 20 LBS.
CARROTS	— 33 LBS.
BREAD	— 10 LOAVES
ROLLS	— 200
BUTTER	— 3 LBS.
POTATO SALAD	— 12 QUARTS
FRUIT SALAD	— 20 QUARTS
VEGETABLE SALAD	— 20 QUARTS
LETTUCE	— 20 HEADS
SALAD DRESSING	— 3 QUARTS
PIES	— 18
CAKES	— 8
ICE CREAM	— 4 GALLONS
CHEESE	— 3 LBS.
OLIVES	— 1 3/4 LBS.
PICKLES	— 2 QUARTS
NUTS	— 3 LBS. SORTED

To serve 50 people, divide by 2
To serve 25 people, divide by 4

how to make
26
new fillings

fillings

**make the
sandwich**

QUANTITY
AND
FAMILY SIZE
RECIPES

for lunch boxes

for outdoor eating

HAWAIIAN HAM SANDWICH		6 SERVINGS	24 SERVINGS
Mix Well	Ground ham	I cup	I quart
	Drained crushed pineapple	½ cup	2 cups (No. 2 can)
	Brown sugar	I tablespoon	¼ cup
	Cloves	⅛ teaspoon	½ teaspoon

O'HARA'S SANDWICH			
Mix Well	Corned beef, chopped	I cup	I quart
	Chopped onion	¼ cup	I cup
	Chopped Kosher pickle	¼ cup	I cup
	Tomato juice	¼ cup	I cup

TANGY TONGUE SANDWICH			
Mix Well	Sliced tongue	¾ pound	3 pounds
	Cream cheese, softened	3-oz. package	¾ pound
	Horseradish	I tablespoon	¼ cup

CHEESE PIMIENTO SANDWICH			
Mix Well	Shredded nippy cheese	I cup	I quart (I pound)
	Chopped pimiento	2 tablespoons	½ cup
	Salad dressing	2 tablespoons	½ cup

EAST COAST SANDWICH		6 SERVINGS	24 SERVINGS
Mix Well	Frankfurters, thinly sliced	3	12 (1½ lbs.)
	Baked beans	½ cup	2 cups (I lb. can)
	Chopped onion	2 tablespoons	½ cup
	Chili sauce	I tablespoon	¼ cup

ALL AMERICAN FAVORITE			
Sliced roast beef	¾ pound	3 pounds
Sliced sweet onion	I onion	4 onions

STUDDED PEANUT BUTTER SANDWICH			
Mix Well	Peanut butter	¾ cup	3 cups
	Diced crisp bacon	¼ cup (8 slices)	I cup (about 1½ lbs.)

for quick 'n' easy snacks

SANDWICHES
QUANTITY and FAMILY SIZE RECIPES

LIVER SAUSAGE SALAD SANDWICH

		6 SERVINGS	24 SERVINGS
	Liver sausage	½ pound	2 pounds
	Chopped celery	¼ cup	1 cup
	Chopped sweet pickle	¼ cup	1 cup
Mix Well	Chopped onion	1 tablespoon	¼ cup
	Hard cooked egg, chopped	1	4
	Salad dressing	3 tablespoons	¾ cup

TASTY TREAT HAMBURGER

		6 SERVINGS	24 SERVINGS
	American cheese, grilled on hamburger bun	6 1-ounce slices	24 1-ounce slices (1½ pounds)
	Ground beef	¾ pound	3 pounds
	Chopped onion	¼ cup	1 cup
Mix Well	Chili sauce	2 tablespoons	½ cup
	Worcestershire sauce	½ teaspoon	2 teaspoons
	Salt and pepper to taste		

SPICY HAM SANDWICH

	6 SERVINGS	24 SERVINGS
Sliced boiled ham, simmered 15 minutes with:	¾ pound	3 pounds
Tomato sauce	1 cup (8-oz. can)	1 quart
Cloves	⅛ teaspoon	½ teaspoon

CREAM CHEESE CRUNCH

		6 SERVINGS	24 SERVINGS
	Cream cheese, softened	2 3-ounce packages	3 8-ounce packages
Mix Well	Diced crisp bacon	¼ cup (8 slices)	1 cup
	Sliced stuffed olives	½ cup	2 cups

CANADIAN DOUBLE DECKER

	6 SERVINGS	24 SERVINGS
First Layer—		
Cheddar cheese	6 1-ounce slices	24 1-ounce slices (about 1½ pounds)
Tomato, sliced	1 medium (6 slices)	4 medium 24 slices
Second Layer—		
Fried Canadian bacon	6 slices	24 slices (1½ pounds)

CHAMPION TWO STORY

		6 SERVINGS	24 SERVINGS
	First Layer—		
	Sliced cooked chicken	½ pound	2 pounds
	Second Layer—		
	Hard cooked eggs, chopped	4	16
	Chopped celery	2 tablespoons	½ cup
Mix Well	Chopped olives	2 tablespoons	½ cup
	Chopped sweet pickle	1 tablespoon	¼ cup
	Salad dressing	2 tablespoons	½ cup
	Prepared mustard	2 teaspoons	3 tablespoons

FOR SMALL FRY

BANANA PEANUT BUTTER WINNER

	6 SERVINGS	24 SERVINGS
Peanut butter	¾ cup	3 cups
Banana, sliced	3 medium	12 medium

SUNSHINE SPECIAL

		6 SERVINGS	24 SERVINGS
	Chopped dates	1 cup	1 quart
Mix Well	Shredded carrots	1 cup	1 quart
	Chopped nuts	½ cup	2 cups
	Salad dressing	½ cup	2 cups

CALIFORNIA DELIGHT

		6 SERVINGS	24 SERVINGS
	Peanut butter	¾ cup	3 cups
	Orange juice	½ cup	2 cups
Mix Well	Shredded orange rind	1 tablespoon	¼ cup
	Shredded coconut	½ cup	2 cups

APPLE CHEESE TOASTY

	6 SERVINGS	24 SERVINGS
Apple sauce, topped with:	½ cup	2 cups
American cheese, melted in broiler	6 1-ounce slices	24 1-ounce slices (about 1½ pounds)

CHICKEN WALDORF SANDWICH

		6 SERVINGS	24 SERVINGS
	Cooked, diced chicken	1 cup	1 quart
	Chopped celery	½ cup	2 cups
Mix Well	Chopped apple	½ cup	2 cups
	Chopped nuts	¼ cup	1 cup
	Salad dressing	3 tablespoons	¾ cup

SANDWICHES

QUANTITY and FAMILY SIZE RECIPES

for hearty lunching

°OPEN FACE°

Arrange ingredients on buttered bread in order listed. Place under broiler about 10 minutes or until toasted

ROYAL LIVER SAUSAGE SANDWICH	6 SERVINGS	24 SERVINGS
Liver sausage	½ pound	2 pounds
Tomato, sliced	1 medium (6 slices)	4 medium (24 slices)
Bacon	6 slices (¼ pound)	1 pound (24 slices)

FRANKFURTER CHEESE GRILL

	6 SERVINGS	24 SERVINGS
Frankfurters, sliced lengthwise	6 (about ¾ pound)	24 (about 3 pounds)
American cheese	6 1-ounce slices	24 1-ounce slices (about 1½ pounds)

SEAFOOD SUPREME

Crabmeat salad:

Mix Well

	6 SERVINGS	24 SERVINGS
Flaked crabmeat	1 cup	1 quart
Chopped green pepper	¼ cup	1 cup
Salad dressing	3 tablespoons	¾ cup
Lemon juice	1 tablespoon	¼ cup
Tomato, sliced	1 medium (6 slices)	4 medium
American cheese	6 1-ounce slices	24 1-ounce slices (about 1½ pounds)

CHEF'S CHICKEN SANDWICH

	6 SERVINGS	24 SERVINGS
Sliced cooked chicken	½ pound	2 pounds
Cooked asparagus spears	18 (about 1 pound)	6 dozen (about 4 pounds)
Cheese sauce	1½ cups	1½ quarts

ROCKY MOUNTAIN SANDWICH	6 SERVINGS	24 SERVINGS
Eggs, scrambled	6	2 dozen
Sausage meat, browned	¼ pound	1 pound
Chopped onion	¼ cup	1 cup
Chopped green pepper	¼ cup	1 cup
Salt and pepper to taste		

Mix Well

*BAKED SANDWICHES°

HEAVENLY HAMBURGER BAKE	4 Servings	24 Servings
Enriched bread	8 slices	48 slices
Butter or margarine	1 tablespoon	¼ cup
Ground beef	½ pound	3 pounds
Chopped onion	¼ cup	1½ cups
Chopped celery	2 tablespoons	¾ cup
Prepared mustard	1 tablespoon	6 tablespoons
Shredded American cheese	1 cup	1 quart
Eggs, beaten	2	1 dozen
Milk	1 cup	1½ quarts

Spread half of bread lightly with butter or margarine. Arrange 4 slices in bottom of 8-inch square baking dish. (For 24 servings, arrange 8 slices in bottom of each of 3 pans, 11x16x2½ in.) Toast lightly in moderate oven (350°F.) about 15 minutes. While bread is toasting, brown meat with onion and celery. Mix in prepared mustard. Spread meat mixture over toasted bread. Sprinkle shredded cheese on top of meat. Cover with remaining bread slices to make sandwiches. Combine egg and milk and pour over bread. Bake in moderate oven (350°F.) about 45 minutes.

TUNA SOUFFLE SANDWICH	6 SERVINGS	24 SERVINGS
Enriched bread	8 slices	48 slices
Flaked tuna	1 cup (7-ounce can)	6 cups (3 13-ounce cans)
Chopped celery	¼ cup	1½ cups
Chopped green pepper	¼ cup	1½ cups
Shredded American cheese	½ cup	3 cups (¾ pound)
Eggs, beaten	3	1½ dozen
Milk	1½ cups	2 quarts
Salt	1 teaspoon	2 tablespoons
Paprika	⅛ teaspoon	¾ teaspoon

Arrange 4 slices bread in bottom of greased 8-inch square baking dish. (For 24 servings, arrange 8 slices in bottom of each of 3 greased pans, 11x16x2½ in.) Combine tuna, celery and green pepper and spread over slices of bread. Sprinkle cheese over all. Cover with remaining bread slices to make sandwiches. Combine eggs, milk and salt and pour over bread. Sprinkle with paprika. Bake in moderate oven (350°F.) about 45 minutes.

6 Easy Steps

TO THE

1 The ingredients for the perfect pie crust: 1 teaspoon salt, 2/3 cup vegetable shortening. 2 cups flour, and cold water.

2 Cut shortening into flour and salt mixture with a fork or pastry blender until crumbs are coarse and granular.

3 Add 3 to 6 tablespoons cold water, a little at a time. Mix quickly and evenly through the flour until the dough just holds together.

Perfect Pie

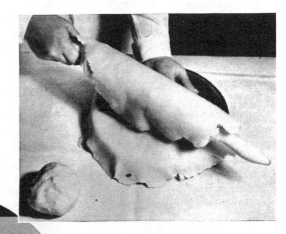

4 Roll half the dough to about one-eighth inch thickness. Lift edge of pastry cloth and roll crust onto rolling pin. Line pie pan, allowing one-half inch crust to extend over edge.

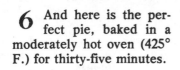

5 Add filling. Roll out top crust, making several gashes to allow escape of steam. Place over filling. Allow top crust to overlap lower crust. Fold top crust under the lower and crimp edges.

6 And here is the perfect pie, baked in a moderately hot oven (425° F.) for thirty-five minutes.

YOU can Reduce---
with SAFETY and COMFORT

If you really want to reduce, the best diet is one that is adequate in all respects, except that it is low in energy value. On such a diet excess fat will be used to supply your energy requirements for work and play.

This diet is based on the results of a study conducted at Rush Medical College, Chicago. On such a diet a large number of patients lost weight consistently while continuing their normal activities. They reported no discomfort from hunger. Many careful tests proved that no harmful effects resulted from staying on this type of diet for a long time.

The diets here outlined are low in calories (the heat units used in measuring energy value of foods) and high in protein (the material which will protect your body while you are taking off weight).

As these are adequate diets, they will provide you with all of the necessary mineral elements and vitamins for the regulation of your body and for the protection of your health.

Just a Word of Caution!

Before going on a diet—
CONSULT YOUR PHYSICIAN

YOUR DIET

If your Ideal Weight is **105** to **125** pounds:

BREAKFAST

Fruit	3½ ounces
Eggs (boiled or poached)	1
Bacon (Canadian-style, broiled)	¼ ounce
Toast	2/3 ounce
Butter	1/6 ounce
Coffee	as desired

LUNCH

Meat (lean)	3 ounces
Vegetable (cooked or salad)	3½ ounces
Bread	2/3 ounce
Butter	1/6 ounce
Milk (skimmed)	7 ounces
Coffee or tea	as desired

DINNER

Clear broth	Optional
Meat (lean)	7 ounces
Vegetable (cooked)	3½ ounces
Salad	3½ ounces
Fruit	3½ ounces
Milk (skimmed)	7 ounces
Coffee or tea	as desired

YOUR DIET

If your Ideal Weight is **125** to **145** pounds:

BREAKFAST

Fruit	3½ ounces
Eggs (boiled or poached)	1
Bacon (Canadian-style, broiled)	1 ounce
Toast	2/3 ounce
Butter	1/6 ounce
Coffee	as desired

LUNCH

Meat (lean)	4 ounces
Vegetable (cooked or salad)	3½ ounces
Bread	2/3 ounce
Butter	1/6 ounce
Milk (skimmed)	7 ounces
Coffee or tea	as desired

DINNER

Clear broth	Optional
Meat (lean)	7 ounces
Vegetable (cooked)	3½ ounces
Salad	3½ ounces
Bread	2/3 ounce
Butter	1/6 ounce
Fruit	3½ ounces
Milk (skimmed)	7 ounces
Coffee or tea	as desired

YOUR DIET

If your Ideal Weight is **145** to **165** pounds:

BREAKFAST

Fruit	3½ ounces
Eggs (boiled or poached)	2
Bacon (Canadian-style, broiled)	1 ounce
Toast	2/3 ounce
Butter	1/6 ounce
Coffee	as desired

LUNCH

Meat (lean)	5 ounces
Vegetable (cooked)	2 ounces
Salad	3 ounces
Bread	2/3 ounce
Butter	1/6 ounce
Fruit	3½ ounces
Milk (skimmed)	7 ounces
Coffee or tea	as desired

DINNER

Clear broth	Optional
Meat (lean)	9 ounces
Vegetable (cooked)	3½ ounces
Salad	3½ ounces
Bread	2/3 ounce
Butter	1/6 ounce
Fruit	3½ ounces
Milk (skimmed)	7 ounces
Coffee or tea	as desired

YOUR DIET

If your Ideal Weight is **165** to **185** pounds:

BREAKFAST

Fruit	3½ ounces
Eggs (boiled or poached)	2
Bacon (Canadian-style, broiled)	2 ounces
Toast	2/3 ounce
Butter	1/6 ounce
Coffee	as desired

LUNCH

Meat (lean)	6 ounces
Vegetable (cooked)	3½ ounces
Salad	3½ ounces
Bread	2/3 ounce
Butter	1/6 ounce
Fruit	3½ ounces
Milk (skimmed)	7 ounces
Coffee or tea	as desired

DINNER

Clear broth	Optional
Meat (lean)	9 ounces
Vegetable (cooked)	3½ ounces
Salad	3½ ounces
Bread	2/3 ounce
Butter	1/6 ounce
Fruit	3½ ounces
Milk (skimmed)	7 ounces
Coffee or tea	as desired

HELPFUL INFORMATION
vvvv

FRUITS
3½ ounces = approximately ½ cup

BREAD
2/3 ounces = 1 thin slice

BUTTER
1/6 ounce = ½ pat

MEATS
4 ounces = piece 4x3x1 inches

MILK
7 ounces = 1 glass

VEGETABLES
3½ ounces = approximately ½ cup

Age	WEIGHT RECORD			
	Date	Weight	Date	Weight
Height				
Weight				
Desired Weight				

INSTRUCTIONS FOR WEIGHING

Weigh yourself at least twice a week at the same time of day and on the same scale. Wear the same type of clothing if possible.

Suggested Menus For Your Diet

MONDAY

Breakfast
Orange juice
Soft boiled egg
Broiled Canadian-style bacon
Toast   Butter
Coffee

Lunch
Cold roast beef
Cauliflower
Cucumber salad
Bread   Butter
Baked apple
Milk   Tea

Dinner
Clear tomato bouillon
Broiled lamb chops
String beans
Head lettuce salad
Whole wheat bread   Butter
Sliced peaches
Milk   Coffee

TUESDAY

Breakfast
Pineapple juice
Coddled egg
Broiled Canadian-style bacon
Toast   Butter
Coffee

Lunch
Hamburger patty
Baked onion
Sliced tomatoes
Bread   Butter
Plums
Milk   Tea

Dinner
Baked liver
Julienne carrots
Celery and radishes
Whole wheat bread   Butter
Pears
Milk   Coffee

WEDNESDAY

Breakfast
Tomato juice
Poached eggs on toast
Broiled ham
Coffee

Lunch
Broiled luncheon meats
Seven minute cabbage
Endive Salad
Bread   Butter
Grapes
Milk   Tea

Dinner
Clear broth
Broiled steak
Baked squash
Mixed vegetable salad
Bread   Butter
Pineapple
Milk   Coffee

THURSDAY

Breakfast
Orange slices
Soft boiled egg
Broiled Canadian-style bacon
Toast   Butter
Coffee

Lunch
Green peppers stuffed with
ground meat
Apple and celery salad
Bread   Butter
Milk   Tea

Dinner
Beef bouillon
Corned beef
Cabbage
Tossed salad
Rye bread   Butter
Sliced peaches
Milk   Coffee

FRIDAY *

Breakfast
Grapefruit juice
Egg in nest on Canadian-
style bacon
Toast   Butter
Coffee

Lunch
Tongue and spinach
Pickled beet salad
Pumpernickel   Butter
Raspberries
Milk   Tea

Dinner
Consommé
Lamb shanks
Broccoli
Carrot sticks and celery curls
Bread   Butter
Honeydew melon
Milk   Coffee

SATURDAY

Breakfast
Tangerine juice
Poached eggs
Broiled Canadian-style bacon
Toast   Butter
Coffee

Lunch
Veal luncheon meat
Stewed tomatoes
Red cabbage and apple salad
Bread   Butter
Milk   Tea

Dinner
Jellied consommé
Pork tenderloin
Diced turnips
Asparagus salad
Bread   Butter
Apricots
Milk   Coffee

SUNDAY

Breakfast
Grapefruit sections
Broiled ham with poached egg
Whole wheat toast   Butter
Coffee

Luncheon or Supper
Assorted cold meats
Tossed green salad
Rye bread   Butter
Strawberries
Milk   Tea

Dinner
Consommé
Roast beef
Asparagus tips
Beet and onion salad
Bread   Butter
Cherries
Milk   Coffee

*For Meatless Fridays ---
    Egg, cottage cheese, fresh and canned fish dishes are used.

Suggested Menus For Your Diet

MONDAY

Breakfast
Orange juice
Poached egg   Frizzled dried beef
Toast   Coffee

Lunch
Cold roast veal
Stewed tomatoes
Endive salad
Bread   Butter
Grapes
Milk   Tea

Dinner
Barbecued pork hearts
Mashed rutabagas
Hearts of lettuce salad
Whole wheat bread   Butter
Broiled grapefruit
Milk   Coffee

TUESDAY

Breakfast
Honeydew melon
Soft boiled egg
Broiled Canadian-style bacon
Toast   Coffee

Lunch
Broiled sweetbreads
Broiled tomatoes
Pineapple and cottage cheese
Bread   Butter
Milk   Tea

Dinner
Roast leg of lamb
Brussels sprouts
Bread   Butter
Blueberries
Milk   Coffee

Breakfast
Cantaloupe
Shirred eggs with diced ham
Whole wheat toast   Butter
Coffee

WEDNESDAY

Breakfast
Grapefruit juice
Coddled egg   Broiled ham slice
Toast   Coffee

Lunch
Cold roast lamb
String beans   Carrot sticks
Bread   Butter
Steamed apple
Milk   Tea

Dinner
Consomme
Veal steak with stewed tomatoes
Mixed green salad
Rye bread   Butter
Sliced peaches
Milk   Coffee

THURSDAY

Breakfast
Apricots
Poached egg on toast
Broiled Canadian-style bacon
Coffee

Lunch
Assorted cold meats
Pickled beets
Artichoke hearts
Bread   Butter
Pineapple
Milk   Tea

Dinner
Beef pot roast
Whole carrots
Assorted relishes
Bread   Butter
Raspberries
Milk   Coffee

SUNDAY

Luncheon or supper
Broiled frankfurters
Beets
Cole slaw
Bread   Butter
Plums
Milk   Tea

FRIDAY *

Breakfast
Orange juice
Baked egg in Canadian-style bacon cup
Toast   Butter
Coffee

Lunch
Deviled beef slices
Seven minute cabbage
Carrot and celery salad
Bread   Butter
Grapes
Milk   Tea

Dinner
Clear broth
Broiled beef steak
Baked onion
Sliced tomato salad
Rye bread   Butter
Watermelon
Milk   Coffee

SATURDAY

Breakfast
Tomato juice
Soft boiled eggs
Broiled Canadian-style bacon
Whole wheat toast   Butter
Coffee

Lunch
Broiled kidney
Diced carrots
Mixed vegetable salad
Bread   Butter
Cherries
Milk   Tea

Dinner
Tomato bouillon
Meat loaf
Asparagus spears
Cauliflower on tomato salad
Bread   Butter
grapefruit
Milk   Coffee

Dinner
Clear vegetable soup
Rolled shoulder of veal
Baked eggplant
Celery curls   Radish roses
Bread   Butter
Strawberries
Milk   Coffee

* For Meatless Fridays ---
Egg, cottage cheese, fresh and canned fish dishes are used.

Protein Content and Caloric Value of Foods for Your Diet

Food	Approx. Weight (Oz.)	Approximate Measure	Protein (Gm.)	Calories
MEAT				
Beef				
Corned	4	2 sl. 7" x 2" x ¼"	19.0	346
Pot Roasts				
Chuck	4	Pc. 2½" x 2" x 1½"	22.3	262
Round	4	Pc. 3½" x 2½" x ½"	23.2	233
Shank	4	Pc. 3¼" x 2½" x ⅝"	24.4	194
Roasts				
Chuck	4	Sl. 4" x 3½" x ½"	22.3	262
Loin	4	Sl. 5½" x 3" x ½"	20.3	352
Rib	4	Sl. 5½" x 3" x ½"	20.9	332
Round	4	Sl. 5" x 3½" x ¼"	23.2	233
Steaks				
Club, T-bone, porterhouse, sirloin	4	Pc. 4¼" x 2" x 1"	20.3	352
Flank	4	Pc. 3" x 2¾" x ¾"	23.9	181
Rib	4	Pc. 5" x 3½" x ½"	20.9	332
Round	4	Pc. 3" x 3" x ½"	23.2	233
Stews				
Chuck	4	3 pc. 1½" x 1¼" x 1¼"	22.3	262
Shank	4	3 pc. 1¼" x 1¼" x 1¼"	24.4	194
Stew meat (av.)	4	3 pc. 1¼" x 1¼" x 1¼"	19.0	400
Lamb				
Chops				
Loin or rib	4	1 loin or 2 rib 1" th.	17.9	421
Shoulder	4	Pc. 4" x 3" x ⅝"	18.7	348
Roasts				
Leg	4	Sl. 4" x 3" x ½"	21.6	276
Shoulder	4	Sl. 5" x 3" x ½"	18.7	348
Pork, fresh				
Chops and steaks				
Leg (ham)	4	Pc. 3½" x 3" x ½"	18.2	408
Loin	4	Chop ¾" th.	19.7	349
Shoulder	4	Pc. 4½" x 3½" x ⅜"	16.1	464
Roasts				
Boston butt	4	Sl. 4½" x 3½" x ⅜"	19.9	327
Loin	4	Sl. ¾" th.	19.7	349
Tenderloin	4	2 pc. 1" dia. x 3" lg.	23.9	172
Pork, cured				
Bacon, Canadian style	1	Sl. 2½" dia. x 3/16" th.	6.6	68
Ham (boiled)	2	Sl. 4¼" x 4" x ⅛"	10.6	147
Veal				
Chops				
Loin	4	Chop ⅝" th.	23.0	211
Rib	4	Chop ¾" th.	22.6	241
Roasts				
Leg	4	Sl. 4" x 2½" x ½"	22.9	223
Loin	4	Sl. 4" x 2½" x ½"	23.0	211
Rib	4	Sl. 4" x 2½" x ½"	22.6	241
Shoulder	4	Sl. 5" x 3" x ½"	23.3	202
Steaks				
Cutlet (round)	4	Pc. 4" x 2½" x ½"	23.4	191
Shoulder	4	Pc. 5" x 3" x ½"	23.3	202
Sirloin	4	Pc. 4" x 2½" x ½"	23.0	211
Stew (breast)	4	4 pc. 2½" x 1" x 1"	22.0	271
Variety Meats				
Brains (beef)	4	2 pc. 2½" x 1½" x 1"	12.6	152
Heart (av.)	4	⅓ ht. 3" dia. x 3½" lg.	19.7	157
Kidney (av.)	4	3 sl. 3¼" x 2½" x ¼"	20.0	161
Liver				
Beef	3	2 sl. 3" x 2½" x ⅜"	17.7	119
Lamb	3	2 sl. 3½" x 2" x ⅜"	18.9	118
Pork	3	2 sl. 3½" x 2" x ⅜"	17.7	116
Veal	3	2 sl. 3" x 2½" x ⅜"	17.1	122
Sweetbread	4	Pc. 4" x 3" x ¾"	18.2	216
Tongue	3	3 sl. 3" x 2" x ¼"	15.7	191
Sausages and Cooked Specialties				
Bologna	1	Sl. 4½" dia. x ⅛" th.	4.4	65
Frankfurter	2	2 5½" lg. x ¾" dia.	9.1	121
Liver sausage	1	Sl. 3" dia. x ¼" th.	5.0	77
Luncheon meat	1	Sl. 4" x 3½" x ⅛"	4.6	81
Vienna sausage	1	2 pc. 2" lg. x ¾" dia.	5.8	76
POULTRY				
Chicken				
Liver	3	4 av.	19.9	122
Roast				
Breast	3	½ breast	21.0	110
Leg	2⅓	1 av.	14.7	88
Thigh	2⅓	1 av.	15.8	95
Wing	1	1 av.	7.0	37
Stewed				
Dark meat	3½	⅓ c. (diced)	23.1	139
Light meat	3	½ c. (diced)	20.3	106
Turkey				
Roast				
Dark meat	3½	Sl. 4" x 3" x ½"	23.2	177
Light meat	3½	Sl. 4" x 3" x ½"	24.5	139

Food	Approx. Weight (Oz.)	Approximate Measure	Protein (Gm.)	Calories
FISH				
Bass	4	1 sm. fish	27.3	113
Clams	3½	5 med.	12.8	77
Cod	3½	Pc. 4" x 2¼" x ¾"	16.5	70
Crab, canned	3	⅔ c.	16.1	94
Finnan haddie	3½	¾ c.	23.2	96
Flounder	3½	Pc. 4" x 3" x ⅜"	19.0	79
Haddock	3½	Pc. 3½" x 3" x ¾"	17.2	72
Halibut	4	Pc. 4" x 3" x ½"	20.4	133
Herring, fresh	4	1 fish 7" lg.	22.8	163
Lobster				
Canned	3	½ c.	15.6	74
Fresh	2⅓	1 av.	12.2	63
Mackerel	2⅓	¼ fish 7" lg.	14.3	119
Oysters	3½	5 med.	6.0	50
Perch	4	2 fish 4½" lg.	23.4	102
Salmon				
Canned	3½	⅔ c.	24.7	203
Fresh	3	Pc. 2½" x 2½" x ⅞"	15.7	196
Shrimps, can'd	2	⅜ c. or 12 pc. 1" dia.	10.7	49
Trout	3	Pc. 6" lg.	16.1	80
White fish	4	Pc. 3¼" x 3" x ½"	25.2	165
MILK AND DAIRY PRODUCTS				
Butter	⅓		.1	73
Cheese, cottage	2	¼ c.	9.6	51
Cream, coffee	½	1 T	.4	29

HEIGHT, WEIGHT, AGE TABLE*

For Adolescents and Young Adults (Ages 15-24 Years)

* Metropolitan Life Insurance Company statistics.

MEN

Height Ft.	In.	Weight 15-19	20-24
4	11	111	117
5	0	113	119
5	1	115	121
5	2	118	124
5	3	121	127
5	4	124	131
5	5	128	135
5	6	132	139
5	7	136	142
5	8	140	146
5	9	144	150
5	10	148	154
5	11	153	158
6	0	158	163
6	1	163	168
6	2	168	173
6	3	173	178

WOMEN

Height Ft.	In.	Weight 15-19	20-24
4	11	110	113
5	0	112	115
5	1	114	117
5	2	117	120
5	3	120	123
5	4	123	126
5	5	126	129
5	6	130	133
5	7	134	137
5	8	138	141
5	9	141	145
5	10	145	149
5	11	150	153
6	0	155	157

Protein Content and Caloric Value of Foods for Your Diet

Food	Approx. Weight (Oz.)	Approximate Measure	Protein (Gm.)	Calories	Food	Approx. Weight (Oz.)	Approximate Measure	Protein (Gm.)	Calories
Milk					**Lettuce**				
Buttermilk	7	1 gl.	7.0	72	Head	3½	¼ head 4" dia.	1.2	18
Evaporated	4	½ c.	8.4	167		½	1 leaf	.2	3
Skim	7	1 gl.	7.0	72	Leaf	⅓	2 leaves	.1	2
Whole	7	1 gl.	7.0	138	Mushrooms	3½	5 caps 2¼" dia.	2.6	15
Eggs	1⅔	1 med.	6.4	79	Okra	2	5 pods	1.0	21
POTATOES.					**Onions**				
White	2	1 small 2½" lg. x 2" dia.	1.2	51	Dried	3	1 onion 2" dia.	1.2	42
VEGETABLES					Green	⅓	3 med.	.2	7
Artichokes	3½	½ lge.	2.9	63	Parsley		2 sprigs	.1	1
Asparagus	3½	7 stalks 6" long	2.3	27	Pumpkin	3½	¼ c.	1.2	36
Beans, string	3½	⅔ c.	2.4	42	Radishes	1	3 radishes 1" dia.	.4	7
Beet greens	3½	½ c.	2.0	33	Rutabagas	3½	½ c.	1.1	41
Beets	3½	⅔ c. or 2 1¾" dia.	1.6	46	Sauerkraut	3½	⅔ c.	1.1	18
Broccoli	3½	2 stalks 5" lg.	3.3	37	Spinach	3½	¾ c.	2.3	25
Brussels sprts.	3½	⅔ c.	4.4	58	**Squash**				
Cabbage	3½	1/5 hd. 4½" dia.	1.4	29	Summer	3½	½ c.	.6	19
Carrots	3½	2 carrots 5" lg.	1.2	45	Winter	3½	½ c.	1.5	44
Cauliflower	3½	⅔ c.	2.4	31	**Tomatoes**				
Celery	½	Pc. 8½" lg. or 2 hts.	.2	3	Canned	3½	½ c.	1.2	25
Chard, Swiss	3½	½ c.	1.4	25	Fresh	3½	1 tomato 2" dia.	1.0	23
Chicory	1	10 sm. leaves	.4	7	Juice, canned	4	½ c.	1.2	28
Cucumbers	2	8 sl. ⅛" th.	.4	7	Turnip greens	3½	½ c.	2.9	37
Eggplant	2	Sl. 3½" dia. x ⅜" th.	.7	17	**Turnips**				
Endive, French	2	2 stalks	.8	11	White	3½	⅔ c.	1.1	35
Green pepper	½	⅛ c. or pc. 4" x 1¼"	.2	4	Yellow (see rutabagas)				
Kohlrabi	3½	⅔ c. (diced)	2.1	36	**PICKLES**				
					Olives				
					Green	1/6	1 med.	.1	7
					Ripe	½	1 lge.	.2	23
					Pickles				
					Dill	2	½ pkle. 5" lg. x 1½" dia.	.3	7
					Sweet	½	1 pkle. 2½" lg. x ¾" dia.	.2	21

BREAD AND CEREAL PRODUCTS

Food	Approx. Weight (Oz.)	Approximate Measure	Protein (Gm.)	Calories
Cereals				
Bran, whole	⅔	½ c.	2.5	67
Cornflakes	⅔	⅔ c.	1.3	56
Farina, enriched	⅔	½ c. (sc. 2 T. dry)	2.3	71
Oatmeal	⅔	⅔ c. (¼ c. dry)	3.1	77
Rice				
Puffed	⅓	¾ c.	.7	36
White	1	⅔ c. (2 T. dry)	2.3	105
Wheat				
Flakes	⅔	¾ c.	2.4	74
Puffed	⅓	¾ c.	1.2	37
Shredded	1	1 biscuit	2.9	103
Breads				
Rye	⅔	Sl. 4" x 3½" x ⅛"	1.2	50
Wheat				
Melba toast	1/6	Sl. 3" x 2" x ¼"	.6	19
White, enrch	⅔	1 sl. (com'l) thin	1.6	50
Whole wheat	⅔	1 sl. (com'l) thin	1.8	50
Crackers				
Graham	½	1 cracker 3" sq.	1.0	54
Saltine	¼	1 cracker 2" sq.	.4	17
Soda	1/5	1 cracker 2¾" x 2½"	.6	25
Zwieback	¼	1 pc. 3¼" x 1¼" x ½"	.9	33
BEVERAGES				
Carbonated	6	1 small bottle		82
Coffee, black			0	0
Tea, plain			0	0
FRUITS				
Apples	3½	1 apple 2¼" dia.	.3	65
Apricots	1	1 med.	.4	20
Blackberries	3½	⅔ c.	1.2	62
Blueberries	3½	⅔ c.	.6	68
Cantaloupe	4	¼ melon 5" dia.	.8	29
Cherries, sweet	3½	15 cherries ⅞" dia.	1.2	87
Grapefruit	3½	½ med. 3⅝" dia.	.5	44
Grapes				
Concord	3½	34 av.	1.4	78
Green s'dless	3½	40 sm.	.8	74
Malaga or Tokay	3½	21 av.	.8	74
Honeydew melon	4	1½" sl. 7" melon	.9	48
Oranges	3½	½ orange 4" dia.	.9	52
Peaches	3½	1 med.	.5	51
Pears	3½	1 sm.	.7	70
Pineapple	3½	1 sl. 4" dia. x ½" th.	.4	58
Plums	2½	1 plum 1¾" dia.	.5	39
Raspberries	3	⅔ c.	1.1	64
Strawberries	3½	10 strawberries 1" dia.	.8	41
Watermelon	5	½ sl. 6" dia. x ¾" th.	.8	51
FRUIT JUICES				
Grapefruit, can'd	4	½ c.	.6	49
Orange	4	½ c.	.7	66
Pineapple, can'd	4	½ c.	.4	65
Tomato (see vegetables)				

IDEAL WEIGHTS FOR ADULTS*
Ages 25 Years and Over

MEN

Height (With shoes)		Weight in Pounds (As Ordinarily Dressed)		
Ft.	In.	Small Frame	Medium Frame	Large Frame
5	2	116-125	124-133	131-142
5	3	119-128	127-136	133-144
5	4	122-132	130-140	137-149
5	5	126-136	134-144	141-153
5	6	129-139	137-147	145-157
5	7	133-143	141-151	149-162
5	8	136-147	145-156	153-166
5	9	140-151	149-160	157-170
5	10	144-155	153-164	161-175
5	11	148-159	157-168	165-180
6	0	152-164	161-173	169-185
6	1	157-169	166-178	174-190
6	2	163-175	171-184	179-196
6	3	168-180	176-189	184-202

WOMEN

Height (With shoes)		Weight in Pounds (As Ordinarily Dressed)		
Ft.	In.	Small Frame	Medium Frame	Large Frame
4	11	104-111	110-118	117-127
5	0	105-113	112-120	119-129
5	1	107-115	114-122	121-131
5	2	110-118	117-125	124-135
5	3	113-121	120-128	127-138
5	4	116-125	124-132	131-142
5	5	119-128	127-135	133-145
5	6	123-132	130-140	138-150
5	7	126-136	134-144	142-154
5	8	129-139	137-147	145-158
5	9	133-143	141-151	149-162
5	10	136-147	145-155	152-166

Freezing Prepared Foods

PACKAGING MATERIALS

Materials used for packaging foods for freezing should keep the air out and the moisture in so select containers that are moisture—vapor resistant or the food will dry out.

Waxed papers, household aluminum foil, and cartons for cottage cheese and ice cream are *not suitable*, because they are *not* moisture-vapor-resistant.

Select a *size* that will hold enough vegetable or fruit for a meal for your family.

Select containers that pack easily into a little space.

Consider cost of containers and if they are reuseable, or not. If they are reuseable, a high initial cost may be justified.

Rigid containers are made of aluminum, glass, plastic, tin or heavily waxed cardboard. They can be used for vegetables, fruits, cooked foods or liquids.

Non-Rigid containers—as sheets and bags of cellophane, heavy aluminum foil, plastic film, polyethylene, or laminated paper are used for foods that are firm but irregularly shaped, like poultry, meat, and baked goods.

Bags are generally used inside cartons as moisture resistant liners.

There is no economy in using poor quality packaging materials.

Fill packages carefully, allowing for the necessary head space for the particular kind of food.

Force or draw out as much air as possible, seal tightly, label, freeze immediately, and store at 0° F or lower.

Foods should be frozen in amounts which will ordinarily be eaten in one meal. To treat light colored fruits to prevent darkening, use ascorbic acid. When freezing fruit in sugar syrup, add ½ teaspoon ascorbic acid for each quart syrup. When freezing fruit in dry sugar, sprinkle ascorbic acid dissolved in water over fruit before adding sugar. Use ¼ teaspoon ascorbic acid in ¼ cup cold water to each quart of fruit.

Freezing Prepared Foods May Not Save Time. It May Allow Time To Be Used To Better Advantage.

GENERAL INFORMATION

Prepare the dish as if it were to be served right away, but do not cook quite done. Reheating for serving will finish the cooking.

Cheese or crumb toppings are best added when the food is reheated for serving.

Pastry crumbs frozen unbaked are more tender, and flaky, and have a fresher flavor than those baked and then frozen.

Cool the cooked food quickly. Pour out in shallow pans or place the uncovered pan of food in iced or very cold water; change water to keep it cold.

As soon as the food is cool—60° F or less, pack promptly into moisture-vapor-resistant containers or packaging material. Pack tightly to force out as much air as possible.

To have the food in desired amounts for serving and for quicker defrosting, separate servings with 2 pieces freezer paper.

Since many main dishes are semi-liquid it is desirable to pack them in rigid containers. Foods frozen in containers with wide-mouthed openings do not have to be thawed completely to remove from container.

Some main dishes may be frozen in the containers in which they were baked.

Freezer weight foil (.0015 gauge) may be used to line the baking dish or pan. After the main dish is frozen (unwrapped) in this container, remove from the baking dish and package. The food may be reheated by slipping it and the foil into the baking pan.

Allow head space for freezing liquid and semi-liquid foods. Seal; label; freeze quickly and store at 0° F or lower.

Most precooked, frozen, main dishes are reheated, either in the oven or on top of the range. Reheating in the oven takes little attention and usually preserves the texture of the food better. Reheating on top of the range in a double boiler or a saucepan is faster. When using a double boiler, start with warm, not hot, water in the lower pan so the food won't stick. Food reheated over direct heat needs to be stirred. This stirring may give a less desirable texture.

If partial thawing is necessary, before the food can be removed from the package, place in lukewarm water for a few minutes. Complete thawing should be done in the refrigerator. If it takes more than 3 or 4 hours, thawing at room temperature may cause dangerous spoilage.

It is best to freeze meat pies and turnovers unbaked.

You can use any good meat loaf recipe for freezing. Just make enough for several meals instead of one and freeze the extra loaves.

Nuts are likely to discolor and become bitter when frozen in a salad mixture.

Suggested Maximum Home-Storage Periods To Maintain Good Quality in Purchased Frozen Foods

Food	Approximate holding period at 0° F.	Food	Approximate holding period at 0° F.
Fruits and vegetables		**Meat—Continued**	
Fruits:	*Months*	Cooked meat:	*Months*
Cherries	12	Meat dinners	3
Peaches	12	Meat pie	3
Raspberries	12	Swiss steak	3
Strawberries	12		
Fruit juice concentrates:		**Poultry**	
Apple	12	Chicken:	
Grape	12	Cut-up	9
Orange	12	Livers	3
Vegetables:		Whole	12
Asparagus	8	Duck, whole	6
Beans	8	Goose, whole	6
Cauliflower	8	Turkey:	
Corn	8	Cut-up	6
Peas	8	Whole	12
Spinach	8	Cooked chicken and turkey:	
		Chicken or turkey dinners (sliced meat and gravy)	6
Baked goods		Chicken or turkey pies	6
Bread and yeast rolls:		Fried chicken	4
White bread	3	Fried chicken dinners	4
Cinnamon rolls	2		
Plain rolls	3	**Fish and shellfish**	
Cakes:		Fish:	
Angel	2	Fillets:	
Chiffon	2	Cod, flounder, haddock, halibut, pollack	6
Chocolate layer	4	Mullet, ocean perch, sea trout, striped bass	3
Fruit	12		
Pound	6	Pacific Ocean perch	2
Yellow	6	Salmon steaks	2
Danish pastry	3	Sea trout, dressed	3
Doughnuts:		Striped bass, dressed	3
Cake type	3	Whiting, drawn	4
Yeast raised	3	Shellfish:	
Pies (unbaked):		Clams, shucked	3
Apple	8	Crabmeat:	
Boysenberry	8	Dungeness	3
Cherry	8	King	10
Peach	8	Oysters, shucked	4
		Shrimp	12
Meat		Cooked fish and shellfish:	
Beef:		Fish with cheese sauce	3
Hamburger or chipped (thin) steaks	4	Fish with lemon butter sauce	3
Roasts	12	Fried fish dinner	3
Steaks	12	Fried fish sticks, scallops, or shrimp	3
Lamb:		Shrimp creole	3
Patties (ground meat)	4	Tuna pie	3
Roasts	9		
Pork, cured	2	**Frozen desserts**	
Pork, fresh:			
Chops	4		
Roasts	8		
Sausage	2		
Veal:			
Cutlets, chops	9	Ice cream	1
Roasts	9	Sherbet	1

How To Convert To Metric System

	WHEN YOU KNOW:	YOU CAN FIND:	IF YOU MULTIPLY BY: *
LENGTH	inches	millimeters	25
	feet	centimeters	30
	yards	meters	0.9
	miles	kilometers	1.6
AREA	square inches	square centimeters	6.5
	square feet	square meters	0.09
	square yards	square meters	0.8
	square miles	square kilometers	2.6
MASS	ounces	grams	28
	pounds	kilograms	0.45
LIQUID VOLUME	ounces	milliliters	30
	pints	liters	0.47
	quarts	liters	0.95
	gallons	liters	3.8
TEMP:	degrees Fahrenheit	degrees Celsius	5/9 (after subtracting 32)

● Metric weights and measures go up (and down) by tens.

Here are some examples :

kilo means a thousand.
Example : a kilometre is a thousand metres.

centi means a hundredth.
Example : a centimetre is a hundredth of a metre.

milli means a thousandth.
Example : a millimetre is a thousandth of a metre.

metre	for length
litre	for liquids
kilogram	for weighing
°C	for temperature

MEASUREMENTS AND WEIGHT

Equipment

3 teaspoons	15 ml	=	1 tablespoon	15 ml
4 tablespoons	60 ml	=	¼ cup	60 ml
5-1/3 tablespoons	79 ml	=	1/3 cup	79 ml
8 tablespoons	118 ml	=	½ cup	118 ml
16 tablespoons	237 ml	=	1 cup	237 ml
1 fluid ounce	30 ml	=	2 tablespoons	30 ml
8 fluid ounces	237 ml	=	1 cup	237 ml
16 fluid ounces	473 ml	=	2 cups or 1 pint	473 ml
32 fluid ounces	946 ml	=	4 cups or 1 quart	946 ml

Food

1 cup butter or margarine	237 ml	=	½ pound	227 g
1 cup Cheddar cheese grated	237 ml	=	¼ pound	114 g
1 cup eggs	237 ml	=	4-5 whole eggs or 8 egg whites or 12 egg yolks	
1 cup all-purpose flour	237 ml	=	¼ pound	114 g
1 envelope of gelatin (unflavored)		=	¼ ounce or 1 tablespoon	7 g 15 ml
1 cup lard or solid vegetable fat	237 ml	=	½ pound	227 g
1 medium lemon (juice)		=	1 ½ fluid ounces (3 tablespoons)	45 ml
1 cup chopped nut meats	237 ml	—	¼ pound	114 g

Dry Measure

0.035 ounces	1 gram	g
1 ounce	28.35 grams	g
1 pound	453.59 grams or 0.45 kilograms	kg
2.21 pounds	1 kilogram	kg

Liquid Measure

1 teaspoon	4.9 milliliters	ml
1 tablespoon	14.8 milliliters	ml
½ cup	118.3 milliliters	ml
1 cup	237 milliliters	ml
1.06 quarts	1000 milliliters or 1 liter	l

To Remove **STAINS** *From Washables*

ALCOHOLIC BEVERAGES

Pre-soak or sponge fresh stains immediately with cold water, then with cold water and glycerine. Rinse with vinegar for a few seconds if stain remains. These stains may turn brown with age. If wine stain remains, rub with concentrated detergent; wait 15 min.; rinse. Repeat if necessary. Wash with detergent in hottest water safe for fabric.

BLOOD

Pre-soak in cold or warm water at least 30 minutes. If stain remains, soak in lukewarm ammonia water (3 tablespoons ammonia per gallon water). Rinse. If stain remains, work in detergent, and wash, using bleach safe for fabric.

CANDLE WAX

Use a dull knife to scrape off as much wax as possible. Place fabric between two blotters or facial tissues and press with warm iron. Remove color stain with non-flammable dry cleaning solvent. Wash with detergent in the hottest water safe for fabric.

CHEWING GUM

Rub area with ice, then scrape off with dull blade. Sponge with dry cleaning solvent; allow to air dry. Wash in detergent and hottest water safe for fabric.

CHOCOLATE AND COCOA

Pre-soak stain in cold or warm water. Wash in hot water with detergent. Remove any grease stains with dry cleaning solvent. If color remains, sponge with hydrogen peroxide, wash again.

COFFEE

Sponge or soak with cold water as soon as possible. Wash, using detergent and bleach safe for fabric. Remove cream grease stains with non-flammable dry cleaning solvent. Wash again.

CRAYON

Scrape with dull blade. Wash in hottest water safe for fabric, with detergent and 1-2 cups of baking soda.
NOTE: If full load is crayon stained, take to cleaners or coin-op dry cleaning machines.

DEODORANTS

Sponge area with white vinegar. If stain remains, soak with denatured alcohol. Wash with detergent in hottest water safe for fabric.

DYE

If dye transfers from a non-colorfast item during washing, immediately bleach discolored items. Repeat as necessary BEFORE drying. On whites use color remover.
CAUTION: Do not use color remover in washer, or around washer and dryer as it may damage the finish.

To Remove **STAINS** *From Washables*

EGG

Scrape with dull blade. Pre-soak in cold or warm water for at least 30 minutes. Remove grease with dry cleaning solvent. Wash in hottest water safe for fabric, with detergent.

FRUIT AND FRUIT JUICES

Sponge with cold water. Pre-soak in cold or warm water for at least 30 minutes. Wash with detergent and bleach safe for fabric.

GRASS

Pre-soak in cold water for at least 30 minutes. Rinse. Pre-treat with detergent. Wash, using detergent, hot water, and bleach safe for fabric. On acetate and colored fabrics, use 1 part of alcohol to 2 parts water.

GREASE, OIL, TAR

Method 1: Use powder or chalk absorbents to remove as much grease as possible. Pre-treat with detergent or non-flammable dry cleaning solvent, or liquid shampoo. Wash in hottest water safe for fabric, using plenty of detergent.
Method 2: Rub spot with lard and sponge with a non-flammable dry cleaning solvent. Wash in hottest water and detergent safe for fabric.

INK—BALL-POINT PEN

Pour denatured alcohol through stain. Rub in petroleum jelly. Sponge with non-flammable dry cleaning solvent. Soak in detergent solution. Wash with detergent and bleach safe for fabric.

INK—FOUNTAIN PEN

Run cold water through stain until no more color will come out. Rub in lemon juice and detergent. Let stand 5 minutes. Wash.
If a yellow stain remains, use a commercial rust remover or oxalic acid, as for rust stains. *CAUTION:* HANDLE POISONOUS RUST REMOVERS CAREFULLY. KEEP OUT OF REACH OF CHILDREN. NEVER USE OXALIC ACID OR ANY RUST REMOVER AROUND WASHER AND DRYER AS IT CAN DAMAGE THE FINISH. SUCH CHEMICALS MAY ALSO REMOVE PERMANENT PRESS FABRIC FINISHES.

LIPSTICK

Loosen stain with a non-flammable dry cleaning solvent. Rub detergent in until stain outline is gone. Wash in hottest water and detergent safe for fabric.

MEAT JUICES

Scrape with dull blade. Pre-soak in cold or warm water for 30 minutes. Wash with detergent and bleach safe for fabric.

MILDEW

Pre-treat as soon as possible with detergent. Wash. If any stain remains, sponge with lemon juice and salt. Dry in sun. Wash, using hottest water, detergent and bleach safe for fabric.
NOTE: Mildew is very hard to remove; treat promptly.

To Remove **STAINS** *From Washables*

MILK, CREAM, ICE CREAM

Pre-soak in cold or warm water for 30 minutes. Wash. Sponge any grease spots with non-flammable dry cleaning solvent. Wash again.

NAIL POLISH

Sponge with polish remover or banana oil. Wash. If stain remains, sponge with denatured alcohol to which a few drops of ammonia have been added. Wash again. Do not use polish remover on acetate or triacetate fabrics.

PAINT

—oil base
Sponge stains with turpentine, cleaning fluid or paint remover. Pre-treat and wash in hot water. For old stains, sponge with banana oil and then with non-flammable dry cleaning solvent. Wash again.
—water base
Scrape off paint with dull blade. Wash with detergent in water as hot as is safe for fabric.

PERSPIRATION

Sponge fresh stain with ammonia; old stain with vinegar. Pre-soak in cold or warm water. Rinse. Wash in hottest water safe for fabric. If fabric is yellowed, use bleach. If stain still remains, dampen and sprinkle with meat tenderizer, or pepsin. Let stand 1 hour. Brush off and wash. For persistent odor, sponge with colorless mouthwash.

RUST

Soak in lemon juice and salt or oxalic acid solution (3 tablespoons oxalic acid to 1 pint warm water). A commercial rust remover may be used.
CAUTION: HANDLE POISONOUS RUST REMOVERS CAREFULLY. KEEP OUT OF REACH OF CHILDREN. NEVER USE OXALIC ACID OR ANY RUST REMOVER AROUND WASHER OR DRYER AS IT CAN DAMAGE THE FINISH. SUCH CHEMICALS MAY ALSO REMOVE PERMANENT PRESS FABRIC FINISHES.

SCORCH

Wash with detergent and bleach safe for fabric. On heavier scorching, cover stain with cloth dampened with hydrogen peroxide. Cover this with dry cloth and press with hot iron. Rinse well.
CAUTION: Severe scorching cannot be removed because of fabric damage.

SOFT DRINKS

Sponge immediately with cold water and alcohol. Heat and detergent may set stain.

TEA

Sponge or soak with cold water as soon as possible. Wash using detergent and bleach safe for fabric.

Words

The six most important words in the English language:
I admit I made a mistake
The five most important words: You did a good job.
The four most important words: What is your opinion?
The three most important words: If you please.
The two most important words: Thank you.
The one most important word: We.
The one least important word: I.

More Words

Happiness is like potato salad — when you share it with others, it's a picnic.

Just about the time you think you can make ends meet, somebody moves the ends.

Be careful how you live — you may be the only bible some people read.

A recipe that is not shared with others will soon be forgotten but when it's shared, it will be enjoyed by future generations.

Birthdays

Monday's child is fair of face,
Tuesday's child is full of grace,
Wednesday's child is loving and giving,
Thursday's child works hard for a living.

Friday's child is full of woe,
Saturday's child has far to go,
But the child that is born on the Sabbath day
Is brave and bonny, and good and gay.

PERPETUAL CALENDAR

SHOWING THE DAY OF THE WEEK FOR ANY DATE BETWEEN 1700 AND 2499

Table of Dominical Letters								Month				Dominical Letter						
Year of the Century ——— *Denote Leap-Years				Centuries				January, October Feb., Mar., Nov. Jan., Apr., July May June February, August Sept., Dec.				A D G B E C F	B E A C F D G	C F B D G A	D G C E A F B	E A D F B G C	F B E G C A D	G C F A D B E
				1700, 2100	1800, 2200	1900, 2300	2000, 2400	1	8	15	22	29	Su	Sa	F	Th	W	Tu	M
0	*28	*56	*84	C	E	G	A	2	9	16	23	30	M	Su	Sa	F	Th	W	Tu
1	29	57	85	B	D	F	G	3	10	17	24	31	Tu	M	Su	Sa	F	Th	W
2	30	58	86	A	C	E	F	4	11	18	25		W	Tu	M	Su	Sa	F	Th
3	31	59	87	G	B	D	E	5	12	19	26		Th	W	Tu	M	Su	Sa	F
*4	*32	*60	*88	E	G	B	C	6	13	20	27		F	Th	W	Tu	M	Su	Sa
5	33	61	89	D	F	A	B	7	14	21	28		Sa	F	Th	W	Tu	M	Su
6	34	62	90	C	E	G	A												
7	35	63	91	B	D	F	G												
*8	*36	*64	*92	G	B	D	E												
9	37	65	93	F	A	C	D												
10	38	66	94	E	G	B	C												
11	39	67	95	D	F	A	B												
*12	*40	*68	*96	B	D	F	G												
13	41	69	97	A	C	E	F												
14	42	70	98	G	B	D	E												
15	43	71	99	F	A	C	D												
*16	*44	*72		D	F	A	B												
17	45	73		C	E	G	A												
18	46	74		B	D	F	G												
19	47	75		A	C	E	F												
*20	*48	*76		F	A	C	D												
21	49	77		E	G	B	C												
22	50	78		D	F	A	B												
23	51	79		C	E	G	A												
*24	*52	*80		A	C	E	F												
25	53	81		G	B	D	E												
26	54	82		F	A	C	D												
27	55	83		E	G	B	C												

EXPLANATION

Find first the *Year of the Century* and in line with that figure at the right, in the proper column under the heading *Centuries*, will be found the Dominical Letter of the year. Then in the table headed *Dominical Letter* and in line with the proper *Month* find the letter previously determined. Run down this column until you are in line with the proper Day of the Month and at the intersection you will find the Day of the Week.

In Leap-Years the Dominical Letters for January and February will be found in the lines where these months are printed in *italics*.

EXAMPLES

On what day of the week did January 5, 1891, fall? For 1891 the Dominical Letter is "D." After finding this letter opposite January in the upper right hand table, and running down that column until you are opposite 5 (the day of the month), you will find Monday. For *January* 1, 1876, the Dominical Letter is "A." Under "A," and in line with 1 is Saturday.

FIRST AID FOR POISONING

In ALL cases it is important to get the poison out or to dilute the poison. **REMEMBER** — If anyone swallows poison it is an emergency. (Any non-food substance is a potential poison). Always call for help promptly.

CALL YOUR PHYSICIAN OR POISON CENTER PROMPTLY

SWALLOWED POISONS
1. Make patient vomit, if so directed, **BUT NOT IF:**
   - Patient is unconscious or is having fits.
   - Swallowed poison is a strong corrosive such as acid or lye. Give liquids.
   - Swallowed poison contains kerosene, gasoline, lighter fluid, furniture polish or other petroleum distillates (unless it contains dangerous insecticides as well, which must be removed). Give liquids.
2. Directions for making patient vomit (if physician orders):
   - Give one tablespoonful (one-half ounce) of Syrup of Ipecac for child one (1) year of age, plus at least one cup of water. If no vomiting occurs after 20 minutes, this dose may be repeated one time only.
   - If no Syrup of Ipecac is available, give water and then try to make patient vomit by gently tickling back of throat with spoon or similar blunt object. Place patient in spanking position when vomiting begins.
3. Do not waste time waiting for vomiting, but transport patient, if indicated, to a medical facility. Bring package or container with intact label and any vomited material.

EYE OR SKIN CONTACT — Wash thoroughly with tap water.

INHALATION — Remove from exposure to fumes.

CALL FOR HELP PROMPTLY

These common household substances are poisonous.

Group 1	Group 2
Induce Vomiting	**Do Not Induce Vomiting**
alcohol	fuel oils
ammonia	furniture polishes and waxes
bleaches	kerosene, gasoline, lighter fluid
cosmetics (including nail	lye and other caustics
polish, hair sprays, and	paint removers
permanent wave solutions)	paints
detergents	paint thinners, turpentine
fertilizers	pesticides
medicines (including aspirin)	weed killers

FIRST AID IN HOUSEHOLD EMERGENCIES

POISONING: When a poison has been taken internally, start first aid at once. Call doctor immediately.

● *Dilute* poison with large amounts of liquids — milk, or water.

● Wash out by inducing vomiting, when not a strong acid, strong alkali or petroleum.

● For acid poisons do not induce vomiting, but neutralize with milk of magnesia. Then give milk, olive oil or egg white. Keep victim warm and lying down.

● For alkali poisons such as lye or ammonia, do not induce vomiting.

● Give lemon juice or vinegar. Then give milk and keep victim warm and lying down.

● If poison is a sleeping drug, induce vomiting and then give strong black coffee frequently. Victim must be kept awake.

● If breathing stops, give artificial respiration.

SHOCK: Shock is brought on by a sudden or severe physical injury or emotional disturbance. In shock, the balance between the nervous system and the blood vessels is upset. The result is faintness, nausea, and a pale and clammy skin. Call ambulance immediately. If not treated the victim may become unconscious and eventually lapse into a coma.

● Keep victim lying down, preferably with head lower than body.

● Don't give fluids unless delayed in getting to doctor, then give only water. (Hot tea, coffee, milk or broth may be tried if water is not tolerated.)

● Never give liquid to an unconscious person. Patient must be alert.

● Cover victim both under and around his body.

● Do not permit victim to become abnormally hot.

● Reassure victim and avoid letting him see other victims, or his own injury.

● Fainting is most common and last form of shock. Patient will respond in 30-60 seconds by merely allowing patient to lie head down if possible on floor

FRACTURES: Pain, deformity or swelling of injured part usually means a fracture. If fracture is suspected, don't move person unless absolutely necessary, and then only if the suspected area is splinted. Give small amounts of lukewarm fluids and treat for shock.

BURNS: Apply or submerge the burned area in cold water. Apply a protective dry sterile cloth or gauze dry dressing if necessary. Do not apply grease or an antiseptic ointment or spray. Call doctor and keep patient warm (not hot) with severe burns.

● If burn case must be transported any distance, cover burns with clean cloth.

● Don't dress extensive facial burns. (It may hinder early plastic surgery.)

WOUNDS: Minor Cuts—Apply pressure with sterile gauze until bleeding stops. Use antiseptic recommended by your doctor. Bandage with sterile gauze. See your doctor. **Puncture Wounds**—Cover with sterile gauze and consult doctor immediately. Serious infection can arise unless properly treated.

ANIMAL BITES: Wash wounds freely with soap and water. Hold under running tap for several minutes if possible. Apply an antiseptic approved by your doctor and cover with sterile gauze compress. Always see your doctor immediately. So that animal may be held in quarantine, obtain name and address of owner.

HEAT EXHAUSTION: Caused by exposure to heat or sun. Symptoms: Pale face, moist and clammy skin, weak pulse, subnormal temperature, victim usually conscious.

Treatment: Keep victim lying down, legs elevated, victim wrapped in blanket. Give salt water to drink (1 tsp. salt to 1 glass water) ½ glass every 15 minutes. Call doctor.

GENERAL DIRECTIONS FOR FIRST AID

1. Effect a prompt rescue.

2. Maintain an open airway.

3. Control severe bleeding by direct pressure over bleeding site. No tourniquet.

4. Give First Aid for poisoning.

5. Do not move victim unless it is necessary for safety reasons.

6. Protect the victim from unnecessary manipulation and disturbance.

7. Avoid or overcome chilling by using blankets or covers, if available.

8. Determine the injuries or cause for sudden illness.

9. Examine the victim methodically but be guided by the kind of accident or sudden illness and the need of the situation.

10. Carry out the indicated First Aid.

Try saying "Good Morning" as though you really meant it

Then (tomorrow, say) try treating some teen-ager like an adult.

Find someone to praise for doing a good job — waitress, bus driver, newsboy, store clerk, anyone.

Show respect for an older person's experience (or fortitude).

Be patient with someone who doesn't understand as quickly as you do.

Write or phone someone having a difficult time. Say you know it's rough, but you have faith in him.

Look pleasant.

Do your job a little better. Maybe you'll get some praise, but certainly you'll get more satisfaction.

Help someone — a cripple across a street, a young man or woman looking for a job (whether you can give it or not, give him hope) or an older one, discouraged in his.

Contribute to some church or charity — money if you can, time if you can't.

It just could be that this sort of *understanding* is what this country needs right now.

Try it tomorrow — all day tomorrow. You might be surprised!

Courtesy THE WARNER & SWASEY COMPANY

INDEX OF RECIPES

APPETIZERS, PICKLES, RELISH

SOUPS, SALADS, SAUCES, DRESSINGS

C

MAIN DISHES--
MEAT, SEAFOOD, POULTRY

D

MAIN DISHES--
CHEESE, EGG, SPAGHETTI, CASSEROLE

E

F

VEGETABLES

G

H

BREAD, ROLLS, PIES, PASTRY

CAKES, COOKIES, ICINGS

J

K

DESSERTS

M

CANDY, JELLY, JAM, PRESERVES

BEVERAGES, MISCELLANEOUS

O

Notes:

TO ORDER

copies of this book, please print your name and
address and send to:

> Logan County Extension Homemakers
> 500 Right of Way Road
> Sterling, CO.   80751

Enclose $6.00 for each copy and add
$2.00 for postage and handling.

1984

JANUARY
S	M	T	W	T	F	S
1	2	3	4	5	6	7
8	9	10	11	12	13	14
15	16	17	18	19	20	21
22	23	24	25	26	27	28
29	30	31				

FEBRUARY
S	M	T	W	T	F	S
			1	2	3	4
5	6	7	8	9	10	11
12	13	14	15	16	17	18
19	20	21	22	23	24	25
26	27	28	29			

MARCH
S	M	T	W	T	F	S
				1	2	3
4	5	6	7	8	9	10
11	12	13	14	15	16	17
18	19	20	21	22	23	24
25	26	27	28	29	30	31

APRIL
S	M	T	W	T	F	S
1	2	3	4	5	6	7
8	9	10	11	12	13	14
15	16	17	18	19	20	21
22	23	24	25	26	27	28
29	30					

MAY
S	M	T	W	T	F	S
		1	2	3	4	5
6	7	8	9	10	11	12
13	14	15	16	17	18	19
20	21	22	23	24	25	26
27	28	29	30	31		

JUNE
S	M	T	W	T	F	S
					1	2
3	4	5	6	7	8	9
10	11	12	13	14	15	16
17	18	19	20	21	22	23
24	25	26	27	28	29	30

JULY
S	M	T	W	T	F	S
1	2	3	4	5	6	7
8	9	10	11	12	13	14
15	16	17	18	19	20	21
22	23	24	25	26	27	28
29	30	31				

AUGUST
S	M	T	W	T	F	S
			1	2	3	4
5	6	7	8	9	10	11
12	13	14	15	16	17	18
19	20	21	22	23	24	25
26	27	28	29	30	31	

SEPTEMBER
S	M	T	W	T	F	S
						1
2	3	4	5	6	7	8
9	10	11	12	13	14	15
16	17	18	19	20	21	22
23	24	25	26	27	28	29
30						

OCTOBER
S	M	T	W	T	F	S
	1	2	3	4	5	6
7	8	9	10	11	12	13
14	15	16	17	18	19	20
21	22	23	24	25	26	27
28	29	30	31			

NOVEMBER
S	M	T	W	T	F	S
				1	2	3
4	5	6	7	8	9	10
11	12	13	14	15	16	17
18	19	20	21	22	23	24
25	26	27	28	29	30	

DECEMBER
S	M	T	W	T	F	S
						1
2	3	4	5	6	7	8
9	10	11	12	13	14	15
16	17	18	19	20	21	22
23	24	25	26	27	28	29
30	31					

1985

JANUARY
S	M	T	W	T	F	S
		1	2	3	4	5
6	7	8	9	10	11	12
13	14	15	16	17	18	19
20	21	22	23	24	25	26
27	28	29	30	31		

FEBRUARY
S	M	T	W	T	F	S
					1	2
3	4	5	6	7	8	9
10	11	12	13	14	15	16
17	18	19	20	21	22	23
24	25	26	27	28		

MARCH
S	M	T	W	T	F	S
					1	2
3	4	5	6	7	8	9
10	11	12	13	14	15	16
17	18	19	20	21	22	23
24	25	26	27	28	29	30
31						

APRIL
S	M	T	W	T	F	S
	1	2	3	4	5	6
7	8	9	10	11	12	13
14	15	16	17	18	19	20
21	22	23	24	25	26	27
28	29	30				

MAY
S	M	T	W	T	F	S
			1	2	3	4
5	6	7	8	9	10	11
12	13	14	15	16	17	18
19	20	21	22	23	24	25
26	27	28	29	30	31	

JUNE
S	M	T	W	T	F	S
						1
2	3	4	5	6	7	8
9	10	11	12	13	14	15
16	17	18	19	20	21	22
23	24	25	26	27	28	29
30						

JULY
S	M	T	W	T	F	S
	1	2	3	4	5	6
7	8	9	10	11	12	13
14	15	16	17	18	19	20
21	22	23	24	25	26	27
28	29	30	31			

AUGUST
S	M	T	W	T	F	S
				1	2	3
4	5	6	7	8	9	10
11	12	13	14	15	16	17
18	19	20	21	22	23	24
25	26	27	28	29	30	31

SEPTEMBER
S	M	T	W	T	F	S
1	2	3	4	5	6	7
8	9	10	11	12	13	14
15	16	17	18	19	20	21
22	23	24	25	26	27	28
29	30					

OCTOBER
S	M	T	W	T	F	S
		1	2	3	4	5
6	7	8	9	10	11	12
13	14	15	16	17	18	19
20	21	22	23	24	25	26
27	28	29	30	31		

NOVEMBER
S	M	T	W	T	F	S
					1	2
3	4	5	6	7	8	9
10	11	12	13	14	15	16
17	18	19	20	21	22	23
24	25	26	27	28	29	30

DECEMBER
S	M	T	W	T	F	S
1	2	3	4	5	6	7
8	9	10	11	12	13	14
15	16	17	18	19	20	21
22	23	24	25	26	27	28
29	30	31				

1986

JANUARY
S	M	T	W	T	F	S
			1	2	3	4
5	6	7	8	9	10	11
12	13	14	15	16	17	18
19	20	21	22	23	24	25
26	27	28	29	30	31	

FEBRUARY
S	M	T	W	T	F	S
						1
2	3	4	5	6	7	8
9	10	11	12	13	14	15
16	17	18	19	20	21	22
23	24	25	26	27	28	

MARCH
S	M	T	W	T	F	S
						1
2	3	4	5	6	7	8
9	10	11	12	13	14	15
16	17	18	19	20	21	22
23	24	25	26	27	28	29
30	31					

APRIL
S	M	T	W	T	F	S
		1	2	3	4	5
6	7	8	9	10	11	12
13	14	15	16	17	18	19
20	21	22	23	24	25	26
27	28	29	30			

MAY
S	M	T	W	T	F	S
				1	2	3
4	5	6	7	8	9	10
11	12	13	14	15	16	17
18	19	20	21	22	23	24
25	26	27	28	29	30	31

JUNE
S	M	T	W	T	F	S
1	2	3	4	5	6	7
8	9	10	11	12	13	14
15	16	17	18	19	20	21
22	23	24	25	26	27	28
29	30					

JULY
S	M	T	W	T	F	S
		1	2	3	4	5
6	7	8	9	10	11	12
13	14	15	16	17	18	19
20	21	22	23	24	25	26
27	28	29	30	31		

AUGUST
S	M	T	W	T	F	S
					1	2
3	4	5	6	7	8	9
10	11	12	13	14	15	16
17	18	19	20	21	22	23
24	25	26	27	28	29	30
31						

SEPTEMBER
S	M	T	W	T	F	S
	1	2	3	4	5	6
7	8	9	10	11	12	13
14	15	16	17	18	19	20
21	22	23	24	25	26	27
28	29	30				

OCTOBER
S	M	T	W	T	F	S
			1	2	3	4
5	6	7	8	9	10	11
12	13	14	15	16	17	18
19	20	21	22	23	24	25
26	27	28	29	30	31	

NOVEMBER
S	M	T	W	T	F	S
						1
2	3	4	5	6	7	8
9	10	11	12	13	14	15
16	17	18	19	20	21	22
23	24	25	26	27	28	29
30						

DECEMBER
S	M	T	W	T	F	S
	1	2	3	4	5	6
7	8	9	10	11	12	13
14	15	16	17	18	19	20
21	22	23	24	25	26	27
28	29	30	31			

The plastic binding on this book will provide years of endless service, but like all plastic material it should not be exposed to excessive heat. Examples of this would be direct sun, left in a hot automobile or near the burners of a kitchen stove.

DATES TO REMEMBER

	1984	1985	1986
NEW YEAR'S DAY	Sunday January 1	Tuesday January 1	Wednesday January 1
LINCOLN'S BIRTHDAY	Sunday February 12	Tuesday February 12	Wednesday February 12
VALENTINE'S DAY	Tuesday February 14	Thursday February 14	Friday February 14
WASHINGTON'S BIRTHDAY (Observed)	Monday February 20	Monday February 18	Monday February 17
ASH WEDNESDAY	Wednesday March 7	Wednesday February 20	Wednesday February 12
ST. PATRICK'S DAY	Saturday March 17	Sunday March 17	Monday March 17
EASTER	Sunday April 22	Sunday April 7	Sunday March 30
PASSOVER (First Day)	Tuesday April 17	Saturday April 6	Thursday April 24
MOTHER'S DAY	Sunday May 13	Sunday May 12	Sunday May 11
NATIONAL MEMORIAL DAY Traditional—Always Observed May 30	Monday May 28	Monday May 27	Monday May 26
FATHER'S DAY	Sunday June 17	Sunday June 16	Sunday June 15
INDEPENDENCE DAY	Wednesday July 4	Thursday July 4	Friday July 4
LABOR DAY	Monday September 3	Monday September 2	Monday September 1
ROSH HASHANAH	Thursday September 27	Monday September 16	Saturday October 4
YOM KIPPUR	Saturday October 6	Wednesday September 25	Monday October 13
COLUMBUS DAY Observed	Monday October 8	Monday October 14	Monday October 13
HALLOWEEN	Wednesday October 31	Thursday October 31	Friday October 31
VETERAN'S DAY	Sunday November 11	Monday November 11	Tuesday November 11
THANKSGIVING	Thursday November 22	Thursday November 28	Thursday November 27
CHANUKAH	Wednesday December 19	Sunday December 8	Saturday December 27
CHRISTMAS	Tuesday December 25	Wednesday December 25	Thursday December 25

We are pleased that we are the world's largest publishers of personalized cook books. If we may have the opportunity to send you information concerning books for your own organization, please write.

CIRCULATION SERVICE, INC.
P.O. BOX 7306 — INDIAN CREEK STATION
SHAWNEE MISSION, KANSAS 66207

Programs of Service and Fund Raising Programs
for Church, School and Civic Organizations